Literacy for Living

A Study of Literacy and Cultural Context in Rural Canadian Communities

William T. Fagan

ISER
Institute of Social and Economic Research

Social and Economic Studies No. 60
Institute of Social and Economic Research
Memorial University of Newfoundland

This book has been published with the help of a grant from the Humanities and Social Sciences Federation of Canada, using funds provided by the Social Sciences and Humanities Research Council of Canada.

Canadian Cataloguing in Publication Data
Fagan, William T.

Literacy for living.

(Social and economic studies ; no. 60)

Includes bibliographical references and index.
ISBN 0-919666-92-2

1. Literacy – Newfoundland. 2. Literacy programs – Newfoundland. 3. Elementary education of adults – Newfoundland. 4. Fishing villages – Newfoundland. I. Memorial University of Newfoundland. Institute of Social and Economic Research. II. Title. III. Series: Social and economic studies (St. John's, Nfld.) ; no. 60.

LC154.2.N53F33 1998 374'.0124'09718 C97-950072-9

Published by the
Institute of Social and Economic Research
Memorial University of Newfoundland
St. John's, Newfoundland
A1C 5S7

Printed and bound in Canada

Contents

The name "Bridget's Harbour/St. Bridget's Parish" was chosen for the area in which I conducted my research. Bridget has long been a popular name in my family. One grandmother insisted that St. Bridget was a true Irish woman while St. Patrick's lineage was questionable (St. Patrick being the recognized patron saint of Ireland). I grew up with a number of customs pertaining to St. Bridget; on St. Bridget's night (February 1), crosses were made of wood and placed over the doors before going to bed as St. Bridget's cross was believed to be a protector of houses. Also, bread was hung on a fence overnight with the belief that St. Bridget blessed it during the night; this bread was used for making poultices for the many infections that the fishermen experienced with fish bones, hooks, and the like.

This book is dedicated to the memory of two important Bridgets in my family: a grandmother (Bridget Butler Rousell) and a great-grandmother (Bridget Dobbin Drohan).

Acknowledgements

No author stands alone in the production of a book, and I am no different. A big thank you is due the Social Sciences and Humanities Research Council of Canada, which provided the research grant (SSHRC–410-92-0798) without which it would not have been possible to gather the data for this book. Memorial University of Newfoundland was most helpful in providing me the use of office space and in allowing me to be part of a supportive academic community during the period I was conducting the research.

Special thanks are due the women who were the interviewers and interpreters. I am indebted to those many people who took time to be interviewed and to the many people with whom I conversed, who contributed their time, who expressed their gratitude for an opportunity to share their views, who provided many insightful, dynamic, and poignant ideas, descriptions, and arguments, and who often "clinched" these contributions through humorous stories and anecdotes.

The publication of this book has been made possible by a grant from the Social Sciences Federation of Canada. A committee of this organization that evaluated the book for this purpose provided many helpful suggestions for improving the text. A vote of thanks is also extended to the staff of ISER Publications and to the editor, whose work in preparing a book for publication is of greater significance than I had even realized. For this support I am indebted.

Preface

The writing of this book actually began the day I started to do the research. Yet, while I constructed many ideas and many hypotheses and heard numerous anecdotes and explanations, I did not know the form the text would take until I began to commit my thoughts to paper. My decision for the present organization was based on a number of reasons.

Trueba (1993) stated that the main purpose of ethnography is to interpret the meaning of behaviour by providing an appropriate social and cultural context, and by building theoretical models or mental constructs or explanatory artifacts. Giroux (1983) indicated that we can take a romantic view of behaviour (data) so that the experience and not the interpretation of experience receives high priority. I had read many phenomenological studies, that while detailing interesting and captivating experiences, often left me with a sense of "so what?" Because of the exciting behavioural events and anecdotes from my research, I was tempted to write in this vein, and still hope to do so for another purpose and a different audience. But the respondents in my study had messages that went far beyond Bridget's Harbour in their applicability and impact. They sparked related theories and conceptualizations that I would never have thought of without these messages as inspirations or cues. As I tried to express what the respondents were saying, I was actually providing interpretation and explanation from a variety of sources. The respondents of Bridget's Harbour allowed me to synthesize this information and to provide a focus—cultural values and literacy (education). Therefore, while grounded in ethnography, this text is not an ethnographic report. The interview data helped capture many generalizations; however, these cannot be separated from the context of the people's lives, and in many cases quantifiable data provided in table form are discussed with the addition of data obtained through participant-observation.

The purpose of the text is to show how literacy cannot be understood in isolation from the larger sociocultural context, how individuals construct their image within the reality of their culture, and how they live this reality. While they may talk about literacy (in response to questions) and even provide definitions for it, its meaning is only possible in the context of the social, economic, educational, and political realities of the people involved. This book is designed to engender discussion and action. It provides suggestions or a basis for action on developing effective adult literacy programs, on integrating literacy/academic upgrading and trade/skills instructional programs, on the necessity for leadership training, on the need for evaluation and accountability, on the necessity of understanding one's total context in making decisions and allowing the individual to contribute to the decision-making. It portrays images of competency while provoking one to reflect on the fatalism of a people in the face of bureaucracy.

I had promised anonymity and for this reason I changed place names. If these names should be synonymous with those of any other communities, this is purely coincidental. To illustrate points, I chose anecdotes and expressions that could not be identified with the source. Names used for people are fictitious.

I deliberately interchanged various terminology since labels were used interchangeably by the respondents and are so often used by the academic community, especially terms like "literacy" and "education," "adult literacy" and "adult basic education," and "vocational skills" and "trades skills instructional programs." The point was not to get caught up in semantic precision but to focus on a construct that seemed relevant to the study participants.

The text is directed to a number of audiences. It should be of great interest to literacy policy-makers, program developers, educators and adult literacy/ABE (adult basic education) instructors, management and unions, and trade skills instructors because it provides insights that are essential in providing meaningful adult literacy (and even child literacy) programs. It is of interest to university educators and graduate students for the data "jolt" a number of beliefs that have been perpetuated in the literature about adult literacy without being empirically tested. Politicians would do well to read it and listen to the "messages" that originate from the people. Finally, for those interested in adult literacy, it should provide that larger and encompassing framework, the culture of a people, with its economic, political, social, and religious innuendo. Only within such a context can literacy ever make sense or can it be determined if people are literate or not.

The text is unique in a number of ways. It is not an argument for a sociocultural interpretation of literacy; the importance of this concept has been argued in other writings. Rather, it is a study within a particular sociocultural context of the lives of people who are affected by the totality of their own local culture and that of the larger society of which their community is a small part. It is an attempt to interpret their lives within a larger framework, which is made possible by using current theory or explanation and by constructing new theory and explanation. In short, it is an attempt to use the actual data to suggest interpretation and to use theory to explain the living of literacy in the particular communities.

The present work represents a combination of methodologies. The first year of the study on which the data are based was totally participant-observation, with perhaps equal emphasis on participating and observing. Observations during that year led to the construction of an interview questionnaire that was administered concurrently with the collection of other ethnographic data. While the tables throughout the text present questionnaire results, discussion of these results often includes data obtained through participant-observation, followed by theoretical insights. The purpose throughout has been to provide description and insight into the lives of a group of people in which literacy competed with many other cultural factors for priority and time, and to provide theoretical interpretation that might form the basis for thought and action.

The text shows how people—many of whom would be labelled less literate than most Canadians—function adequately within their immediate sociocultural context. It is about the intelligence, wit, and insights of these people. It is also about leadership, authority, and decision-making, about how people make decisions on matters perceived to be under their control and how bureaucrats and other government officials decide on matters beyond the people's control. It shows the helplessness of people against bureaucracy, a helplessness that literacy will not remove since the central struggle for control is about power, not literacy.

Literacy for Living is about the importance of leadership, about people who believe that the way to a better future is through capable leaders. It focuses on action rather than reaction. When certain descriptions/issues suggest implications for a course of action, the implications are addressed at that point. It is about hope in the face of adversity.

Introduction 1

"It's hard to come at it if you don't know what you're looking for."

Perhaps one of the biggest tribulations among people in the world today is lack of mutual understanding. While such misunderstanding is so very common, it is hardly ever seriously thought about, even among the educated. What is "chalk" to one person may be "cheese" to another. The story goes that Jack was walking past the priest's house in Bridget's Harbour one day as it was pouring rain. The old priest, out on his verandah, shouted to him, "Jack, my boy, you should run or you'll get wet." "Ah Father," replied Jack, "there's just as much rain in front of me as there is behind me and it's just as wet too." Certainly, what the old priest had in mind for Jack's welfare was not to Jack's advantage as he perceived it. And so it is with policy and practice concerning a multitude of social factors, including literacy. An institution, like the old priest, tells the learners what is good for them and develops literacy programs to operationalize the institution's intent. Whether this has the perceived effect on the learners is another matter. Perhaps, even more unfortunately, the learners may not be as smart as Jack about what is realistic for their welfare and may believe without question what the institution says. Nevertheless, institutions and agencies dealing with literacy can meet the learners halfway and make an attempt to understand what literacy means to them, what they perceive to be the advantages.

LITERACY

Literacy is perhaps one of the terms most disagreed on regarding its meaning or meanings. In fact, some writers and researchers refuse to define it and leave it to the readers to decide what it should mean. Regardless of the ease or difficulty of defining literacy, "the study of literacy has become a major academic growth area in the West during recent years" (Lankshear and Lawler, 1987). This is especially true for Canada, where two major national surveys (Southam Literacy Survey, 1987; Statistics Canada, 1990) and one international literacy survey involving Canada (OECD and Statistics Canada, 1995) have been conducted within the past decade. All of these surveys have highlighted the low levels of adult literacy across the nation. Levels of adult literacy decrease from west to east, and both surveys single out Newfoundland as the province with the highest illiteracy rate.

In spite of the ease with which the authors of the surveys draw conclusions, one of the difficulties in interpreting the results is the lack of a consistent definition of literacy. Does literacy mean being able to read, being able to write, or both? At what level of reading and writing must a person function to be considered literate and how is level defined? Does it make a difference as to the nature of the material read or written, whether it is a book with contrived language patterns (The fat cat sat on the mat), a newspaper article, a short story, a scientific article, a letter to a company regarding an unsatisfactory product, a job application form, or a personal diary? And does it make a difference whether the material read or written has any personal meaning for the reader/writer?

In more recent years the term "functional literacy" has been used widely, to the point that it has lost any specific meaning. Some define functional literacy as "practical," that is, accomplishing a particular task, such as reading a bus schedule or filling out a cheque. But what about the person who picks up a Harlequin romance to read; is this not functional for that person since it provides enjoyment and also functions to pass the time pleasurably? "Multiple literacies" has also found its way into the literature. Yet, does this term mean anything more than multiple materials to be read or written, or multiple contexts in which literacy occurs?

Does it really make a difference how or if literacy is defined? It does! If we are to understand what is being said or written about literacy we must know what the authors mean by the term. For example, Jennings and Purves (1991: 40) tell us that by the year 2000, the total number of illiterates in the world will surpass one billion; one third of the adult world and four out of ten children in developing countries will not complete primary education. Coupled with such statements on the magnitude of illiteracy is the exhortation to do something about it. Jennings and Purves (1991) remind us that "As fortunate possessors of the ability to read and write, our duty to those less fortunate looks transparently clear, help the 'illiterate' learn to do what we can do. We think our life is better than theirs and we want to share the specific ability that we take to be the cause of the betterness."

And this leads to the crux of the problem. To improve the status of literacy, we are bound by policy and practice (program). Now, policy and program *are* based on a particular definition of literacy. How do we sort out programs unless we understand what literacy means to the policy-makers or program developers? Whether or not there are multiple literacies, there are certainly multiple literacy programs. In one program a definition of literacy as mastering the alphabet and sound associations will confine learners to a highly analytical and parts-to-whole focus; in a second program, a definition of literacy as empowerment will involve learners in taking political action such as writing members of government about issues affecting their lives; in yet a third program, a focus on levels of attainment in specific reading/writing skills (such as finding a main idea, identifying syllables in a word) will focus on a mastery of such skills to the required level. A definition of literacy also interacts with the meaning of adult basic education (ABE), a popularly used label for adult educational upgrading. Some policy-makers equate ABE with literacy, while others define ABE as also including the study of factual content (science, social studies); still others believe that literacy is only pertinent at the very initial level of ABE (Level 1) while at the highest level, which approximates a school-leaving certificate, literacy is considered to be non-important and it is assumed that learners merely need to *know* information or *perform* mathematical computations, while ignoring their need to read evaluatively and critically and to write for action and empowerment.

Another appropriate use of the term "multiple" in discussing literacy is to conceptualize societies or subcultures. Canada is a mosaic of societies/cultures. The key, then, to understanding literacy and its development and use may not be in seeking to provide a specific definition of literacy but in defining literacy generally as the ability to use print/writing to construct meaning, and in focusing on the socio-political-economic context (and religious, where significant) to understand how people within that context conceive and use literacy. The importance of studying context in understanding literacy has been emphasized by Fingeret (1983), Heath (1980), and Lankshear and Lawler (1987). Lankshear and Lawler argue that "literacy *is* the uses to which it is put"; this definition then allows one "to entertain the possibility that the forms reading and writing take in daily life are related to the wider operation of power and patterns of interest within society" (p. 50). Consequently, instead of describing levels of reading and/or writing competencies and/or the extent to which individuals can read tasks "functional" to others and imposed by them, it would make more sense to study the sociocultural base of the power and patterns of literacy (Olson, 1990).

The argument that literacy is best understood within a particular sociocultural context is further strengthened by the fact that literacy cannot be separated from oral language use (Olson, Torrance, and Hildyard, 1985). This is especially so when a particular culture has its roots in oral rather than written language. Such is the case of the Newfoundland culture in which storytelling, recitation, and song were for years the mainstay of social interaction within most communities. The culture is known for its quips, puns, and jokes, and for the immediate recording in song of any significant or unusual local event. What becomes of interest, then, is whether the people are able to make a ready transition from oral to written language and the manner in which oral language interacts with written language as people meet the challenge of literacy tasks in the day-to-day life of their community.

CULTURE

While culture, like literacy, defies precision in meaning, there is general agreement that it constitutes a bond or force among a community of people. Spradley (1974: 2, 3) describes it as a "cognitive map" – the categories, plans, and rules that such individuals "use to interpret their world and act purposefully within it. . . . Culture thus becomes a meaning system by which people design their actions and interpret the behavior of others."

Within the concept of culture, the notion of "value" is important since values determine how the culture is oriented and how it works. If literacy is a value, then the people will be involved in literacy acts. A value, according to Spradley (1974: 5), "is an arbitrary conception of what is desirable in human experience." A system of values underlies the rules, norms, and behaviour patterns of a cultural group. However, while some values are common or universal to a culture, there is also variation in values held by particular individuals (Gillin, 1948; Swartz and Jordan, 1980; Vivelo, 1978). The commonality of a culture is what tends to stand out. Only after having developed a sense of what constitutes a culture do exceptions or variations become obvious. Spain (1975: 31) explains the overall force of the culture as follows: "One of the most significant facts about us may finally be that we all begin with the natural equipment to live a thousand kinds of life, but end in the end having lived one."

Initiation into a culture, whether through birth or integration, involves being privy to what is significant as the essence of that culture. Spain (1975) points out that cultural significance may be exemplified in many ways – speech, print, drawings, gestures, musical sounds, and mechanical devices; in fact, any act or action (including literacy) that occurs repeatedly in the culture indicates significance. In addition, the significance of events cannot be understood in isolation but only in interaction with other events and behaviours. To determine the meaning of literacy within a particular sociocultural context and whether individuals shall be classed as literate or not, it is not sufficient, desirable, or valid to do that solely on the basis of literacy tests. The role(s) of literacy and the status of an individual as literate or not can only be understood when the social, political, economic, and religious contexts are taken into account. Consequently, literacy cannot be studied apart from the various acts and actions that give meaning and purpose to individuals' lives. Various acts and actions may be in harmony, conflict, or contradiction, or may merely be contiguous with literacy events.

METHODOLOGY

While the goal to understand literacy by attempting to understand the society or culture in which it is used may appear straightforward, there is the question of how this is best done.

The research methodology that best lends itself to understanding and interpreting values and actions within a larger context is ethnography. Ethnography takes its identity from cultural anthropology (Stuckey, 1991). As Ellen (1984) points out, it is not a method but rather a genre that includes a variety of methods. According to Smith (1986: 264), "people by and large act rationally in that their behavior and point of view are grounded in an attempt to make sense of the world they are experiencing." The task of ethnography, therefore, is to seek an explanation for that behaviour. Smith cautions that to explicate the meaning of literacy-related issues to participants, the researcher must not have preconceived notions, including a strongly held definition of literacy. The researcher must constantly ask, "What is going on? What does this mean in the lives of the people involved?" Through ethnography, the researcher "seeks these answers by participating in their lives while at the same time observing and interpreting from the outside." Another interesting way of explaining ethnography is provided by Wagner (1993), who states that the role of researchers falls into two general categories – filling in blank spots and filling in blind spots. Blank spots mean that questions are known and the goal is to find the answers; blind spots mean that neither the questions nor answers are known. The goal of ethnography is to make sense out of a complex situation; it is an attempt to fill in the blind spots.

Smith (1986: 271) argues that ethnography can provide a different understanding of literacy/illiteracy from that of other research methods. Part of this argument is phrased as follows:

> An ethnography of literacy (or illiteracy) that is true to its cultural roots will examine, without preoccupation, both the social consequences of the particular illiteracy under investigation and its various levels of meaning to individuals. It will be sensitive to the entire web of relationships human beings find themselves enveloped in. It will not, a priori, control out any segments of this web no matter how trivial they seem. Such rich understandings will not always lead to solutions that are essentially technological, i.e. that consist of more responsive or efficient methods of teaching. Rather they will promote serious questioning of basic assumptions and examination of the invisible consequences of behaviors and relationships.

Methodological Decisions

Ellen (1984) maintains that one of the conditions for ethnography is long-term residence within a group and knowledge of the language of the group. Thus, for two years I spent one or two days a week in the rural region in which my study was focused (Bridget's Harbour). I resided in the St. John's area and since many people originally from Bridget's Harbour lived there or visited there I also interacted with these. The population of St. Bridget's parish, including Bridget's Harbour, is about 1,600. It is located approximately 120 km from St. John's.

The primary research method in ethnography is participant-observation (Smith, 1986). Trueba (1993) adds a number of other methods involved in gathering data: interviews, life histories, vignettes, note-taking, video-taping, audio-taping, photography, case studies, journals. Lather (1986a) maintains that in order to establish validity for the data, several methods and data sources must be used.

Since ethnography involves interpreting data in progress, various research methods cannot be chosen a priori. The decision to use interviews, for example, occurred at the end of the first year of the study. During the first year the research focus was mainly participant-observation and the collection of anything in print that was accessible – local newspapers, flyers, memos, bulletins, etc., plus the author's attending card games, bingos, and concerts. Smith (1986: 264) claims that participant-observation is necessary for "it is only possible to understand the worlds of participants and the meaning of phenomena in those worlds through first-hand experience by participating in those worlds." Such participation occurred in a number of venues – meeting people on the road, giving someone a lift, in driveways, and, most importantly, in people's kitchens. The kitchen is still the focal part of the house in rural Newfoundland and "dropping in" is the norm. I dropped in on a number of people and sometimes others were already in the kitchen or arrived after me. In this way, parents, spouses, grandparents, siblings, children, friends, and neighbours became respondents.

Ogbu (1981: 421) states that because of the relativity of literacy, "standardized groups" cannot be used as the basis for understanding it. He would consider the kitchen scene as an example of cultural ecology, which he defines as "the study of the way a population uses natural environment influences and is influenced by its social organization and cultural values and how the relationship between the personal attributes and behaviour of its members and their environment is to be found in the strategies or tasks they have devised for coping with their environmental demands." Many interesting concepts arose from the kitchen. Once, in a discussion about why people who were quite dissatisfied with the action of church officials and who complained loudly among themselves would not go public, one person explained it as "kitchen talk" – that is, talk meant to be kept within the confines of the kitchen and not to be part of the public context, or at least not part of public context with particular names associated with it.

The kitchen groups also allowed for a form of reciprocity, as proposed by Lather (1986b). She conceives reciprocity as engendering an awareness in the respondents of their situation and of alternative modes of behaviour. This often calls for the researcher to take a stand opposite that of the respondent. In the kitchen scene, because different viewpoints were often expressed, respondents were forced to debate the pros and cons. At times I was brought into the controversy when my opinions of a particular issue were sought. For example, two major issues at the time of the study were the proposed privatization of the government hydro facilities and a teachers' strike. One day as I walked into a kitchen one person said, "We have just been talking about the privatization of hydro and the teachers' strike. Now sit down and tell us your views." Since my views corresponded with those of some of the people present and clashed with others, a lively discussion ensued as to the bases for holding a particular belief.

Kazemek (1984: 66) points out the significance of attitude in a setting such as the kitchen. He says that the researcher must understand people's lives without searching for what he/she thinks should be there. "The researcher should be willing to listen long and carefully to people. . . . The researcher should be open to the experiences and wisdom of those he/she talks to."

After a year of taking the role of participant-observer, I became aware that a number of concerns/issues/questions kept reoccurring. To determine if these were reflective of various cohort groups, I designed a questionnaire based on these. The questionnaire also provided a mechanism for checking whether people who had been observed participating or not participating in literacy events would express views consistent with the observed actions.

A major decision was which cohorts would be selected from which to gather survey type data within the ethnographic study and which would reflect the contexts of the communities in which the people lived. From my notes I identified instances of people being referred to as groups or as possessing common attributes – teachers, high school students, and seniors were readily identified. The remaining adults were grouped on the basis of age (young adults and mid-age adults). In order to choose a cross-section of adults from these groups, during my kitchen discussions I raised the question of who speaks for the parish, whose views are respected, and who are unlikely to be heard. This provided a sense of a cross-section of people who should be included. Since the study was about cultural values and literacy, an effort was made to identify a group who had completed high school versus a group who had not completed grade 9. This was possible at the young adult level and two groups differentiated on literacy/educational levels within that age group were identified.

Four women from the area acted as interviewers but also as interpreters and respondents. The cod moratorium, supplementary income, and lack of clarity about earning additional income eliminated most residents as potential interviewers. The four women lived in different areas of the parish and had access to all eligible participants. They collected data from those people who lived in their area or with whom they were familiar. They ranged in age from late teens (one interviewer) to mid-forties. The interview data were collected over a period of five months. The researcher met with the interviewers every week or two, depending on how many people had been interviewed, collected completed questionnaires, and monitored the progress of the project. No changes were made in the format of the questionnaire during the interviewing period.

Since they knew their respondents much better than I did, I relied on them in obtaining another level of data. They were able to put into a larger context various statements as well as share observational data. As an example of the latter, they told me that the seniors were most comfortable with the oral language interaction of the interview and tended to sit back and relax, and while they had lots to tell, they were not always sure of their choice of words and would often say, "You help me say it right." The literate young adults and the teachers were more inclined to be "print bound" and would ask to see the questions in print. After they were asked a question, "Let me see that," was a common request of those who had experienced most success with literacy.

Interpreting the Data

Three aspects to interpretation were interactive and interdependent. Trueba (1993: 2) states that "the main purpose of ethnographic research is to interpret the meaning of behaviour by providing its appropriate social and cultural context." If I had merely asked respondents in an interview what literacy meant to them, I would have received (and actually, did receive) a range – narrow rather than broad – of meaning. To understand these sayings more fully it was necessary to see why and how and when the respondents engaged in literacy tasks. In this way ethnography became the basis for interpreting what was said. This also provides a unique "marrying" of ethnographic and survey data, thereby allowing for contextual understanding and explanation. I was also able to observe how adults engaged in literacy tasks with their children.

A second aspect of interpretation is following leads arising from the data during the process of the study. Trueba (1993: 4) elaborates: "the actual data gathered impacts continuously the research goals and the nature of the inquiry itself which are restructured with new information obtained. New questions are asked to get to the bottom of new data and new goals are constructed as relevant to the new line of inquiry if they prove to be emically significant, that is, functionally relevant to the ethnographer's understanding of the culture and behaviour of the people under study." There were two major digressions in the study. At one point I became fascinated with how effectively people seemed to be able to read sales flyers and achieve economic as well as literacy goals (Fagan, 1993). Also, I became aware that literacy is not the only voice for empowerment and that the people in my study effectively used song. I pursued the study of song as a form of literacy and empowerment (Fagan, 1994a). These research digressions involved expanding the context focus and also included people and materials outside of St. Bridget's parish.

A third aspect of analysis is "to build theoretical models or mental constructs, or explanatory artifacts to make sense of behaviour" (Trueba, 1993: 3). Lather (1986b: 67) cautions about the danger of too much conceptual determinism on the part of the researcher, suggesting that when theory is developed interactively with the data, it must illuminate the lived experiences and be illuminated by them. She states, "Building empirically grounded theory requires a reciprocal relationship between data and theory. Data must be allowed to generate propositions in a dialectical manner that permits use of a priori theoretical frameworks but which keep a particular framework from becoming the container into which the data must be poured." In order to provide a theoretical interpretation it was necessary to read hundreds of books and articles with the general sense of the data in mind. Deciding which theoretical constructs might provide an interpretation for the data was based generally on insight. This seemed to become a rather significant aspect of data interpretation, at least for this text, since the goal was to show how the behaviour of the participants provided the basis for theoretical insights and generalization, on one hand, and how the resulting theory was grounded in a particular context, on the other.

The Researcher

The researcher must always be aware of the limitations of a particular methodology. Trueba (1993: 4) states that "The ethnographer is the weakest link in the ethnographic inquiry. . . . The context may be accessible, rich and clearly pointing in some interpretational direction. Yet the ethnographer may be blind, biased and unwilling to consider certain contextual factors as relevant or significant in order to make inferences."

I approached the situation with two, often conflicting orientations. It was difficult to accept the illiterate label applied to Newfoundlanders and the stigma accompanying this label – that illiterates are poor, dependent, helpless, hopeless, in danger of causing accidents, in danger of poisoning themselves by not being able to read medicine labels, ignorant of world affairs, unable to take part in civic affairs, unable to take a job, sad, depressed, unenlightened, and unempowered. On the other hand, I had memories of growing up in rural Newfoundland and of people who readily pronounced that literacy and education were a necessity, while the school drop-out rate was high, there was no public library, and often little evidence existed of literacy in action.

Because of the beliefs and biases that researchers bring to a situation it is necessary to be aware of and share those that doubtless influence the interpretation of data in spite of the researcher's efforts to describe each event as objectively as possible. One of my biases was that Newfoundlanders are intelligent, hardworking, adaptable, and independent. Another bias of which I was aware was my dislike of the "outside-in" approach to literacy programs in which educators/academics from outside a community arrive in the community with their packaged programs ready to implement. A belief similar to this was my dislike for the "one-size-fits-all" approach to literacy, the belief that the same program is good for everyone. Finally, the belief that literacy programs should result in a positive and observable change was constantly uppermost in my mind. In order to provide some objectivity in understanding an adult educational upgrading program in which many of the respondents were enrolled, it was necessary to suspend this belief and try to describe the situation as the respondents experienced and described it.

A second limitation suggested by Trueba is that the ethnographer may lack a sense of the historical/theoretical context and misunderstand various concepts within the culture. Since I had grown up within the culture being investigated and had always been keenly interested in the historical factors of the area, I do not think this constituted a problem.

However, a limitation of ethnography raised by Gaffney (1982: 210) must be considered, that ethnography, "no matter how holistic in treatment or holocultural in content, is a distortion, in some cases, an exaggeration, and in others, an understatement." While what is focused on may represent a significant slice of the cultural experiences of the participants, it still is restricted in terms of the full life these participants live. Szwed (1987: 11) makes a similar point even more forcefully:

> Only a charlatan or a fool would claim that he had definitely understood the culture of a people because he has developed a model that is explanatory and predictive. . . . To be sure the anthropologist's model should be more complex, more sophisticated than any held by the participants in the culture. . . . But the organization of data, the interrelationships of parts into wholes, all are finally carried out in the personal sphere of the anthropologist's mind.

REPORTING THE DATA

As indicated in the Preface, a major decision I had to make was how to report the data. While ethnographic data usually lead to ethnographic reporting and survey data to survey reporting, since this study included both, some sort of compromise had to be reached. My bias was against reporting the details of a way of life that, while giving readers a "picture" of lived experiences, would remain as "narrative" and would not provide a theoretical interpretation or explanation of people's behaviour. Besides, there were too many participants for such ethnographic description. While I could have been selective, I hesitated to do this because I had promised anonymity, and behaviour and events would have easily led to the identity of respondents. I was interested in how literacy and cultural values interacted in people's lives. Thus, while needing a contextual base within which the data could be shaped, I also needed to portray a broad perspective of belief and thinking on the part of the participants. Consequently, I decided to meld ethnographic and survey data in the report. The theoretical insights were largely based on data arising from participant-observation while the degree of commonality of beliefs was possible through the data obtained from interviews. Tabulated data cannot be interpreted outside of the community context, and information obtained outside of interviews is used to provide additional meaning.

I did not feel constrained by the source of the data in deciding how it should be reported. The overall goal of the study was to understand how cultural values related to literacy. Both ethnographic and interview (survey) data seemed appropriate for fleshing out the nature of this relationship. While the interview data highlighted certain beliefs and trends in people's thinking, the contextual data is always present to provide a background against which this makes most sense.

BRIDGET'S HARBOUR AREA AND THE PARTICIPANTS

The study was conducted in a rural Newfoundland area on the Avalon Peninsula. The particular area under investigation constituted a parish, referred to as St. Bridget's parish. The major community is Bridget's Harbour. Seven smaller communities – Gull Cove, Long Beach, Wild Cove, Kerry's Path, Camper's Brook, Alice Arm, and Caplin Bight – are also in the parish and were included in the field research. Settlement in the area was founded on the fishery, and at the time of the study a moratorium on fishing for cod, the main form of fishing in the area, had been implemented. The fisherpeople and plant workers were being compensated with an income program known as TAGS (The Atlantic Groundfish Strategy) or "The Package" and had to make one of four choices regarding their future: retire, leave the fishery, retrain for work outside the fishery, retrain for work within a revamped fishery whenever such would return. An adult education program was established in the parish for academic upgrading.

Bridget's Harbour was settled in the early 1600s by the Basques, later to be followed by the English and then the Irish, who arrived towards the end of the eighteenth century. The economy has always been focused on the fishery and formerly this was very successful. The area is replete with remnants of history, from 140-year-old houses to cannons, the latter reminders of the struggles in times past for control and protection. The overall population in the parish at the time of the study approximated 1,600. The religion is predominantly Roman Catholic, although a number of people are no longer churchgoers. All except one are native English speakers. Other demographic information on the area is given in Table 1.

Table 1

Demographic Information on St. Bridget's Parish (Statistics Canada, 1991)

Male	49.6%
Female	50.4%
Homes owned	94.4%
Two-parent families	91.5%

Four of the groups who were respondents to a structured questionnaire interview approximated four generations: high school students, young adults, mid-age adults, and senior adults. The three adult groups would be considered "illiterate" according to the Statistics Canada census criterion of literacy since they had not completed grade 9. A second young adult group, who had completed high school and who would meet the literacy criterion, was also interviewed. The final group consisted of the teachers in the parish. Information on the interview respondents is given in Table 2.

The overall percentages of male and female interview respondents were 44.8 and 55.2, respectively; if the teachers' data were removed, the percentages would be 48.1 and 51.9.

Table 2

Data on Interview Respondents

	Seniors	Mid-age Adults	Young Adults	Young Adults (high school)	Teachers	Youth
Number	25	25	25	25	27	30
Mean age	74.6	52.1	33.7	34.5	39.9	17.6
Male (no.)	12	12	13	11	8	14
Female (no.)	13	13	12	14	19	16

Sense of History

The people of the Bridget's Harbour area, like many Newfoundlanders, have a strong sense of history and pride in that history. While Newfoundland first received European settlers around the year 1000, it has been a Canadian province for just over forty years. The senior adults and the mid-age adults all remember a time when they were not Canadians. As an independent country prior to the 1930s (at that time, due to economic hardships, independent rule was suspended in Newfoundland and it was ruled by a commission made up of members from Britain and Newfoundland), Newfoundland had its own flag, its national anthem, and its own currency. The strong identity of being a Newfoundlander still exists and is aptly projected by Pol Chantraine, a journalist who recently authored *The Last Codfish: Life and Death of a Newfoundland Way of Life* (1993). He describes a scene at the St. John's waterfront when a fleet of boats sailed for the Grand Banks in a gesture of reasserting Newfoundland's claim to its fish stocks. Prior to the sailing, there were speeches and homilies, followed by prayer and the Canadian national anthem. At the very end, the former Newfoundland national anthem was sung. Chantraine (p. 102) describes it:

> The Ode to Newfoundland was announced. Now heads rose and from every throat the melody and words poured out. From the docks full of people rose a powerful, proud clamour that buried the voice of the person singing at the microphone, rolling along the slopes of the old fjord that forms the harbour, spreading beyond the Battery and the Narrows to mix with the sharp cries of the gulls and the murmuring of the waves.

The staunch pride of Newfoundlanders in their history is due to many factors, one being that the province of Newfoundland is relatively isolated (made up of the island of Newfoundland, plus Labrador), another its bonds across generations. Young and old intermingle, apparently without noticing age differences. It was not unusual for retired fishermen and children who would "drop in" to chat about the fishing activities of the day, the size of catches, and any other related news. It was not unusual, when dances (reels) such as lancers and square dances were held in the parish hall, for twenty-year-olds to ask sixty- and seventy-year-olds to dance, and vice versa. While there have been many changes, the closeness of the community and its people is still obvious. The people still have a distinct cultural heritage. Freire (1970) reminds us that people are very different from animals in that the latter have no historical sense and therefore no value system and resulting options. People, on the other hand, are the products of their past, whether they admit it or not. But Freire points out that for a literate culture, people must understand their relationship to the world, *including their past*. This can only be done, he says, by constantly raising questions about the present and how it came to be, and about the role the past played in the construction of the present. Street (1984) tells us that an important part of being literate is being able to function effectively in one's culture; this means understanding the sociocultural context and the roles of the participants.

One example of such functioning in Bridget's Harbour comes from a time past when religious days were of great significance. One important religious day was Ash Wednesday, when all the community attended Mass and at the end had ashes applied to their foreheads to remind them of their mortality. Children attended Mass before going to school. On this one Ash Wednesday, one young boy had slept in. An older man coming from Mass met him rushing to school but crying because he feared being punished by the nuns for not having attended Mass. The absence of ashes on his forehead would be a dead giveaway. The man consoled him and stooping down, picked up some soft dirt and put it on his forehead. "There," he said, "she'll never know the difference." With the coming of the Irish, the Catholic Church became a strong presence and remained so until about two decades ago when, with the shortage of priests and the closure of convents, its presence became less obvious. While Catholicism is still the only religion in the area, a large number of people are not regular churchgoers, although attendance at weddings and funerals is large.

In earlier days many of the people left in search of a better life, usually for the United States until 1949 when Newfoundland became a province of Canada, after which time they migrated mainly to Ontario, Alberta, and British Columbia. By the 1950s the population of Bridget's Harbour was slowly decreasing; by the 1960s and 1970s, however, more young people were staying at home and more houses were built. The younger generation was usually employed in the fishery, which at that time also began to employ women, so that for many families there were two incomes.

Changes - Language

There have been many changes in Bridget's Harbour over the years, especially in the relationship between generations. While generational bonds may be of different types, one obvious one is that of language. To get an idea of how far removed the younger and older generations were in terms of knowledge of certain words peculiar to the area (and maybe Newfoundland in general) a word meaning test of twenty words was devised. These words were selected from notes taken during the first year of the study based on conversation with residents eighty years of age and older. These were all words I had remembered from my youth. They were checked against the *Dictionary of Newfoundland English* (Story, Kirwin, and Widdowson, 1990). All but four words were included. The fact that four words were not included indicates the uniqueness and peculiarity of linguistic expressions in different areas of the province. A knowledge of those words by the interview respondents is provided in Table 3.

The results show that those words were still very much integral to the culture for the senior and mid-age groups of adults. Except for two words, the teachers also displayed a working knowledge of them. There is a definite progression of the unfamiliarity of these words from the young adults to the high school students. While about five words were no longer prevalent in the listening vocabulary of the young adults (using a 75 per cent criterion), the number of such words rose to eighteen for the youth; in other words, only two of these terms, "mug-up" and "splits," were still understood to any extent by the younger generation. This was a test of understanding through listening and not of use. However, if there is a decline in the listening understanding of the younger generation, it might be hypothesized that these terms are being less and less used in the respondents' speaking vocabularies, a hypothesis borne out by the responses of 12 per cent or more of all groups that these terms are not commonly used today. While many of the words unique to the culture appear to be dying out, these are being replaced by another corpus of words common in everyday conversation – words acquired in association with technological advances, transportation, and communication, particularly via the media.

Table 3

Word Meanings (percentage who knew meaning)

	Seniors	Mid-age Adults	Young Adults	Young Adults (high school)	Teachers	Youth
mug-up	100	100	100	100	100	100
gaching	80	88	76	84	81.5	13.3
darbies	100	100	100	92	81.5	66.6
blubber	92	92	76	72	96.3	16.6
box-car	100	96	92	96	92.6	16.6
sleeveen	84	96	80	76	100	20
grub	100	100	100	96	81.5	76.6
pinny	100	88	28	64	88.9	13.3
scuff	88	85	96	92	100	20
barking (twine)	92	92	56	60	70.3	0
drought	100	100	88	88	100	23.3
rampse	88	88	80	92	96.3	6.6
splits	100	100	96	96	100	86.6
flake	100	100	100	96	100	70
winkers	96	96	92	80	92.6	3.3
jawed	100	100	92	92	96.3	23.3
sqyuall	100	100	96	88	100	43.3
"up in G"	80	80	28	36	33.3	6.6
handbarrow	96	88	84	76	96.3	16.6
glauvauning	84	76	44	48	51.9	3.3
Mean score:	94	93.2	80.2	81.2	87.9	31.3

There appears to be a feeling of contentment and satisfaction and a feeling of restlessness and concern occurring simultaneously in Bridget's Harbour. The older generations regret the many changes that see cherished values slipping away, yet at the same time they appreciate the amenities that modern conveniences provide. The younger generations, while feeling secure in the structure and tradition of their community, know that they can never return to the past. They try to cope with an unstable present and an uncertain future.

ORGANIZATION OF THE TEXT

The remaining chapters are arranged to lead readers to the people's thinking about literacy, to understand facets of their lives and the manner in which literacy impacts these. Chapter 2 focuses on definitions of literacy that commonly occur in the literature and then looks at the meanings of literacy for the Bridget's Harbour respondents in light of these definitions. Chapter 3 addresses the "doing" of literacy by the respondents, which does not always correspond to what they say literacy is, a phenomenon that may be explained by media influence. The central concern of the Bridget's Harbour people was employment. Chapter 4 discusses the relationship of literacy and work and provides models for more effective training in literacy and trade/skills programs. The focus in Chapter 5 moves to change and people's perceptions of how change has made Bridget's Harbour a different place. The theme of change is continued in Chapter 6, but here the attention is on the school, the community, and the parents and their roles in education. It allows readers to obtain a glimpse of the Bridget's Harbour setting as it supports literacy development. Chapters 7 and 8 provide images of a self-sufficient, independent, and competent people who have learned well from their culture and who do not suffer because of limited "formal" literacy attainment. Life is much broader than literacy and images of their worth as people are affected by this broader life. Chapter 9, while based on information obtained from and observations of the Bridget's Harbour respondents, addresses issues that are often controversial within literacy/ABE programs and issues that transcend the themes of the various chapters. A number of implications or suggestions are presented here, some very directly. However, this is not the only chapter that raises implications from the data. Finally, since one purpose of this text is to inspire others to thought and action, an Appendix contains exercises for discussion and action for each chapter as starting points for this purpose.

Literacy: What Do You Mean? 2

Valentine (1985) bemoans the confusion resulting over the lack of a definition of literacy. It is perhaps ironic that the experts on literacy (the literate) cannot agree on what it means to be literate. In the meantime the term "literacy" has become a catch word that is used *ad nauseam*. An analysis of the literature and of discussions and comments on literacy in the print media provided the following list of terms of which literacy is a part.

Cultural literacy	Civic literacy
Ecological literacy	Scientific literacy
Musical literacy	Computer literacy
Moral literacy	Religious literacy
Biblical literacy	Visual literacy
Financial literacy	Technological literacy
Fiscal literacy	Automotive literacy
Xerox literacy	Amish literacy
Emergent literacy	General literacy
Basic literacy	Functional literacy
Advanced literacy	Marginal literacy

In other words, literacy means nothing more than knowledge. Qualifying the word "literacy" with another word somehow supposedly gives that word an aura of significance, and seems to embody a goal that people should strive for, a goal not easily attained that, when reached, marks off the achievers as a privileged class. Snow and Dickinson (1991: 180) comment that "the term *literacy* has achieved such popularity that it has come to be used in ways that ignore tradition and etymology, and that threaten to undermine communities." Newman and Beverstock (1990: 43) conclude that "If everything becomes a literacy, literacy itself is in danger of becoming lost among its hyperdefinitions."

Clark (1984) tried to make sense out of the myriad definitions by suggesting four categories of literacy definition: statistical, traditional, functional, and contextual. However, other terms have been used synonymously with some of Clark's labels, and concepts have been coined to extend some categories. For example, while Clark speaks of "traditional literacy," other writers refer to this category as "basic" or "conventional"; either synonymous with or as a subset of traditional literacy is "survival literacy."

STATISTICAL LITERACY

While statistical literacy is easily defined as providing a number or statistic of how many people attain a certain *level* of literacy, there is little consensus over what that level should be. Furthermore, the level of attainment fluctuates over time and across regions; for example, several decades ago, the ability to write one's name was indicative of being literate. Today in Canada, grade 9 is a recognized level for being classed as literate, while in the United States the preferred level is completion of high school. To add to this confusion one may question what it means to complete high school; for example, does the person who engages in a rigorous program of studies based on the sciences have the same level of literacy as a graduate from a program with a school-leaving equivalency certificate based on a knowledge of some math, English conventions, and memorized scientific and social studies facts?

Smith (1986) cautions that singling out a grade level, assuming that there is agreement over a measure of grade level, cannot separate literates from illiterates. He points out that one cannot designate people below a certain level, such as grade 5, as illiterate because of the complexity and intricacies of modern-day society. Reder (1987) maintains that in focusing on level, level itself as an esoteric concept becomes important rather than the actual literacy practice or what takes place in the name of literacy.

Determining literacy by a statistic of level attained identifies literacy "as an absolute concept once and for all, where is and as is" (Jennings and Purves, 1991: 4). They question whether it is possible to isolate literacy as an absolute without reference to function, context, and the individual. They question, too, whether a statistical measure of literacy is actually a convenience for those people who abhor the idea of illiteracy, who often, like reformed smokers, have attained a level of accomplishment (no smokes) and feel that everyone else who falls below that level (whether two cigarettes or two packs a day) must be rescued.

Literacy surveys provide statistics or a measure of the literacy health of a nation. Such statistics may be a measure of convenience for fund-raisers and politicians. After all, if one can promote the illiteracy rate as 44 per cent of the population, surely this necessitates a call for drastic action. This action usually occurs in the form of public awareness efforts, literacy promotional campaigns, or literacy program blitzes. Galtung (1981:129) points out that "illiteracy campaigns are conducted very much in the same manner as anti-smallpox and anti-malaria campaigns; illiteracy has to be eradicated so that the country can claim that the territory is free from the plague." Galtung adds that the alternative to smallpox or malaria is clear – a state of no smallpox and no malaria, that is, no sickness. But he questions what the alternative to illiteracy might be? On the surface it would appear to be literacy, but this takes us back to the beginning of the circle – what is literacy? Statistical notions of literacy, while perhaps serving political ends, mean little for the reality of the individual as literate.

It is rather interesting that after the completion of literacy blitzes we hear little about the change in statistics. Millions of dollars, for example, were spent on educational/literacy programs in Atlantic Canada under the TAGS agreement during the cod moratorium. How have these programs impacted the literacy levels of people in that area? What are the statistical differences for literacy levels prior to and after the money invested from this federal program? Even if such statistics were available, for them to make sense we would have to know the definition of level from which these statistics were derived. Current surveys maintain that the ensuing statistics are based on levels of functional literacy, a claim that is questioned later in this chapter.

TRADITIONAL/CONVENTIONAL/BASIC

Still another synonym for traditional/conventional/basic is "school literacy." This does not mean that this is how literacy in school should be but how it often is. In fact, there are great efforts under way to change school literacy.

Nevertheless, school literacy, according to Street (1984: 48), may be best defined within an autonomous model; from this perspective, literacy is somehow seen as "independent – somehow divorced from the social and ideological contexts that gave it meaning." While school literacy, like statistical literacy, involves measuring levels of attainment, unlike statistical literacy, the content or what shall be measured is clearly defined. School children are generally required to know certain information about reading and writing and language. School-age learners are expected to learn such skills as:

- recognize letters of the alphabet randomly
- recognize that letters combine to form words
- recognize and pronounce long vowels
- locate common prefixes in everyday vocabulary and show how they change the meaning of root words
- identify closed and open syllables
- define new words
- recognize and use common abbreviations
- recognize that words combine to form sentences
- print and write letters of the alphabet in upper and lower case
- print and write sentences from typed copy
- form plurals
- form possessives
- use a dictionary or spell check to find or check spelling
- define and identify nouns and verbs
- use commas correctly
- combine simple sentences to form compound and complex sentences
- skim text
- follow directions
- locate specific information from text
- identify likenesses and differences among characters and situations
- identify sequences
- classify and categorize information
- recognize explicit statements of opinion
- recognize prior knowledge of the topic and relate it to the task of selecting appropriate text
- organize randomly selected newspaper ads into categories
- generate and organize ideas using brainstorming, semantic mapping, notetaking, and outlining techniques
- recognize explicit statements of opinion
- write first draft of paragraph with topic sentence, supporting detail, and concluding sentence

Very often such skills are arranged in a hierarchy with the letter and word skills being taught before the more general text-meaning skills. Venezky (1990) refers to this type of literacy as "vanilla literacy," in that it represents a generic brand without being related to any specific task or function. For example, when would someone need to follow directions and what specific directions would be meaningful for them to follow, or even why would anyone need to organize randomly selected newspaper ads into categories?

The context for measuring literacy in national literacy surveys in Canada and the United States is similar in some ways to that of school-based literacy. Literacy, from survey data, is identified by a number of levels, so that I may be performing at Level 1 while you are clearly a Level 2 performer. Rather than measuring specific skills as indicated above, respondents are expected to demonstrate competency in reading various kinds of text (which embody some of the skills listed above) and in various writing tasks. Text embodying the above skills is known as prose literacy. Another type of reading involves document literacy, that is, the reading of text with such formats as job application forms, tax forms, television schedules, advertisements, and product labels. Skill in mathematics or numeracy is also measured.

One advantage of viewing literacy from a school-based perspective is that it is easy to separate the literates from the illiterates, or even the basic illiterates from the functional illiterates from the marginal illiterates from the fuller illiterates (Southam Literacy Survey, 1987) or, in a less pejorative and stigmatizing designation of literacy, by level (1, 2, 3, or 4) (Statistics Canada, 1990). Survey authors also identify "false illiterates" and "false literates." Performance on specific reading/writing tasks is combined with the statistical measure of literacy for this purpose. Those who perform lower than would be expected based on years of schooling are false literates, while those who perform higher are false illiterates.

A major implication of defining literacy as basic/conventional/traditional/school is that adult literacy programs are not distinguished from school-based programs. For the latter, the assumption is that children must learn certain reading, writing, and language skills over a twelve-year period; the same assumption erroneously sometimes underlies adult literacy programs. However, adults cannot enrol in upgrading programs for twelve years. Such an assumption also ignores the fact that adults have many more life experiences, including exposure to print (whether successful in its mastery or not), have more responsibilities in life, and are more immediate goal-directed.

A companion implication is that instructors in adult education programs are often recruited from having been trained for school-based literacy programs; consequently, they bring their beliefs and skills to the adult education program and may argue for more time for the adult to learn a well-defined body of literacy skills. Adult literacy instructors and school teachers are similar in that their goal is to "cover the curriculum," which is generally followed by a test (or periodic tests) of what has been mastered.

FUNCTIONAL/PRAGMATIC

One of the problems of language is that concepts are defined in terms that lack precise definition themselves. For example, in discussing school-based literacy above, I consciously avoided using the term "functioning" and instead used "performing" in the phrase "performing at Level 1," since I knew that in this section the term "functional" is being defined specifically with regard to literacy. In a general sense, functional/pragmatic literacy means that literacy is *for* something; it is a means to an end. Rather than learning how to classify newspaper ads (school/traditional literacy), for example, Mrs. Brown may clip four ads on job opportunities and pin them together for her son, William (functional literacy).

The UNESCO definition of literacy has frequently been used by those who define literacy in terms of its functionality. UNESCO defines a functionally literate person as one who is able "to engage in all those activities in which literacy is required for effective functioning in his group and community and also for enabling him to continue to use reading, writing and calculation for his own and the community's development" (UNESCO International Literacy Year Secretariat, 1990: 8).

A key question raised by a number of educators, especially Levine (1982), is *who* are these literacy activities for? This is a problem that promoters of functional literacy tasks in surveys face. What is functional as literacy tasks in such surveys is often decided by a panel, which in some cases is minimally representative of the general population. This panel decides what literacy tasks shall be functional for a nation. To consider this seriously is ludicrous. Functional, by its very nature, indicates that it is person-specific, and what may be functional for one person may constitute a very unfamiliar task for another. Panels that decide on the functional literacy tasks for a nation are actually adopting a holier-than-thou attitude. Because I need to read a bus schedule in Toronto or Winnipeg or Clarenville does not mean that all people in Canada need to read bus schedules, or even that they have buses. Such panels are often blinded by the assumed homogeneity of literacy and of a nation. A point that I have made on a number of occasions (see, e.g., Fagan, 1988, 1990, 1994b) that would enhance the validity of statistical survey data is simply to ask the respondents if and when they last engaged in the literacy task they are being given to complete.

The pertinence of literacy to one's specific context is highlighted by Smith (1987), who tells of two successful businessmen who came to a literacy centre seeking help. If, as he says, functional illiteracy means not reading at a high enough level to function in the workplace, these men, in spite of their low levels of literacy, could not be considered functionally illiterate. After all, he continues, they were successful in their work, comfortable in their communities, and participated fully in personal relationships. Sadder, perhaps, is Smith's final comment that for them illiteracy was a serious social fault, and they arrived at the literacy centre not for remediation but for redemption. This redemption was exemplified in the form of a certificate they would receive after having completed a course at the centre.

The fallacy of functional literacy is often compounded by the belief that without certain literacy skills, people are dysfunctional. As an example, in *Broken Words* (Calamai, 1987), the journalistic booklet accompanying the Southam Literacy Survey report, a picture of a woman shopping and holding two cans in her hand is accompanied by the sensationalist caption: "Woman comparing Raid and PAM, both in yellow-and-red aerosol cans with red caps, illustrates one of the many potential dangers to people who can't read" (p. 33). There were also containers of Ivory detergent pictured on the shelves. When I showed this picture to a number of low-literate adults, explained what was happening, and asked if they would be in the same situation as the woman shopper, they all gave similar responses – No store would ever put Raid, PAM, and Ivory detergent on the same shelves." These people may have had low reading skills, but they were not stupid.

Biggs (1991: 7) raises the notion of personal theories of literacy that affect the expectations of individuals regarding the meaning of literacy, and ultimately, the literacy tasks in which they engage. Consequently, "literacy for each person is, or may be, quite different from literacy for groups and subgroups. Literacy is situated in the present; *it is not an abstraction*" (emphasis added). Stuckey (1991: 17) emphasizes this point in her statement that functional literacy is "the possession of skills perceived as necessary by particular persons and groups to fulfill their own self-determined objectives as family, community members, citizens, consumers, job holders, and members of social, religious, or other associations of their choosing." Purves (1987) suggests that one measure of functional literacy might be the number of people with drivers' licences, since to obtain a driver's licence the applicant would have to read part of the test, and even in situations when the written portion of the qualifying test may be given orally, the person must be able to read road and highway signs, directions, etc. A check with the Newfoundland and Labrador Motor Vehicle Registration Division indicated that as of 31 December 1993, 336,958 people in the province held motor vehicle licences. This number constituted 76.5 per cent of those fifteen years old and older. A person must be sixteen years of age to hold a motorcycle licence and seventeen to hold a passenger vehicle licence. This percentage of licensed drivers is high considering that a number of places in Newfoundland and Labrador are not accessible by road and vehicle licences are irrelevant. While the contact person at the Motor Vehicle Registration Division did not have figures on the number of people who had taken the driver's test orally, he stated that the total was minimal. While it is difficult to construct a common test of literacy that is truly functional (that is, both meaningful for the individual and for the nation), the notion of a functional literacy task for an individual is easy to grasp.

An added confusion to a functional definition of literacy is that some policy-makers have tried to equate ability to perform specific tasks with the levels definition of literacy. In fact, UNESCO suggests that a grade 9 level of schooling would indicate that the person was functionally literate. This criterion was also adopted within Canada and the rationale for this was that since schooling is generally compulsory until age sixteen, there is the societal expectation that young people of this age would have completed 9 years of school (Cairns, 1988). This involves a rather circular reasoning, but one can see the benefits for politicians: since 9 years of schooling corresponds to functional literacy, and since we require our youth to stay in school long enough to attain grade 9, then our young people of school-leaving age are functionally literate.

This combination of functional literacy with levels of literacy also throws confusion into literacy evaluation. Based on the conclusion that grade 9 equals functional literacy, then it is only necessary to count the number of years in school to determine the level of functional literacy. This is inappropriate according to Reder (1987), who maintains that the literacy practice itself, and not the inferred level of an individual's reading or writing skill, must be the primary unit of analysis in literacy evaluation.

LITERACY IN CONTEXT

According to Street (1984: 49) literacy in context is best described within an ideological model that concentrates on the practices or tasks of reading and writing *and* also on the culturally embedded nature of such practices. It distinguishes levels of literacy accomplishment from the real significance of literacy for social groups. It acknowledges the interaction of oral and written language modes.

Literacy in context stresses collaboration or collectivism rather than individualism. Smith (1987) says that school literacy is very much an individualistic enterprise, so much so that schools often overlook what young children entering school have learned within the context of the home. Langer (1987: 4) stresses that literacy takes place within contexts for particular purposes. As a collective and purposeful activity, literacy must also encompass thinking: "people read, write, talk and think about real ideas and information in order to ponder and extend what they know, to communicate with others, to present their points of view, and to understand and be understood."

Paris and Wixson (1987: 37) argue that since literacy must be viewed as contextual, it is impossible to agree on a single definition of literacy attainment; rather, being literate must be considered relative since "the attributes and standards of literacy are relative to the context in which literacy is observed." For a similar reason, Langer (1987: 2) maintains that it is illogical to distinguish between literacy and illiteracy; she favours the notion of "literacy profiles based on the variety and contexts of literacy use." Literacy in context means intelligently using knowledge constructed via print. Freire and Macedo (1987) believe that reading (or writing) in context implies an effort on the part of people to weigh meaning generated from text against other textual material and against the *reality* of the person doing the reading and writing. Knowledge of the word cannot be separated from a knowledge of the world. Stuckey (1991) also stresses the necessity of understanding one's world in order to understand meanings via print; she maintains that word and world knowledge must proceed simultaneously. While world knowledge can range across various spheres, Purves (1987: 217) contends that the community as context becomes focal in making sense out of print. For one thing, the community is a collection of individuals who at least share a common interpretative system based on commonality of language and a common semantic space, including common denotations, connotations, and idioms. Purves is also convinced that oral language is bound by similar community constraints.

Discussing the closing of a fish plant in a small community based on information in print documents can only provide a limited understanding of this issue. The issue can only be best understood against a background of all factors within the community that impinge on the plant closure, not only people and their relationships, support structures, and conditions of the present, but also past traditions, values, and experiences, as well as concerns for and insights into the future. New information provided by bureaucrats or outsiders can only make sense when weighed, analysed, and considered vis-à-vis the life space of the people at the centre of the plant closure.

Within context, literacy takes on a collaborative stance. As Reder (1987) points out, collaboration can take many forms. It means that several individuals jointly construct meaning by weighing information conveyed through reading and writing against the contextual backdrop of their existence. Because of the collaborative value of literacy in context, outsiders often fail to make inroads or to initiate change, whether in action or in thinking. Reder tells of an Eskimo fishing village in south-central Alaska where outsiders organized a town meeting on the traditional model of forming people into groups with a group secretary. They were not successful because this organization was not familiar to the local people. In fact, this form of organization had a negative social meaning for the inhabitants.

Small rural communities tend to have well-developed "grapevines" so that any issue/event is quickly known throughout the community. However, both information and misinformation may be spread, and misinformation, once initiated, may become accepted so that it thwarts any efforts to address an issue/event by outside agents until it has first been dealt with. Not understanding the power of this grapevine, the outside officials are defeated before they start. This is a classic case of Freire and Macedo's and Stuckey's admonition of failing (or being unable) to relate world and word, a common error of bureaucrats and outsiders.

Ironically, the need for higher standards of literacy is usually not based on a contextual interpretation of literacy but on a traditional definition of literacy, and to a lesser extent, on a functional literacy definition popularized in literacy surveys. Campaigns for higher literacy standards often ignore the context in which literacy occurs and communities often suffer from the fallout of such campaigns. As Mace (1992) points out, illiteracy in our culture is associated with strong negative emotion – shock, contempt, disbelief, anger, shame, and pity. This only serves to divide people, and people who ordinarily might have enrolled in a literacy course tend to shy away because of the stigma attached.

Cairns (1988) reminds us of the myriad of federal and provincial publications from the 1970s onward which have heralded major social and economic costs of illiteracy. One thing the authors of these publications neglect is to relate world and word. Such pronouncements on the debilitating state of illiterates ignore the contexts of literacy. While there is no doubt that when people with education compete with those lacking this expertise, when education is a key criterion the former are generally at an advantage. But what is the situation when the literates and illiterates are not in competition? Furthermore, is the state of the illiterate in downtown Toronto without a family or community support system the same as that of a similarly illiterate person in a small rural community?

A second factor ignored by promoters of the drastic state of illiteracy and its concomitant ills is that education, like money, is subject to inflation. Why, for example, is grade 12 necessary in order to be a janitor, waiter, or sanitation engineer? Cairns (1988) suggests that grade 12 or higher educational qualifications do not necessarily relate to the job to be done, but simply serve as a criterion to sort out applicants. It is also likely that high school graduates are hired over non-graduates because they have proven they can work within a bureaucracy for at least 12 years and therefore may be more amenable to authority, more reliable, more pliable, and punctual.

Since literacy is a relative term, according to Winterowd (1989: xii) "Its meaning depends on individual needs and values and the norms and expectations of the social groups of which the individual is a part." As an example, he cites an episode of a teenager who could understand instructions on a job application form and could fill it out but who had problems reading the daily paper. This teenager, according to Winterowd, might consider himself/herself literate and be so considered by family and peers. But if the teenager were placed in another context with people who highly valued daily newspaper reading, he/she might be labelled as illiterate. Not only is one's illiteracy status relative, but so also is one's literacy. As I have pointed out elsewhere (Fagan, 1993), outsiders to a community, not privy to the oral language networks and necessary prior knowledge, while they might be considered literate according to statistical, traditional, and functional definitions of literacy, find themselves experiencing difficulty in constructing meaning from print in that local context.

It must be emphasized that the individual is not subservient to the context. Rather, the individual interprets context, including cultural wisdom, in creating his/her own role. Individuals within context must strive to be consciously aware of their role and their identities, and must seek to control any changes affecting their status; "who is learning precedes what is learned" (Doyle, 1983: 7). In this way individuals strive for empowerment. However, empowerment, a commonly used term in discussions on literacy, does not always mean "getting the upper hand"; it may involve action against an external agent but may also involve inner control, a greater understanding of how the individual locates him/herself within the community amidst present circumstances, perhaps shaped by past values and traditions.

Duke (1983: 77) points out that research has failed to prove that adult education reduces poverty or is essential to its reduction. Adult education, he maintains, may be effective only in the presence of other conditions (context). He concludes that "Adult education is a necessary but not sufficient condition for the reduction of the poverty of groups, communities, and classes." A similar point is made by Giroux (1988: 65):

> To be literate is *not* to be free; it is to be present and active in the struggle for reclaiming one's voice, history, and future. Just as illiteracy does not explain the causes of massive unemployment, bureaucracy, or the growing racism in major cities in the United States, South Africa, or elsewhere, literacy neither automatically reveals nor guarantees social, political or economic freedom.

Literacy without context defies interpretation!

"I MEANS TO SAY"

The expression "I means to say" as used by residents of Bridget's Harbour has two meanings. One meaning is "I intend to say something"; the other is "I am getting to the bare bones of the matter without qualification and elaboration." The interview respondents in the study were asked three questions about what literacy meant to them. The questions and responses are shown in Tables 4, 5, and 6. Percentages in a column do not add to 100 because a single person may have given more than one response.

There was general agreement among all respondents that the basis of literacy is reading and writing; this belief was more pronounced among the more literate respondents. In one sense this reflected a self-fulfilling prophecy – "I can read and write, therefore I am literate; I am literate, therefore I can read and write." Conceptualization of literacy as reading and writing reflects a traditional definition of literacy. Only the teachers, and only 15 per cent of these, indicated that literacy was functional. On the basis of further probing, defining literacy as reading and writing belies the meaning of the expression "I means to say" since many of the respondents admitted they were verbalizing what they heard or read about literacy in the media, particularly in television ads.

Table 4

How Do I Understand Literacy? (percentage of people responding)

	Seniors	Mid-age Adults	Young Adults	Young Adults (High school)	Teachers	Youth
Reading and writing	64.0	76.0	64.0	100	100	96.6
Education	36.0	28.0	28.0	16.0	22.2	6.6
Intelligence	—	4.0	—	—	—	—
Financially well off	—	—	4.0	—	—	—
Ability to communicate	—	—	—	—	18.5	3.3
Function meaningfully in one's world	—	—	—	—	14.8	—
Enables professional development	—	—	—	—	14.8	—
Understands basic math	—	—	—	—	3.7	—
Not sure/vague responses	12.0	—	4.0	—	—	13.3

A significant minority of all respondents except the high school students ("youth") also indicated that literacy was synonymous with education. The meaning of education will be pursued below. It is interesting that the youth viewed literacy most narrowly as reading and writing, which raises the issue of knowing by authority and knowing by personal action. Since the youth did not as yet have many out-of-school work and life experiences, it was natural for them to describe literacy based on their experience, the world of school literacy and of authority. The teachers as a group gave a greater variety of responses; there is also the possibility that these, too, were influenced by experience in university and in-service training, and through reading – all also reflecting the voice of authority. Interesting as well is that the senior adults, those with most work and life experiences, were more inclined to view literacy broadly as education.

In order to further pursue the two major categories of meaning for literacy, the respondents were further questioned on what literacy could do as reading and writing and as education. The responses are summarized in Tables 5 and 6.

Table 5

How Can Literacy (as Reading and Writing) Help a Person? (percentage of people responding)

	Seniors	Mid-age Adults	Young Adults	Young Adults (high school)	Teachers	Youth
Get work	40.0	40.0	52.0	36.0	48.2	34.4
Engage in reading/writing activities	28.0	48.0	44.0	32.0	37.0	100
Perform specific tasks	18.0	24.0	32.0	28.0	22.2	10.3
Personal/social skills	20.0	—	8.0	20.0	48.1	13.7
Further education/ knowledge	—	—	4.0	12.0	—	6.8
Self-confidence	—	—	—	—	14.8	—
Help others	—	—	—	—	—	6.8
Other	—	—	—	—	—	6.8

When lines 2 and 3 of Table 5 are combined, it appears that the respondents' contention is that literacy allows one to engage in reading and writing activities in general, and to perform specific reading and writing tasks in particular (functional). The youth were least likely to see literacy as functional with respect to particular reading and writing tasks. This is understandable, for the youth are still experiencing school literacy that focuses on general reading and writing activities.

From one-third to one-half of the respondents in the various groups believed that literacy as reading and writing is a passport to getting a job. When the statistics are stated in reverse, this point is even more revealing: from one-half to two-thirds of the respondents by group believed that literacy did not lead directly to a job. In other words, they believed that literacy as reading and writing was a necessary but not a sufficient condition for obtaining work. As one respondent explained, "Well, it's like this. You can't do much with your grade 12 certificate these days. But it's a start."

Table 6

How Can Literacy (as Education) Help a Person? (percentage of people responding)

	Seniors	Mid-age Adults	Young Adults	Young Adults (high school)	Teachers	Youth
Get good jobs/ good income	72.0	76.0	84.0	100	74.0	100
Better life	48.0	20.0	—	—	—	3.3
Better reading/ writing skills	8.0	28.0	24.0	—	3.7	10.0
Greater confi-dence/personal satisfaction/ communication	—	12.0	8.0	24.0	37.0	26.6
Increased knowledge/ function better in society	4.0	4.0	20.0	20.0	18.5	56.6
Help children/ others	—	8.0	12.0	8.0	—	—
Contribute to personal/ economic growth of area	4.0	—	12.0	—	14.8	10.0

The teachers were more likely to comment on the relationship between literacy and personal/social skills. Such skills largely deal with the ability to communicate, to take part in meaningful conversations, and to use appropriate language in different contexts, such as job interviews versus visiting a friend in hospital. Teachers were more likely than any other group to see an interrelationship between written and oral language. One wonders why the students were not being likewise influenced by this perspective?

Literacy as education was conceived of much more broadly in its impact than literacy as reading and writing. From three-quarters to all respondents in each group believed that literacy as education would lead to a job. The senior and mid-adult groups also pointed out that a better education led to a better life. They were easily able to narrate examples of people who, because of their education, had been able to live comfortably.

Literacy as education was not always equated with school, while literacy as reading and writing was. As one informant noted, "Take Jack Quinn! He never got much past the ninth grade but he's never missed a day's work in his life. And he has a nice home to show for it." The respondents believed that literacy as education continued to develop beyond school years. Literacy as education also resulted in other broad attainments – developing greater confidence in oneself, greater personal satisfaction, better communication ability, increased knowledge, and a better ability to function in society.

Those respondents enrolled in the academic upgrading program set up in response to the cod moratorium expressed two views about their program and its functionality. To some it represented literacy as education; it provided knowledge (science), was personally satisfying, and engendered greater confidence. Their expectation was that it would lead to a "better life." As one of the students said, "Well, we're learning all this stuff like the circulatory system of the body. It all has to come to something. It's bound to pay off."

Others, however, were less sure of how to conceptualize the program. While the emphasis according to them was on knowledge (English, math, science, and computers) it was reflective of the school program they had encountered years ago, which they didn't buy into then and refused (although often passively) to buy into now. They did not see it as an opportunity to increase their reading and writing skills. Yet, because they were told that income (fisheries compensation) was tied to attendance, some went for this reason; a few, not seeing any value for them as individuals, attempted to withdraw by staying away from classes. But due to the power of the grapevine (and possibly, misinformation) that those receiving income as part of the compensation for the fisheries closure either attended school or lost their income, these few returned to school. They consoled themselves by the fact that they could absent themselves from instruction to have a cigarette or to play pool. What is interesting is that both those who valued the academic upgrading experience for whatever reason and those who did not and attempted to withdraw were seeking to empower themselves, to gain control over their lives – but they were doing so very differently. Each group interpreted the adult education program within a larger context, including knowledge of their goals, abilities, and circumstances, yet they came to different conclusions as to what it meant for their particular lives.

WHAT DO I THINK?

Because the literacy definitions that respondents gave and their knowledge of the use to which literacy could be put were influenced by authority or outside agents, an attempt was made to determine the respondents' awareness of media in promoting literacy and to seek their opinion on this information and its implications. The topics or questions and resulting responses are given in Tables 7 and 8.

Table 7

Awareness of Literacy Standards Through Media Ads (percentage of people responding)

	Seniors	Mid-age Adults	Young Adults	Young Adults (high school)	Teachers	Youth
Yes	60.0	64.0	72.0	80.0	85.1	76.6
No	40.0	36.0	28.0	20.0	14.9	22.4

The majority of respondents in all groups were aware of media reports on literacy; this was especially true of the younger adults who had completed high school, the teachers, and the students. Also, a majority believed that the problem was as serious as reported; however, the mid- and senior adults were less convinced of the seriousness of the problem. The high school students were more sensitive to the presence of a literacy problem. Their view regarding the state of the literacy problem was much more pessimistic compared to older adult groups. It seems that media reports regarding the status of literacy in the province were having a powerful impact on the people of Bridget's Harbour, especially the younger generations.

People's reactions to media reports of literacy standards ranged from explaining why the literacy rate was so high to expressing negative emotions often found in the literature in reaction to low literacy standards. A significant percentage of all groups understood that the literacy statistics included older adults who had not had an opportunity to attend school. A small percentage of the high school students pointed out that literacy must be understood within its cultural context, that any standard of literacy can only be interpreted within such a context.

Table 8

Do You Believe the Problem is as Serious as Reported? (percentage of people responding)

	Seniors	Mid-age Adults	Young Adults	Young Adults (high school)	Teachers	Youth
Yes	56.0	56.0	68.0	64.0	62.9	76.6
No	40.0	32.0	28.0	32.0	33.3	22.4
Don't know	4.0	12.0	4.0	4.0	3.8	—

When those who agreed with the severity of the literacy problem were questioned about their reasons for this agreement, about one-half of respondents in all groups pointed out that older adults in Newfoundland, not having had schooling opportunities, would be functioning low on the literacy scale. Just over 76 per cent of the seventeen teachers who agreed that a serious problem existed also stressed that the education system must be changed to accommodate individual needs and reflect society; this percentage represents thirteen or approximately one-half of the twenty-seven teachers. Teachers were more likely to indicate more reasons for the state of illiteracy. In addition to the education system not meeting needs, they also listed lack of interest, lack of effort, no perceived immediate use, learning problems, and external social and cultural pressures. Almost one-fifth of the high school students also questioned the non-immediate functionality of literacy.

Those respondents who disagreed with the media reports questioned the figures and the manner in which they were obtained, and pointed out the limitations of literacy statistics as not accounting for intelligence, ability, experience, and effort, and that literacy is not always a criterion as to whether or not people function productively in society. As one person explained, "It's hard to measure literacy until you see what it means to the people – what they are using it for. Like you can give my buddy and me a test and we might measure the same but until you see what we do with it you really haven't measured much, have you?"

Table 9

Reaction to Information on Literacy Standards (percentage of people responding)

	Seniors	Mid-age Adults	Young Adults	Young Adults (high school)	Teachers	Youth
Older adults never had the opportunity	32.0	28.0	16.0	24.0	22.2	23.3
Unfortunate for those affected	36.0	32.0	16.0	20.0	14.8	26.6
Need to raise standards	12.0	20.0	12.0	4.0	29.6	30.0
Difficult to believe	16.0	24.0	12.0	16.0	22.2	3.0
Terrible	—	12.0	28.0	28.0	18.5	46.6
Education system needs changing	—	—	12.0	4.0	37.0	3.3
Must understand the cultural context	—	—	—	—	—	13.3
Other	4.0	—	8.0	—	14.8	17.6

A final question on people's thoughts about low literacy standards concerned the "victims," those at the centre of the literacy controversy. An interesting step progression based on age and literacy level (see italic figures in table) resulted, as shown in Table 10.

While the senior adults believed that the individual suffered most, the next two groups (mid-age adults and young adults without high school) also believed in a generational connection that when parents had low literacy levels, children, too, were likely to suffer. The three literate groups added that low literacy standards affect society as a whole. The seniors seemed to buy into the school-based literacy model of individual responsibility for literacy attainment, while the remaining groups expanded their vision somewhat, with the three most literate groups viewing literacy in a much larger context. The differential impact of context was noted by one person: "It goes both ways – no different ways, actually. Take the fishery now; some of the people thrown out of work and with no skills would go to the mainland to get a job even if it meant uprooting the family. And then there's some jobs locally that suffer because people haven't got the skills to take them."

Table 10

Who Suffers Most When Literacy Standards Are Low? (percentage of people responding)

	Seniors	Mid-age Adults	Young Adults	Young Adults (high school)	Teachers	Youth
The Individual	*76.0*	52.0	32.0	24.0	55.5	36.6
Children	12.0	*32.0*	*40.0*	52.0	14.8	43.3
Everybody/ society	12.0	12.0	16.0	*40.0*	*68.0*	*36.6*
Poorer people	4.0	8.0	—	—	11.1	—
Family	—	16.0	20.0	—	18.5	—
Others	—	—	4.0	4.0	—	6.6

SUMMARY

While "*a* definition" of literacy is not important, nor perhaps possible, what is important is "*the* definition" of literacy underlying policy and program (practice). Without this information, it is difficult to assess the instructional procedures, materials, merits, and impact of a program.

My bias is that literacy, to make sense, must be understood within the sociocultural context in which it is embedded, since it is the people (the learners) who become the focus, not the program. While the respondents of Bridget's Harbour expressed their understanding of literacy from a school/traditional perspective, there were two basic interpretations: literacy as reading/writing and as education. The first was conceived of rather narrowly and was specific to engaging in reading/writing tasks. Literacy as education was conceived of in a much broader fashion and was seen to have a more expansive impact on a person's life, such as getting good jobs and, in general, attaining the "good life."

One important issue arising from this chapter is the basis that leads to certain statements, such as statements of literacy definition. The respondents were often influenced by external sources, such as the media, in stating what they believed literacy was. This seemed to be more pronounced among individuals with higher levels of literacy, with teachers, for example, often giving definitions learned in books or in university courses. This raises the question of whether a person's statement of belief is ever truly removed from external and authoritative influences. Of course, people will be influenced by ideas (arguments, slogans, etc.), but will they narrate these in response to a question or, after having reflectively considered them in relation to their own experiences, provide a truly personal meaning? "I means to say" is a significant expression within the culture of Bridget's Harbour. However, in regard to the meaning of literacy, it seems to have been used mainly in conveying belief and conviction influenced by others rather than as coming from the soul, which would reflect its true meaning.

Literacy in My Life 3

> Illiteracy is not primarily a technological but a relational issue. The task of becoming literate should not be viewed as one of merely acquiring a set of skills. The presence or lack of skills is the result of a real or perceived life context that makes their acquisition either worth or not worth the effort. (Smith, 1986: 270)

It is one thing to create a definition of literacy; it is another to situate oneself within an interpretation of literacy. As one respondent said, "It's so much easier to talk about the next fellow than to talk about yourself." In fact, it may not be just a matter of talking about oneself but of understanding oneself in relation to literacy.

The literature is replete with arguments for literacy. D'Angelo (1983: 68) narrates the drawbacks of not being literate: "The literacy of preliterate and non-literate people is concrete, syncretic, diffuse, perceptual, affective, situation-bound, additive, digressive, concerned with everyday events, actions and happenings rather than with abstract ideas." Illiteracy, of course, supposedly condemns people to poverty, hunger, sickness, and crime.

However, arguments against such pronouncements are just as cogent. Erickson (1984) points out that non-literate people are capable of high-level thinking; and thinking, he argues, cannot be separated from the content of thought, the context of use, and the purpose for the thinking. Thinking is a relational act between an individual's intellectual capabilities, the specific material being addressed, and the social situation, including the other players. The illiterate is capable of analysing, synthesizing, drawing conclusions, and making predictions in such situations and is astute in weighing the biases of the participants based on prior knowledge or nonverbal behaviour. As Erickson points out, once one of the social or physical forms of the context are changed, the whole thinking act changes. As an example he points to the research that showed that children could function with arithmetic concepts in a grocery store but not in a classroom. Pictures of coins in math books are not real coins and real items are not being bought; therefore, the context changes and so does the quality of the thinking. Furthermore, in the social context of the classroom, children may feel threatened in the presence of peers or by their teacher for fear of making a mistake.

Lave, Murtagh, and de la Roche (1984) cite similar research on context-related math abilities of adults. I recall similar behaviour of older fishermen who could readily calculate the weights of fish deliveries to fish plants and the value in dollars and they would readily challenge merchants when mistakes were made in calculating value based on weight. Yet these same fishermen would have difficulty in "doing sums on a page" without relevance to a particular life context. Lave, Murtagh, and de la Roche explain the impact of context in terms of problem definition. Within a social context, the individual formulates or defines a problem around him/herself in relation to the other social players. This is vastly different when the problem is formulated by someone else, whether teacher, merchant, or bureaucrat. Once the individual is allowed to shape the problem, he/she takes ownership and the problem is interpreted within a personal value system. This explains why so-called "illiterate" fishermen have no problems in mastering the use of radar and other technological devices on their fishing boats when these are perceived necessary for maintaining one's livelihood. It also explains why the effects of schooling do not always transfer to real-life conditions. For example, one school engaged in a massive campaign on environmental protection with study units, guest speakers, and promotional buttons and badges. Yet the students did not seem bothered by litter along the roadsides in the area, accompanied older siblings or parents who cut Christmas trees in restricted areas or cut several trees and then chose only the one they wanted, and rode bikes across lawns in early spring when vegetation roots were most susceptible to damage. What they had learned was divorced from practice; they did not practise what they had learned.

CONTEXTUAL INFLUENCE

The influence of context in shaping literacy needs, as pointed out in the last chapter, has been emphasized by many writers. As Holzman (1986: 235) phrases it, "literacy is not a felt need in a magical world."

Bourdieu (1991) stresses that reality cannot be an absolute, and reality differs according to the situation or group of which the individual is a part. Heath (1980) describes a low-literate working-class community in the southeastern United States and documents many types and functions of literacy among the inhabitants. Heath identifies seven uses of literacy: (1) instrumental – solving practical problems; (2) social interaction; (3) news related; (4) memory support; (5) substitute for an oral message; (6) creating a permanent record; (7) confirmation – supporting views already held, or checking that directions have been correctly followed.

Becoming part of a community necessitates adopting an acceptable role with regard to literacy use (Purves, 1987). That role, however, may consist of being minimally or non-involved directly with literacy activities. Levine (1982) cautions that literacy, when understood from its contextual identity, involves not just reading and writing ability but also the attitude, norms, and behaviours of a culture. Levine adds that the societal value of literacy cannot be determined by simply aggregating its monetary value across individuals who possess it, or the loss of monetary value based on those who lack it – a common practice among promoters of literacy campaigns who try to equate low literacy standards with loss of money to the economy, or loss of profits to employers, though not necessarily couched in those terms. Levine (1986) advises that the individual and collective value of literacy is relative to political and cultural environments.

School Literacy

The school represents a certain type of political and cultural environment (Gee, 1986) and, consequently, a certain type of literacy. While respondents in the study gave definitions of literacy that often coincided with media reports, their "doing of literacy" and their comments on this doing indicated a different understanding. They distinguished the literacy of schooling from their literacy in the community. Literacy of schooling, to them, was individualistic and each student was considered responsible for his/her becoming literate. While teachers were sometimes rated according to their teaching ability, it was the student who was finally held responsible for learning. Such comments as "Poor child, he's not too smart"; "She never liked school"; "He doesn't take to the books much"; "She doesn't look at a book from Friday till Monday" all exemplified this kind of thinking. The literacy of school was associated with delayed gratification. Respondents, generally, did not expect anything of school literacy until the student had completed high school and had enrolled in a post-secondary institution. Literacy of schooling was sequential and abstract. The definition was certainly of a traditional nature – a body of knowledge to be learned was spread over twelve years, the learning of which depended on regular school attendance, commitment, and involvement. This definition was intertwined with "education," a broader base of knowledge to be used at a later time in life.

Community/Collective Literacy

On the other hand, the cultural and political context of the adults engendered another type of literacy, one often not recognized as literacy by the participants themselves. They were more likely to refer to it as oral language. They often engaged in literacy collectively, including sharing and discussion. The word "collective" rather than "collaborative" was chosen because the literacy event was more likely to be spontaneous than planned or deliberately initiated: a husband might pass his wife a paper and pencil to compile a grocery list; a person finishing writing a letter might ask a friend who had just dropped in to address an envelope; a person knowing that a certain news item would be in the newspaper might ask another to read it out loud; a person may read a newspaper item to illustrate a point in a discussion; a person may read a newspaper item or announcement silently and then phone a friend to share or discuss the information. A good example of collective literacy occurred at the time that the fisherpeople and plant workers of Bridget's Harbour had to make a decision regarding their future. One day I spoke to a woman and, as was common, asked what the news was. She said that she had just come from the parish hall where the union representative had called them together about their decisions. I inquired how many people had been there, expecting over 100, and so was surprised when she said there were about ten present. When I questioned this, she explained that the union representative decided to call them together in small groups so that she could explain the choices and then help them in filling out any necessary forms. The union representative, knowing the sociocultural context and the people, constructed a collective situation to ensure that everything went smoothly. A more likely plan by a bureaucrat or official from outside would have been to call all 100 or so people together, explain the choices they were to make with respect to the closing of the fishery and their future, hand out the appropriate forms for completion, and cause an uproar in confusion and frustration.

Collective literacy was associated with short-term gratification since results were immediately available. This notion of the immediacy of the results of literacy practices made writing letters to the editor non-meaningful for respondents as there was no assurance that the letters would be published, or if they were, the respondents felt that by the time this occurred, the issue would no longer be of immediate concern. This is a point often overlooked or even unknown by newspaper editors.

There is strong support in the literature for the notion that literacy varies according to the in-school and out-of-school cultural contexts. Barnes (1976) distinguished between school knowledge and action knowledge, which Siefert (1979) paraphrased as children learning to read while adults learn to do. What children learn, says Ogbu (1981), is "knowing that versus knowing how," the basis of the former being text and of the latter, task (Purves, 1987). The method by which school literacy is usually achieved, according to Freire (1970), is the "banking method," or providing knowledge to be stored for future use. The reality of the school culture is different from the out-of-school culture. As Ogbu (1981) points out, there are sets of skills for coping with realities, and the level of an individual's functioning depends on his/her acquisition of the skills required by these realities.

Literacy in the school is shaped around roles, particularly the role of a teacher and the role of a learner (Holzman, 1986). These roles are based on the notion of verticality with the individual as the unit (Galtung, 1981). The individual is ranked vertically both within grades and within classes. By attending school, children learn the cultural principles of acting in school-like ways (Erickson, 1984), which are manifested by young children when they "play school." The situation becomes the reality. Myers (1992) argues that school literacy, however, is as authentic for students as personal literacy is for adults; these different literacies, simply, are for different purposes in different contexts. The school becomes the context in which their personal lives as students make sense. Consequently, they identify with the society of the school and their membership in it and engage in strategies and negotiation, collaboration, and circumvention to act as students rather than as children in the community, and their main concern is to meet the literacy needs of school (teachers).

Literacy in out-of-school contexts is bound by a different set of principles, a different reality that some educators find difficult to admit. Illiterate adults are neither dependent (Fingeret, 1983) nor dysfunctional (Tough, 1979), nor deficient (Lytle and Landau,

1987). Fingeret (1983:133-34) points out that such adults often live in interactive and supportive environments. They view reading and writing "as only two of the many instrumental skills and knowledge resources that combined, are required for daily life." Educators are often amazed, even shocked, that illiterate adults have been very resourceful in finding ways to circumvent their lack of skill in reading and writing. Such behaviours are often looked upon with shame by these educators, and the adults, often sensing this attitude, also admit shamefully their "ruses" for dealing with literacy tasks rather than being made to feel proud of their achievements and confident in their ability to function adequately and creatively even without expected literacy skills.

Examples of such resourcefulness are the subject of many literacy stories. Henze (1992: 51) tells the story of Katrina, who had very little schooling so it was expected that family members would always see to Katrina's literacy needs. As Heinze states, "there will always be someone who can do it for her, either in her own household or in the larger network of neighbours, most of whom are also relatives," a grouping of support Henze labels "collective literacy." In my study, a woman with low-literacy skills was asked if she feared making a mistake on the amount of medication she was taking. "Oh no," she replied. "Jenny always measures out what pills I have to take; she's the daughter-in-law you know. And if she's away a few days, she'll line them up in egg cups so I don't mix them up." Then she laughs. "I suppose she could get it into her mind to do away with me," and then adds, "but sure I have nothing to leave her anyway." Fingeret (1983) documented the interdependence of individuals within a particular sociocultural context, literate and illiterate alike. There is a trade-off between the deployment of skills, including literacy, as long as there is a basis of trust. Similar behaviour has been described among prison inmates (Fagan, 1989).

An underlying assumption of literacy use is change (Windham, 1991). As pointed out earlier, in out-of-school contexts, since literacy is generally focused on tasks with immediate gratification, change is easily noted – the task is accomplished or not. Measuring change that occurs for school-based literacy is not as easy and change is often treated merely as a cognitive skill and measured by pencil and paper tests. While out-of-school literacy can be observed in action, literacy in school can only be observed in contrived situations (Mace, 1992).

A major question is whether school and out-of-school contexts should be polarized in terms of the nature of literacy involved. While certain literacy tasks are considered "school-like" and are introduced over a twelve-year period, there is some concern that the gap between the reality of school and the reality outside of school is too great. A landmark study by Scribner and Cole (1981) on the effects of schooling showed that schooling did not stimulate what might be called cognitive competence; rather, it led to the development of a narrow range of skills based on role, such as knowing how to respond to an interviewer. The higher value accorded school-based literacy, or rather the lower value associated with out-of-school literacy, is often due to the biases of the evaluators (Scribner and Cole, 1981). As they point out, assessing literacy competence may be more in the eye or ear and brain of the interpreter than in the mouth and brain of the respondents. Lytle and Landau (1987: 214) argue that "Literacy abilities cannot then be simply ranked along a continuum from the unskilled to the highly proficient, illiteracy to literacy, because of the many possible interactions of readers/writers, text, purpose and context." This is in marked contrast to conclusions of national literacy surveys that purport but fail to do this very thing.

VALUING LITERACY AND MOTIVATION

Langer (1987) notes that literacy behaviours gain their value from the contextual settings that cultures and subcultures provide for their uses. Since school and out-of-school contexts differ in terms of their realities, it would follow that the value placed on literacy in both contexts differs. In school, literacy may be valued in terms of roles, such as completing a task assigned by the teacher or knowing certain information, while in out-of-school contexts, literacy may be valued for what it enables one to do, whether by oneself or collectively with the assistance of others.

The importance of understanding how people value literacy is highlighted by comments from Winterowd and Galtung. Winterowd (1989: 20), who suggests that reading and writing are not so much skills as they are reflections of values and lifestyles, states, "It makes little sense to consider literacy in the abstract. People gain literacy for reasons and these reasons come about because of scenes, situations, social conditions, cultural values, and norms, the ethos of the family." Galtung (1975: 48) maintains that "literacy should be experienced as a magnificent instrument to express and understand important things, not as a goal in itself when it becomes a fetish."

Valuing, of course, is closely tied to motivation, and what is valued provides motivation for involvement. This point has many implications for literacy, whether in school or out of school. While literacy in general may be valued, the specific literacy being offered may not be valued. As Mace (1992) reminds us, adults who drop out of literacy/basic education programs may have developed a positive interest in (value for) other things than literacy. Szwed (1987: 83), for example, notes the value placed on family in a region of Newfoundland. "In general the . . . family is a closely related group that spends a great deal of time together in a great number of activities. As a result of high interaction, their mutual identity is high, and the family unit is the basic unit in parish society." Values, of course, may change or may be expressed in different ways. Harvey (1993), in a study of religious values, noted that the number of people showing no religious affiliation in Canada almost doubled between 1981 and 1991, yet the survey data showed that this did not mean a decline in spiritual values; people were merely fed up with mainstream churches as a vehicle for expressing these values. A problem with literacy is that some educators cannot admit that all others do not value literacy to the same degree and in the same way as they do. Literacy is associated with good and illiteracy with evil. Such values are promoted as slogans like "Open a school, close a jail" (Kandel, 1946) or "Illiteracy may not be a sin but it sure feels like hell." Kandel (1946: 346), writing just after World War Two, also reminds us that the Nazi onslaught on the world was not due to a lack of literacy or knowledge about people and nations. "In the choice between the ideas that knowledge is virtue and knowledge is power, the latter has too frequently prevailed in the national and international fields." Corbett (1982:153) cogently expresses a similar point about valuing literacy and the presumed status of the illiterate:

> I feel sorrow for what our young people will miss out on if they abandon books. But maybe they will find nirvana in other pursuits. If they do, they will have to experience that nirvana firsthand, rather than vicariously, through reading. I wonder if they will ever stand 'silent upon a peak in Darien,' as I have many times done while reading a book. 'Tis a pity. But we always think that people are to be pitied if they do not have what we have had. Maybe we can staunch our bleeding hearts by recalling that paradoxical maxim that we literate people have often read in print: 'Ignorance is bliss.' Wouldn't it be ironical if we were to discover that literacy, after all, is the source of all our woes?

PLACING A VALUE ON LITERACY

There is no doubt that respondents from all groups valued literacy highly, at least in saying that they did (see Table 11). However, it became obvious that valuing is not a dichotomous act; that is, it is not a question of valuing or not valuing but of valuing more or less. Values are prioritized. So while people may verbalize that literacy is important and in all honesty believe this, at times literacy may have to take second or third place to another activity of greater priority.

Table 11

Importance of Literacy to Me (percentage of people responding)

	Seniors	Mid-age Adults	Young Adults	Young Adults (high school)	Teachers	Youth
Very/most/ extremely	80.0	92.0	88.0	92.0	100	100
Important	16.0	8.0	12.0	8.0	—	—
No response	4.0	—	—	—	—	—

Table 12

Mean Ranked Values of Five Factors (Scale 1-5, 1 is highest)

	Seniors	Mid-age Adults	Young Adults	Young Adults (high school)	Teachers	Youth
Family	1.5	1.3	1.1	1.0	1.1	1.7
Work	3.7	2.8	3.0	2.9	2.6	3.7
Friends	2.9	3.2	3.0	3.5	3.3	3.0
Education	3.9	3.7	3.7	3.2	3.6	1.6
Religion	3.0	4.0	4.3	4.4	4.0	4.9

When the respondents were asked to prioritize the value of five factors/events in their lives (Table 12), education/literacy ranked third for young adults with high school, fourth for young adults without high school, mid-age adults, and teachers, and fifth for senior adults. Family, work, and friends, and for the seniors, religion, were more highly valued than education. Again, it is not that literacy is not valued; the data from Table 11 clearly show that it is, but there are only so many hours in a day, and days in a week, and when time must be allotted across several activities, other factors rank higher than education/literacy. The importance of family in western Newfoundland, as noted by Szwed (1987), was also true for the respondents of Bridget's Harbour. Family can be very extensive, including aunts, uncles, cousins, in-laws, and grandparents. Furthermore, while family members may move away from home to other parts of Canada or other countries, they do not sever family ties, and they retain bonds with home not just through letters, phone calls, and occasional visits, but also through being remembered on special occasions and in being sent local preserves, knitting, or crafts. When a person from the community who now lives in a city on the mainland goes home to visit his/her immediate family, it is common for that person to also visit the family of anyone from the community who lives near him/her in the mainland city. It is common when visitors return to carry items and packages to members of other families. Family support is evident in times of births, marriages, sickness, and death. Showers are held for expectant mothers, whether the mother-to-be lives in the community or has moved away to another part of Canada. Consequently, when a significant family event occurs, involvement with education, whether for children or adults, is likely to be "put on the back burner." For example, one parent said to a child: "Now, you won't have much time for your books this weekend [because an older son and his family were arriving from outside the province for a visit] so make sure you put them some place where you can find them for Monday morning."

In contrast to the other cohorts, the youth ranked education first, which is not unusual and is best understood in terms of context/circumstances. The students were interviewed at the end of the school year, the fishery had closed, and they had great concerns for their future. Education was seen as a possible means to their salvation. It is also interesting that for the young people, religion was placed very low on the scale, 4.9 out of 5.0. In fact, some students added that they would rather invest time in additional events, such as sports or TV, rather than in religion. This marks a difference between the youth and the seniors, who ranked religion third, and who regretted that religion was no longer, in their view, given the same emphasis in school as it used to be. They felt helpless as "the young crowd got away from us," meaning that their attempt to transmit their values was interrupted by other values. They singled out TV as having a significant influence on what people valued today and how they thought and acted. As one senior said, "It's that TV. The youngsters know more now that we did as adults. It has their heads turned completely around."

EXPERIENCES WITH LITERACY

All groups except teachers and high school students were asked if they had ever experienced difficulty with reading or writing. Less than 12 per cent of the mid-age adults and young adults with high school diplomas indicated they had experienced difficulty; however, 40 per cent of the other two groups of adults indicated that they had. When questioned about the nature of such difficulty, responses were about evenly divided between needing help with pronouncing words, spelling words, reading aloud with fluency, comprehending, engaging in specialized or technical writing, and, in the case of a few seniors, having forgotten how to write. When further questioned on whether reading/writing ability would prevent them from doing something, from 20 to 36 per cent of the four adult groups (teachers were not asked this question) thought lower skills may interfere with job opportunities or job competition. This percentage increased to 44 per cent for the high school students. All of the high school students expressed caution about the difficulty of programs in post-secondary institutions, especially at university, because they thought they would be challenged there by reading and writing demands. Approximately 28 per cent of the senior adults expressed some concern about the adequacy of their reading level for understanding what they read.

Seventy per cent and more of each group indicated they had at some point helped others with reading and/or writing. Children constituted a large percentage of those helped, but help was also extended to family and friends, a finding that supports the notion of collective literacy, although it must be kept in mind that collective literacy does not necessarily involve a supportive or helping situation. When asked if literacy affected their present lives, the groups responded as reported in Table 13.

Table 13

Does Reading Affect My Life? (percentage of people responding)

	Seniors	Mid-age Adults	Young Adults	Young Adults (high school)	Teachers	Youth
Yes	64.0	64.0	72.0	80.0	92.5	90.0
No	36.0	36.0	28.0	20.0	7.5	10.0

All groups, particularly the younger adults, teachers, and youth, agreed that literacy had an impact on their lives. When probed for the nature of this impact, except for 20 per cent of the senior adults who noted a negative impact (that is, thirteen people), literacy impacted their lives positively (see Table 14).

Table 14

How Reading Affects My Life (percentage of people responding)

	Seniors	Mid-age Adults	Young Adults	Young Adults (high school)	Teachers	Youth
*Work	4.0	20.0	20.0	28.0	66.6	7.4
*Recreation	8.0	20.0	4.0	16.0	37.0	18.5
*Enable learning	20.0	8.0	8.0	16.0	7.4	77.5
*Generally useful	8.0	32.0	32.0	20.0	7.0	40.7
*Help children with homework	—	—	16.0	32.0	7.0	3.7
*Keep in touch	4.0	4.0	4.0	—	11.1	—
**Inadequate skills	20.0	—	—	—	—	11.1

*denotes a positive outcome
**indicates a negative outcome.

Literacy was seen as useful for work, recreation, enabling learning, helping others, and maintaining interpersonal contact. The high school students viewed the influence of literacy more in terms of their school learning than in activities that have been termed functional in the literature.

When asked if literacy affected how they got along with others (see Table 15), while a significant number agreed that it did, the effect was more noticeable for the three groups possessing higher literacy skills. Literacy was seen to have a positive effect on interpersonal relationships, through writing letters, sharing in reading and writing (collective literacy), accessing information (news) for conversation and discussion, and sharpening one's communication skills.

SAYING AND DOING

Engaging in Literacy Activities

There is an old saying that the proof of the pudding is in the eating; likewise, the proof of an expressed value of literacy is engaging in literacy activities. The nature of involvement was expressed in a number of ways. The respondents were asked questions about their involvement in literacy activities; the questions and responses are reported in Tables 16 to 18.

Table 15

Does Reading and Writing Ability Affect How You Get Along with People? (percentage of people responding)

	Seniors	Mid-age Adults	Young Adults	Young Adults (high school)	Teachers	Youth
Positive effect	40.0	28.0	36.0	68.0	85.0	67.8
Negative effect	8.0	16.0	—	—	—	—
Somewhat	12.0	—	—	—	14.9	—
No	40.0	56.0	64.0	32.0	14.9	32.1

Table 16

Would You Read to Pass the Time? (percentage of people responding)

	Seniors	Mid-age Adults	Young Adults	Young Adults (high school)	Teachers	Youth
Yes	76.0	72.0	60.0	68.0	96.2	76.6
Read a book in the past month	36.0	44.0	28.0	44.0	59.2	50.0

The percentage of people who said they would read to pass the time ranged from 60 per cent for the young adults without high school to 96.2 for the teachers. However, when questioned on whether they had read a book for this purpose within the past month, the percentages were much lower. Except for the teachers and high school students, less that one-half indicated they had read a book. This response did not include the reading of magazines or newspapers. These data illustrate the relationship between saying and doing. While the respondents were no doubt sincere in saying that they would read a book to pass the time, other tasks usually consumed the time they would normally devote to reading. One woman explained:

> I don't know where a day goes. By the time I get the children off to school and get the house straightened up, it's dinner time [noon]. Then there is always an odd job like washing or baking to be done

and by that time the children are home from school and it's getting supper ready. Then after I get the small ones to bed and homework done with the others I'm too tired to read for myself and so I might watch television for a while.

People's preferences for language activities, as reported in Table 17, indicate that engaging in oral conversation greatly surpassed reading as a preferred activity, and for the three groups of less literate adults TV was also a higher priority. These findings are consistent with the data on values that indicated the high priority placed on family and family activities. Both conversation and TV involve interactions with or association with family members.

Table 17

Priority of Activities People Would Engage In (percentage of people responding)

	Seniors	Mid-age Adults	Young Adults	Young Adults (high school)	Teachers	Youth
Talking to people	48.0	72.0	72.0	68.0	62.9	73.3
Reading	24.0	16.0	16.0	24.0	40.7	13.0
TV	36.0	20.0	20.0	8.0	7.4	13.3

Table 18

Would You Enrol in a Program to Improve Your Reading/Writing? (percentage of people responding)

	Seniors	Mid-age Adults	Young Adults	Young Adults (high school)	Teachers	Youth
Yes	36.0	44.0	64.0	50.0	36.0	80.0
No	64.0	56.0	36.0	50.0	64.0	20.0
Why Not:						
Age/retired	64.0	20.0	12.0	—	—	60.0
Skills sufficient	—	28.0	24.0	42.0	60.0	—
No immediate need	—	—	—	8.0	—	—
Too busy	—	—	—	—	18.5	—
Not interested	—	—	—	—	—	20.0
Other priorities	—	—	—	—	—	20.0

Improving Literacy Skills

When asked if they would enrol in a program to improve their reading and writing, a sizeable percentage gave a positive response (Table 18). Figures were 64 per cent for the young adults without high school and 80 per cent for the high school graduates. Of those who indicated they would not enrol, the reasons usually indicated that they felt their literacy skills were adequate and therefore did not perceive a need. All of the seniors and 20 per cent of the mid-age adults indicated no need because, as they said, they were retired and did not see a function for increased literacy proficiency in their lives.

A second source of data on the "doing of literacy" came from observation and from logs that all interview respondents kept over the period of one week. While all who were interviewed or observed engaged to some degree in reading/writing, the degree of involvement ranged from minimal to extensive. For example, one adult from the seniors' group had read five books within the past six months (three best-sellers, two biographies), and was a regular subscriber and reader of *Time*, *National Geographic*, *Maclean's*, a local paper, a local newsletter, and the regional daily paper, while another senior reported not engaging in any reading at all.

A large proportion of people in Bridget's Harbour area enrolled in an adult upgrading program as part of the fisheries moratorium financial assistance agreement. The program is a standard ABE program consisting of three levels. Level 1 generally ranges from no to minimal literacy skills, while Level 3 involves working toward the completion of a high school diploma. Enrolling in this program was not always a question of the inherent value of or motivation for increased education since one of the assumed conditions for the financial assistance was that the recipients attend. However, for many individuals, interest in the program developed for a number of reasons. First, it occupied time that was now free since there was no work in the fishery, and in this way it helped participants deal with the additional free time they now had. Also, it was unlike the school organization they had known as children since there were smaller instructor-student ratios and a closer bond between instructor and student. There was also considerable flexibility in engaging in learning tasks over the course of a day; individuals indicated they were free to leave the classroom and go for a smoke or play pool. While the organization of the ABE program was unlike regular schooling, the subjects the students studied, except for computers, seemed strikingly familiar. Science, English, and math generally constituted the curriculum with the memorization of science facts and periodic testing being the norm. The tests became motivational for some students as they represented a challenge, and since they were an integral part of the education program they were therefore considered authentic as schooling (Myers, 1992). That is, they were perceived as essential within the school context and formed the basis upon which the participants measured their success within the school setting.

A big question, of course, is how this program was viewed in terms of its functionality, its attempt to meet specific goals, to provide for transition to jobs outside the fishery, or to re-enter the fishery (should it ever return) as professional fisherpeople. The program was viewed as traditional in nature, as similar to a school program in terms of functionality, that is, certification was the immediate goal which would then hopefully lead to something else. There was no immediate crossover of skills from the program to occupations, in spite of the fact that many of the recipients possessed considerable skill in various areas: plumbing, carpentry, cabinet-making, electrical work, cooking, crocheting, crafts, etc. The school program was oriented towards individual competition rather than to group support. In addition to studying basic school content, there were also guest speakers and field trips. Some respondents felt that their knowledge regarding the topics of guest speakers or the purpose of field trips was not always integrated with these activities, and they either did not get involved or did so (especially field trips) as an opportunity to "do something different." When there was an attempt at what appeared to be a functional application of literacy/education, this was derided by some, especially those who had been minimally involved in the program. One respondent, for example, questioned the practicality of a project in planting potatoes, particularly in light of the fact that the Irish had arrived in Bridget's Harbour and surrounding areas nearly 200 years previously and they and their descendants had continuously and successfully grown potatoes. Furthermore, as the respondent indicated, the potatoes from the experimental plot did not grow.

A key question on the minds of people was what difference would increased education of the people make in the community. The results of a query regarding this are given in Table 19. Only among the high school students, teachers, and seniors did more than one-half suggest that a high school diploma for all would result in change in the community. Sixty per cent or more of the mid-adult and young adult groups were not so convinced. Those who did not foresee a great impact on the community if all people were to obtain a high school diploma were constructing meaning for the question within their sociocultural context as they knew it. They could identify people who had a high school diploma, assess the potential of the area with respect to financial opportunity, narrate the interpersonal and social activities that were not dependent on education, and, consequently, come to this conclusion. There was a lot of realism in the responses of the people. As one person said, "Look at ___! Do you think that a diploma is going to made a big difference for her or for ___ or ___? It's not just the bit of education, it's so much bigger than that. A diploma is not going to make that big a difference."

Table 19

Expectation that a High School Diploma for All Would Change the Community (percentage of people responding)

	Seniors	Mid-age Adults	Young Adults	Young Adults (high school)	Teachers	Youth
Yes	56.0	32.0	32.0	28.0	55.5	66.6
No	44.0	60.0	68.0	72.0	37.0	32.4
Maybe	—	8.0	—	—	—	—
Don't know	—	—	—	—	7.5	—

Those ABE participants who did not choose to become mentally involved in the program (even though they may have made a physical appearance) were generally those who had not identified with schooling as children and who were far removed from the instructional expectations of memorization, homework, tests, and any other form of regimentation that reflected their earlier school experiences. They could not see a relationship between participating in the program and a "better life," and some chose not to live with this conflict and opted out of the program: "Now, look at me! I'm forty-seven. I've always managed quite well with the education I have. I'm not going any place so why am I up there [the adult learning centre] taking up space when I could be home doing my work and having a happier life for myself?"

Some, of course, did become involved and completed a high school certificate. Discussions with several of these suggested a number of reasons. Some, as suggested by Brock (1983), needed to regain confidence. They found themselves in a supportive environment with instructors who reached out to them, who were nice and caring compared to memories of teachers of their youth. As well, they were in the company of peers who congregated as social groups and through frequent testing they received constant feedback from their instructors.

Others saw the program, not as a vehicle for remediation, but for redemption (Smith, 1987). These individuals, as Smith pointed out, felt they had been inadequate in terms of social expectancies, and the attainment of a high school equivalency certificate would now give them a status with others in comparison to whom they had felt socially and educationally inferior. The goal of redemption was sometimes associated with a strong emotion of proving oneself, about showing that "I can do it."

Still another group viewed the program as another hope on the horizon. They reflected the history of Newfoundland in general, and of the region in particular. Historically, the area was marked by a series of ups and downs, and when down, people sought for hope – any glimmer of hope. This was tied to the spirit of survival, the refusal to give up regardless of the odds. While they could not narrate any close connection between what they learned in the program to a future job, they saw the school-leaving certificate as a "lifeline," as something they now had that they did not possess before, a resource that might at some point prove useful. The program represented a "stopgap measure," almost a "continuation of the fishery on hold."

A few respondents saw the completion of school and then a trade as a way out, an opportunity to move elsewhere to make a new start in life. However, few married people migrated out of the area. It was seen more as an opportunity for the younger generation, who were single, to get out and start a new life for themselves. In fact, married people were often upset at what they believed to be the government's hidden agenda to displace them from their community, as one letter to the editor indicated.

> Our reward for being exceptionally good at our trade and one of the best classes ever is a one-way trip to Upper Canada. We do applaud some of the instructors as they are professional people. We lay blame on those responsible for wasting our time and tax dollars in order to shuffle us off to other parts of this country. (*Evening Telegram*, 30 August 1994)

Goals and Needs

What the government intended in setting up educational programs for displaced fisherpeople and the goal(s) pursued by participants were not always compatible. In fact, it was not always clear what the goals of the government were; for example, the notion of professional fisherpeople (also advocated by the fisheries union) was most nebulous (this topic will be discussed in a later chapter). One respondent, summarizing a view held by others, stated that they could see no long-range plan on the part of the government, that the government merely assumed that educational upgrading would lead to jobs; however, they were appreciative of the fact that they were receiving financial assistance and if that meant attending the ABE program, they were not going to question the government's plan, long-term or not. "You don't look a gift horse in the mouth," said one adult.

It must be pointed out that the adult educational program in Bridget's Harbour, like many ABE programs, especially at Levels 2 and 3, was not literacy-based, although some work was done on English exercises and writing. In spite of a large number of respondents (Table 18) who said they would enrol in a program to increase their reading and writing ability, there seemed to be no emphasis on critical and evaluative reading and writing. Any reading taught at Level 1 appeared to be taught within a traditional school-based approach. According to respondents' descriptions, individual involvement, personal control, and empowerment did not seem to be fostered with respect to literacy. Consequent to the ABE program, another TAGS-sponsored project involved displaced fisherpeople in the discussion of the fishery closure and their future. This was criticized by a number of people. The plan seemed to come from outside the community, and was therefore directed from an external source and ended without an action plan. One man said that a big question for many fisherpeople was the role of draggers in a revived fishery, for draggers, they believed, were the main source of the fish stock depletion. They felt this issue needed to be addressed with input from the local fisherpeople and some sort of direction given or policy formulated. The "get-togethers" to talk about the fishery were viewed as another requirement for receiving financial aid rather than as having an impact on their immediate and future lives. As one woman said, "It's great for those who can rent (a building)" for this purpose.

LITERACY FOR OTHERS

The value of literacy may also be noted in terms of its recommended importance for others. When those interviewed were asked whether they would encourage students to finish high school rather than leave to take a good job, the majority of each respondent group were positive in their responses (Table 20). However, a significant minority placed more value on a job. The results are fairly predictable; over 90 per cent of the teachers recommended high school over a job, while almost one-third of the young adults who had not completed high school and who were without a job recommended the job. It is interesting that about 17 per cent of the high school students would have opted for the job rather than finish high school. Decisions to take advantage of a job are understandable when one considers the immediacy of the context, the current economic conditions, and the fact that a high school diploma is not a guarantee for work. This decision further illustrates how people interact with their environment in conceptualizing the significance of literacy and in operationalizing their value system.

Table 20

Would You Encourage Students to Finish High School Over a Good Job (percentage of people responding)

	Seniors	Mid-age Adults	Young Adults	Young Adults (high school)	Teachers	Youth
High school	84.0	80.0	68.0	76.0	92.5	83.3
Job	12.0	20.0	32.0	24.0	7.5	16.7
Not sure	4.0	—	—	—	—	—

A final question dealt with the relationship of leadership and literacy/education. Responses to this question of whether leaders are the most literate are given in Table 21. Significant percentages of each group (more than one-half of three groups) did not believe that leaders were more literate than the general population. The role of leadership varied across generations. The seniors remembered a time when leaders in the community and even in the province were few and clearly defined. They could readily name a person and say "He/she was a great leader." In the community, leadership had been provided by the parish priest, the doctor/nurse, and possibly a teacher. At the provincial level, the premier of the province was a recognized leader, as were the elected government representatives (MHAs – members of the House of Assembly) from the area. As one senior said about leaders, whether local or provincial, "If they were all of high calibre and all pulling together, you had something going for you." He and others narrated accomplishments under good leadership. A local priest stood out as the most significant leader in the memories of the seniors.

A problem with leadership is in getting sufficient support. Local history had it that an elected government member from the district at one time said that the problem in getting anything done in

Bridget's Harbour was that you could never get two people to agree on anything. For this reason, a priest who proved to be a strong leader was more successful because, being strong Catholic believers, "most would not go against the priest."

Table 21

Do You Agree that Leaders are the Most Literate? (percentage of people responding)

	Seniors	Mid-age Adults	Young Adults	Young Adults (high school)	Teachers	Youth
Yes	48.0	60.0	40.0	60.0	55.5	46.4
No	40.0	40.0	60.0	40.0	37.0	53.6
Not sure	12.0	—	—	—	7.5	—

However, younger generations did not have this experience and the role of leadership was now more diverse, with the leadership of priest and doctor/nurse being minimal, and unless teachers were involved in some form of community endeavour, they, too, were not perceived as providing leadership. It was difficult for people to identify current leaders. There was little agreement on who were recognized leaders of the community. A number of people occupied various roles in the community: councils, church organizations, crafts, charitable groups, and various agencies of the provincial government (usually with economic interests). Some of these positions were elected, yet as one person said, "You know who is going to get elected anyhow; it's always the same crowd."

A large percentage of the people viewed leadership/management as something removed from them; they (the people) were merely to accept the decisions. Some respondents, however, were critical of decisions made; one person, for example, discussed the waste of money and pointed to two swimming pools built at considerable cost and now "eyesores," because they were not maintained or were constructed in an area that was difficult for young people to reach. People seemed to have a fatalistic attitude towards leadership/management. One person felt that those in leadership positions were too bound by extended family ties to provide objective support and involvement for all members of the area – it all depended on "what crowd you belonged to." Faris (1973), in his ethnography of Cat Harbour, discussed the various meanings of the word "crowd," one of which, a negative connotation, was applied to particular families (usually across generations) and seemed to constitute a barrier to community cohesion if those in leadership did not relate well to a certain "crowd" regardless of the latter's constructive criticism or willingness to be involved.

The younger generations felt that leaders needed to be well educated and possess managerial and administrative skills as well as out-of-community experience. They preferred long-range (about five-year) action plans, rather than being subjected to *ad hoc* decisions, especially when these decisions involved the spending of money. "You need someone who has vision – someone who can put forth a plan of action for at least five years down the road. This would give us direction and hope; we need hope more than ever these days."

The people felt that the government was hypocritical in its leadership role in promoting literacy development. The general public, in their perception, was cast in an illiterate image, while somehow community and government leaders were assumed to be different from the general public in this regard. They felt that there should be courses (in-service sessions) for leaders. One person said that all the "hullabaloo" about professional fisherpeople should also be applied to leaders and that the government, instead of "throwing money on projects," should help the people come up with solutions to the problems in the area. The seniors felt that people were changing and that more and more were expecting money for anything that was done today, while in times past "people hove together and got the job done." Now there was too much reliance on the government and on money to get things started.

Respondents wanted a say in their future. They had lots of ideas and wanted to make these ideas known. But what they wanted more was for strong leadership to capitalize on these ideas to bring about positive change. They wanted leaders who were intelligent, understanding, supportive of the people, and, in particular, fair. When this did not happen, whether through civic or church leadership, many silently withdrew from any attempts at input and the only time their views were expressed was during "kitchen talk."

LITERACY/EDUCATION AS INVESTMENT

Valuing literacy was tied to one's definition of literacy, whether consciously expressed or through subconscious action. Certainly, literacy of a functional nature, including collective literacy, was valued. However, the doing of literacy of a collective nature was usually at a subconscious level. Respondents read and wrote for a number of reasons and some read extensively, including those with lower standards of literacy. At a conscious level, literacy was still defined from a traditional perspective: learning a myriad of basic skills, from symbol-sound relations to answering questions. While the fisheries education program was not literacy-based, it, too, was viewed in the same way as the literacy/education of schooling. A high school certificate was a ray of hope, something to "tide one over." When it had immediate value it was tied to the notion of social redemption, of having proven oneself within the social milieu and being no longer categorized among the uneducated. As a means to a job it had no immediate functional value; its value lay in its transition to something else. In the case of high school graduates it usually meant enrolling in university (profession) or joining a trade, and in the case of the adults it allowed one to enrol in a trade-preparation program or merely acted as a holding ground until the return of the fishery.

The youth were more concerned about the immediacy of life than about the immediate returns of literacy/education, although there was a connection. Premier Wells (at the time), who was interviewed on CBC radio in March, 1994, was asked by a caller what the purpose of retraining thousands of fisherpeople was when there were no jobs in the province. His reply was that retraining was for life. The questions are "What life?" and "Where will this life be lived?" These were the questions that most haunted the youth of Bridget's Harbour and, most likely, of many other Newfoundland communities.

SUMMARY

While writers have argued over the virtue of literacy, they have seemed to overlook the relationship between context and thinking and thinking and context. Given a particular and pertinent context, high-level thinking can go on regardless of literacy ability, while all kinds of thinking can go on with little or no applicability to real-life circumstances (lack of transfer). The context of school is different from the context of the community with respect to literacy, and the respondents perceived both as having very different roles. The context of the community that fostered collective literacy was associated with, and sometimes not distinguished from, oral language, a valued cultural form of communication. People without literacy usually exemplified intelligence and ingenuity, and not stupidity, a description often levelled by well-meaning but misguided literates. People make decisions, whether about literacy or other matters, in terms of their environmental context, their roles or position within that context, their present and future goals, and their relationships with others. The people of Bridget's Harbour exemplified this socio-cultural-individual relationship; their involvement in and their reflections on literacy were based on common sense. They distinguished the literacy of school from their literacy of use. Their literacy was immediate and task-oriented and usually occurred through interaction with others. They were not dysfunctional in terms of literacy use; in fact, it was impossible to distinguish the more literate from the less literate in this regard. Unfortunately, the academic upgrading of the displaced fishery workers was not always perceived as functional to their lives and some had difficulties conceptualizing this program in terms of their present and their future.

Values are prioritized, not dichotomized. While Bridget's Harbour respondents professed the importance of literacy in their lives, other values, such as family, took on a higher priority. Values influence motivation and involvement, and when there is only so much time in a day, people will only get involved in what they value most. The ranking of values is influenced by experience. The youth ranked education highest among a number of options. However, the youth were not greatly different from the other groups in their lack of literacy involvement, as indicated by one literacy act – reading a book within the past month. Oral language interaction and TV viewing were important to the respondents as these activities were usually intertwined with family socializing. As in most communities, the degree of involvement in literacy activities varied and was not always related to the literacy standards of the individuals.

While a significant minority indicated that at some time in their lives they had experienced difficulty with reading/writing, they did not perceive that this difficulty negatively influenced their lives to any degree. A larger rather than a smaller percentage felt that literacy had positively impacted their lives. The Bridget's Harbour respondents demonstrated considerable realism. They did not see that if everyone had a high school certificate this would necessarily mean change in the community. They knew the community, its past and present, its people, its resources, and its potential. They weighed their responses against a context with which they were familiar. Likewise, not all respondents, especially the young adult groups, would recommend literacy over a job opportunity. Fifty per cent or more of the young adults, however, would enrol in a literacy program. Currently, some of them were involved in an academic upgrading program, which was viewed from a variety of perspectives. To some it meant "school," even though there were many differences from how they had experienced school as children – from the organization of a day schedule to teacher-learner relationships. Yet, they were expected to memorize and write tests on information they did not immediately connect to their lives. For some, a high school equivalency certificate was a stepping-stone to a trade; to others, it was a passport for migration; and to others, high school equivalency became a matter of redemption, of proving oneself. Others were critical of the perceived non-relevancy of various aspects of the program or of related programs.

The relationships of literacy/education to expertise and effective leadership were not always that clear to the respondents. Some felt that there was a double standard on the part of the government in promoting campaigns to "save the illiterates" yet seemingly not investing in leadership training. Anyone who was willing to come forward seemed to be a "recognized" leader. They felt that without innovative, positive, action-oriented leadership, all the literacy in the world was not going to make a difference. The respondents, by and large, sought direction and were prepared to give their support. "We're more than willing to shove," said one man, "but we must have someone at the helm who's going somewhere."

Literacy: Will It Bring Work? 4

Government-sponsored literacy/education upgrading programs, like regular school programs, tend to have a "transition-to-work" agenda. School graduates are expected to go to work at some point and contribute to the economy. The TAGS-supported education program in Bridget's Harbour was also based on education for work, either inside or outside the fishery. A point, however, that has been debated for years is the relationship between literacy and work.

SENSE OF COMMUNITY

The community represents an important context in Newfoundland society (Faris, 1973; Szwed, 1987) and the economy is integral to the sense of community. Some people of Bridget's Harbour, when asked where they are from, will often reply "Bridget's Harbour proper," in this way emphasizing their identity with their community and distinguishing it from the neighbouring communities (Kerry's Path, Caplin Bight, etc.) that make up St. Bridget's parish.

Chantraine (1993:18) predicts that Newfoundland will survive the fishery crisis, largely on the basis of a strong sense of identity, community, and endurance passed down from generation to generation: "Each generation, following in the footsteps of their forebears, found happiness and fulfillment. Knowledge and wisdom were transmitted from old to young through families and through communities that were homogeneous and tightly knit, as if to withstand the cold." Being members of a community, "Newfoundlanders acquired not only strength, endurance, independence, and courage, but also the altruism, sense of community, equanimity, and humour they needed to survive in such harsh conditions" (Chantraine,

1993:28). However, conditions and people are changing and people in their mid-forties and older fear that the younger generation may not have acquired the values and strengths that Chantraine talks about. As one man in his late forties said, "Take me, for example, I can cope with difficult times. I grew up with difficult times. I grew up knowing how to do with little. But what about the young people coming up today? They weren't just born with the silver spoon in the mouth; they haven't taken it out yet."

People were asked to name the main sources of community income to determine their perceptions of their community from an economic standpoint. The results are given in Table 22.

Table 22

Main Sources of Community Income (percentage of people responding)

	Seniors	Mid-age Adults	Young Adults	Young Adults (high school)	Teachers	Youth
"The Package"	48.0	60.0	64.0	72.0	62.9	50.0
Unemployment Insurance	40.0	24.0	32.0	20.0	48.1	25.0
Fishery	24.0	28.0	16.0	16.0	18.5	14.3
Small business	4.0	—	—	—	—	—
Social Assistance	4.0	—	—	—	7.4	3.6
Teaching/ professional	4.0	—	—	—	11.1	—
Pensions	—	—	—	—	3.7	—
Hibernia	—	—	—	—	—	3.6

"The Package," the name given the financial assistance arising from the cod fishery moratorium, constituted the main source of income according to the majority of the people. This was followed by unemployment insurance (UI) and the fishery (for species other than cod). Reactions to the sources of income were mixed and varied by group. The four adult groups (excluding teachers) thought that "The Package" was a good thing to tide people over. As one person said, "That's all there is so we can't complain." A significant number of the teachers and youth were more disparaging in their comments and considered it as another form of welfare or government dependency. About 20 per cent of the four adult groups and 50 per cent of the teachers thought of it as only a short-term solution; however, about

30 per cent of the youth discussed the corollary to this, that there was a need for long-term planning. One youth said, "You just can't live year by year without knowing what's going to come next. And even if you can't know exactly what the future holds, you can have different [contingency] plans." All groups specified the need for a more diversified economy.

When asked to indicate the most pressing needs for the province and the community, a range of responses resulted. These are listed in Tables 23 and 24.

Table 23

Most Pressing Need in Newfoundland (percentage of people responding)

	Seniors	Mid-age Adults	Young Adults	Young Adults (high school)	Teachers	Youth
Employment/ economy	100	96.0	96.0	100	92.5	76.6
Education	4.0	4.0	—	8.0	14.8	26.6
Fishery	4.0	8.0	—	—	—	10.0
Self-initiative/ self-reliance	—	4.0	—	—	7.4	—
Health care	—	—	4.0	—	7.4	—
Child care	—	—	8.0	—	—	—
Government assistance	—	—	4.0	—	—	3.3
Resource management	—	—	—	—	7.4	—

In spite of the range of responses, the message was clear – the most pressing need, both provincially and locally, was employment. A significant minority of the youth (26.6 per cent and 16.6 per cent for provincial and community needs, respectively) felt there was a need for a better education system.

When respondents were asked for their suggestions as to how these needs could be met (Table 25), again the responses were clear – more government investment in creating jobs and effective leadership. These seemed to go hand in hand, as some respondents spoke of job-creation programs that seemed to spend too much money on administration and management and too little on creating jobs. All such programs were seen as make-work projects or stopgap measures that provided minimal pay and were usually tied to "topping-up" UI without any relationship to permanence and productivity.

Table 24

Most Pressing Need in Community (percentage of people responding)

	Seniors	Mid-age Adults	Young Adults	Young Adults (high school)	Teachers	Youth
Employment	84.0	88.0	88.0	92.0	74.0	73.3
Good water supply	16.0	12.0	24.0	12.0	7.4	—
Fishery	4.0	4.0	—	—	—	3.3
Health services	4.0	—	—	4.0	3.7	—
Co-operation	—	4.0	8.0	4.0	—	6.6
Public Library	4.0	—	—	—	3.7	—
Recreation facilities	—	—	16.0	—	7.4	6.6
Better education system	—	—	—	—	11.1	16.6
Self-initiative/ positive attitude	—	—	—	—	7.4	—
Move away from UI dependency	—	—	—	—	3.7	—
Drug and alcohol control	—	—	—	—	—	6.6
Wise use of package income	—	—	—	—	—	3.3

LITERACY AND WORK

While there was no doubt in the minds of the people of Bridget's Harbour that the most pressing need, both at the provincial and community level, was opportunity for work, they did not perceive a straightforward relationship between literacy/education and work. The literacy/education-work relationship is also a controversial issue for many literacy/education experts.

Literacy Levels and Work

A number of people argue that there is no direct relationship between literacy/education and work (Blaugh, 1985; Wagner, 1987). This argument takes two forms: (1) people out of work is more a matter of the economy than it is of education, and (2) levels of education do not equate with job demands. Regarding the first point, Verne (1981: 299) maintains that jobs come first and then the required education: "Education neither creates jobs, nor does it possess the power of conjuring them out of thin air. The main cause of unemployment and of underemployment lies in the existence of more workers than jobs for them." With regard to level of education and job requirements, a major question is who decides what level of education shall be necessary for what job and how this is decided. If one wishes to become a medical doctor, certainly a grounding in physiology, biology, etc. is necessary, and for a carpenter a certain level of mathematical skill is essential. But what level of English and math and science and social studies knowledge is necessary for a painter, janitor, road repair person, garbage collector, home decorator, nursing assistant, groundskeeper, taxi driver, dishwasher, or fisherperson? While technology on one hand makes more demands for improved education, on the other hand it reduces the need for literacy and math skills; for example, cash registers in some outlets are coded in terms of the items served.

Table 25

How Can Needs Be Met? (percentage of people responding)

	Seniors	Mid-age Adults	Young Adults	Young Adults (high school)	Teachers	Youth
Government invest more money	28.0	84.0	56.0	36.0	51.9	40.0
Good leadership	24.0	20.0	20.0	28.0	11.1	13.3
Spend money more wisely	8.0	—	4.0	8.0	7.4	3.3
Private sector become more involved	16.0	8.0	8.0	12.0	22.2	6.6
Co-operative effort	—	16.0	16.0	12.0	7.4	20.0
Education/training programs	—	—	4.0	16.0	29.6	16.6
Changes in attitude of youth	—	—	—	—	18.5	—
Raise taxes	—	—	8.0	—	—	—
Other	4.0	—	—	8.0	7.4	6.6

The grade level chosen as a prerequisite or as entry level into a job is often arbitrary. Sticht (1987: 297-98) gives an example; at a correctional institution, a reading test score at the sixth-grade level was required for entry into the shoe repair training program, while an eighth-grade reading score was required for those who intended to enrol in mechanical drawing. The fallacy of a particular grade level for a certain job was forcefully made in a military experiment described by Braddock (1967). One hundred thousand men with lower than required educational standards were admitted to the American army. These recruits were in competition with those who had the required or higher than required entrance educational levels. Yet at the end of the program, 94.5 per cent or 94,500 of the men had successfully completed the program. In fact, in a U.S. court case challenging the requirements of a certain grade level for a particular job (*Griggs vs. Duke Power Co.*, 1971), the Supreme Court ruled that if literacy tests were to screen applicants for a particular job, the employer must show that the literacy standards clearly relate to the job requirements. Mikulecky (1985) indicates that research has since supported that decision and that workers often score from one to two grade levels higher when reading from job-related materials than from general passages on which they are tested. One wonders when a Canadian citizen will challenge the relationship of educational requirements and job selection in this country!

Heath (1980) points out that a number of studies have challenged the literacy-work relationship. She indicates that the absence of a direct relationship was true in eighteenth-century England and is true today. One reason for the lack of a direct relationship is that many other behaviours, such as those related to moral values and social norms, are often considered more important than education. Blaugh (1966: 405) reminds us that the higher earnings of the more literate do not just simply reflect their level of reading/writing expertise but also "their endowed intelligence, native ability, achievement drive, home background, and possibly their enhanced capacity to benefit from work experience and from training on the job."

The responses of the Bridget's Harbour interviewees were consistent with the points made in the literature about the literacy /education-work relationship. The question asked and a summary of the responses are given in Table 26. Approximately three-quarters or more of all groups, except the youth group, were aware through real-life experiences that education does not necessarily bring work. When questioned about why this was so, the overwhelming reply was that there were too few jobs. A variety of responses given by a smaller number of people included: too many people trained in a particular skill (carpentry, beautician, etc.), unwilling to move, becoming discouraged in job search, overqualified, and do not have the right connections.

Table 26

Do You Know People with a Good Education and No Work? (percentage of people responding)

	Seniors	Mid-age Adults	Young Adults	Young Adults (high school)	Teachers	Youth
Yes	84.0	72.0	84.0	76.0	80.0	56.0

The corollary question to that in Table 26 and the results appear in Table 27.

Table 27

Do You Know People without High School Who Made/Make a Good Living? (percentage of people responding)

	Seniors	Mid-age Adults	Young Adults	Young Adults (high school)	Teachers	Youth
Yes	88.0	80.0	72.0	76.0	85.2	56.6

The results were very similar to those for the previous question. When asked why less educated people would have jobs when educated people were idle, there were two major responses. The first indicated that some people had learned on the job, were quick to pick up skills on their own, and had acquired meaningful experiences; the second focused on people having drive, persistence, and perseverance. As one woman said, "When it comes to jobs, my son, they don't come knocking on your door."

Table 28

Would a Person with Most Education Have First Chance at a Job? (percentage of people responding)

	Seniors	Mid-age Adults	Young Adults	Young Adults (high school)	Teachers	Youth
Yes	44.0	36.0	36.0	20.0	22.2	60.0
No	52.0	56.0	64.0	80.0	74.1	40.0
Possibly	4.0	8.0	—	—	3.7	—

A further question was: All other things being equal, would an educated person and a less educated person have the same chance for a job? The results are shown in Table 28.

Except for the youth, a majority in each group did not believe that education was the sole criterion for getting a job. The percentage thinking so rose to 75 per cent for teachers and 80 per cent for the young adults who had completed high school. The reasons behind their thinking were as follows:

(1) *It depends on the experience a person has.* One woman commented, "St. Paul said, faith without good works, is dead; well education without some experience is just as dead."

(2) *"Connections, b'y, connections.* You have to know the right people. I can name people who have gotten good jobs and it's all because they knew someone, they had someone putting in a good word for them." The respondent narrated specific examples, and it was amazing that the "connections network" was so complex. Having a contact on the "inside" was certainly an advantage. Current workers, usually in administrative positions, often alerted family (extended family) to upcoming opportunities, and these people were then able to capitalize on future initiatives. This was especially noted in reference to capitalizing on funds for educational projects under TAGS. It was also interesting that in spite of the decline of the power of the Catholic Church, church connections were still perceived as of great significance in getting jobs and promotions, especially in the education system.

(3) *People were overqualified* for the jobs that were available. "You wouldn't really expect a university graduate to gut fish!"

(4) *Personality, interpersonal relations.* This was mentioned by over one-half of the youth group and was seen as a significant factor for job interviews. "She might have the education, but there's not much else in her head but herself" was one description of why an educated person might be rejected in favour of a less well-educated person at the interview stage.

(5) Finally, from a local perspective, *make-work programs were often put into place to help the less fortunate*, the less educated, to qualify for UI or to top-up current UI income. Respondents felt that these jobs went to the less educated because of special need. However, there was no negativism connected with this. They actually phrased this as the less educated being given a necessary priority in terms of job opportunity.

When asked to think of a person's best chance for a job, the responses of all groups were similar, except for emphasis placed on different characteristics by the high school students. The profile of the best job prospect, with qualities in order of most to least often cited, was:

- educated
- experienced
- connections
- positive attitude/pleasant personality
- energetic/determined
- self-confident

The high school students placed more emphasis on education compared to other groups. All the students included education; this was 12 per cent more than for the teachers, who rated it next highly, and 32 per cent more than for the young adults with high school. The students had not yet had experience in looking for a job and finding out that education alone is not enough. The youth group also placed more emphasis on attitude/personality in comparison to the other groups. Ogbu (1987) emphasizes that in each community there is a folk theory of how to get ahead. If this includes the importance of factors other than education, such as knowing the right people, then convincing school graduates that education alone will ensure employment is difficult. Another fallout from the folk theory of success is that it is difficult for parents who "have made it" without education to motivate their children that education is the key to success. Or perhaps, even worse, if parents and relatives can manage successfully on government-sponsored assistance, there is little motivation for the younger generation to believe that this will not work for them. A follow-up survey of youth between the ages of eighteen and twenty on the west coast of Newfoundland, sponsored by the Port au Port Economic Development Association and Canada Employment Centre (1983:18), concluded that "Attitudes toward employment are developed in early childhood and adolescence, with youth responding to what they experience through their parents' work habits." Basically, those who had been exposed to models of full-time and committed working parents showed strong and positive attitudes towards employment, while those from homes where social welfare and UI were the main sources of income expressed a very negative attitude towards full-time employment and were content to work only the minimal amount of time to qualify for UI benefits.

Galtung (1981) explains that the economic sector sorts people through "division of labour"; the lowest sector includes people who extract something directly from nature (such as fisherpersons), the second level includes those who process it, and the highest level involves the distribution and administration of the whole process. Countries or regions that are much involved in the primary sector (as was Newfoundland prior to the fisheries moratorium) will have difficulty finding jobs for the better educated and hence they will move away to other regions. An analysis of Statistics Canada data by Norris, Phillips, and Bulcock (1992) showed this to be happening in the case of Newfoundland. It explained why educational standards, compared to those in mainland Canada, were lower in Newfoundland.

Kirsch and Guthrie (1977/78) argue that functional literacy should be distinguished from functional competency. Functional competency may include functional literacy but includes many other skills and abilities as well, particularly metacognition or the ability to size up a situation, to be aware of tasks to be completed, the role of other participants, and the most effective strategies for getting the job done. Research by Norton (1992) on workers with a range of levels of literacy competency confirmed the importance of metacognition in job performance. Wagner (1987: 12) concluded that "the intellectual tide is turning against those who argued that universal literacy would have important economic outcomes."

Overall, the people of Bridget's Harbour were quite realistic about the job situation and about the role of education in getting a job. Education alone was never seen as a job ticket; many other factors had to enter the picture, and these factors sometimes could be more empowering than education itself. The relationship between literacy and work is best summed up by Ogbu (1981), who said that education is no longer a panacea for job-seekers but it expresses hope. This is how many adults in Bridget's Harbour interpreted the high school certificate they obtained via the TAGS-sponsored adult education program.

Literacy/Education Costs and Work Benefits

Windham (1991) points out that if literacy/education programs are to be considered an investment in the economy (leading to work) then the relationship of benefits to costs must be calculated. Cost of literacy/education programs as an investment for employment was uppermost in the minds of the people of Bridget's Harbour and elsewhere in Newfoundland, as reported in the media. Many talked about the cost to taxpayers of providing an adult education program in the community as a result of rent charged by the building's owners, the cost of teachers, and the cost per student, which several people believed to be $75–$80 per day for each person in attendance. According to reports, the number of private institutions offering adult education programs jumped from one, prior to the TAGS money, to over 100 by 1995.

Blaugh (1966) provides a diagram for analysing benefits and costs of education programs. A modified form is reproduced in Figure 1.

Figure 1: Estimating Educational Benefits and Costs

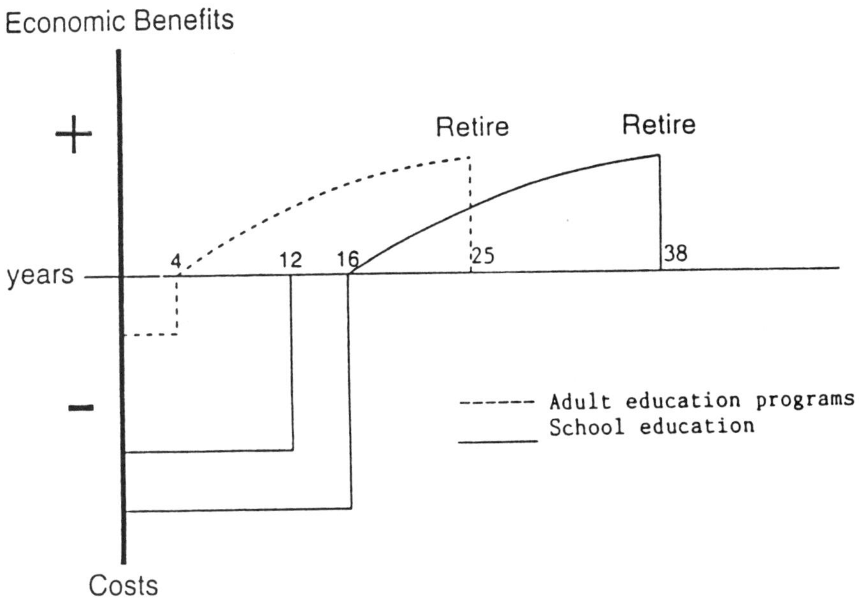

Source: Adapted from Blaugh (1966).

The first three figures on the left of the horizontal axis represent number of years in school/trades instructional program, that is 4, 12, or 16, while the two figures following (25 and 38) indicate the number of years in the workforce after school. The years in school /trades instructional program and in the workforce for adults are shown by a broken line and for regular school students by a solid line. The example for the adult is for a four-year education/trades program. It is assumed that the age of the adult at the end of this time is thirty-five years, and this person will spend about twenty-five years in the workforce after the program before retirement (assuming a retirement age of sixty). It is assumed the cost per year for the adult education program per person is $3,000 and the average salary for the time in the workforce is $30,000. The second example focuses on a high school student who after completing grade 12 would then go on to university for an additional four years (that is, 16 years of schooling in all); the mean age at that time would be 22. Suppose the cost per year for regular schooling is $5,000 and the mean salary for the university graduate is $45,000. As in the case of the adult, the retirement age is sixty. The costs and benefits for the high school student and for the adult are calculated as follows:

High School Student		
Benefits:	$45,000 X 38 =	$1,710,000
Costs:	$5,000 X 16 =	$80,000
Gain:	$1,630,000	
Adult		
Benefits:	$30,000 X 25 =	$750,000
Costs:	$3,000 X 4 =	$12,000
Gain:	$738,000	

These, of course, are not actual costs and salaries, but they do reflect differential expenditure on school versus adult programs and different income based on level of education attained and years worked. Certainly, the net gain of investing in a regular school program is greater than that for an adult education/trades instructional program for the two examples given. Nevertheless, there is a substantial gain for adult education investment, especially when one considers what the alternative may be – unemployment and social welfare.

Of course, the above examples assume that employment follows the completion of a program. Without such employment, the cost-benefit relationship changes and results in a loss to taxpayers. Concerns were being raised by "trainees" in programs funded under the TAGS agreement. Reports in the St. John's *Evening Telegram* on 20 and 22 August 1995 document the story of two former fishplant workers (there were ten people in the project) who were being retrained to make seat-belts for dogs but felt they had attained little training. The amount of funding under TAGS was $175,000, although it was not clear if this covered other costs. When contacted, the TAGS program consultant, according to the newspaper reporter, stated that TAGS does not run such projects. Rather, it supplies funding to someone to provide a product on its behalf. The report further indicated that the consultant would "probably" talk to the two trainees "but certainly I wouldn't characterize it as an investigation." This incident also raises the issue of accountability of tax dollars for educational/training programs.

A cost-benefit model of adult literacy/education is an essential part of the human capital model, which Becker (1975: i) defined as "the present value of past investments in the skills of people." A human capital model or cost-benefits model of adult literacy/ education raises two important issues. (1) It is difficult to calculate simple and straightforward benefits to costs since literacy/education does not necessarily lead to employment – a point repeatedly noted by the Bridget's Harbour respondents. Assessing the value, or even identifying all the other factors that impinge on this relationship, is difficult, if not impossible; some factors that might intervene in the education-work equation have been discussed in previous pages. (2) The human capital model assumes that the only goal of literacy/adult education is employment; this overlooks the many other benefits that may accrue from increased literacy/education and benefits not easily assessed in monetary value.

NATURE OF LITERACY/EDUCATION PROGRAMS

While the conclusion from the literature and from those participants in academic upgrading/trade skills programs in Bridget's Harbour is that there is not a direct relationship between these programs and work, it is important to note that this conclusion is drawn from programs that exemplify a traditional school definition of literacy /education. The expected direction of the relationship to work within this definition of literacy is given in Figure 2. This model of adult education-work relationship is based on the belief that adults must acquire academic knowledge first, usually leading to a GED or school-leaving diploma *before* they can enrol in a trade/skills instructional program that hopefully will lead to work. The diploma becomes the passport to entry into the trade/skills instructional program. The fact that knowledge attained as part of the academic program may be irrelevant to the chosen trade is ignored. Sticht (1987: 298) comments on this model: "A difficulty with the great majority of literacy and technical vocational training programs is that they view literacy and technological knowledge acquisition as two different things. Literacy is something one must first get and then apply to the learning of job technical skills; in fact, nothing could be farther from the truth."

When the Bridget's Harbour respondents were asked if they would enrol in a trade/skills instructional program, their decisions per group ranged from 4 per cent for the seniors to 96 per cent for the two groups of young adults. The percentage for the mid-age adults was 52, for the teachers, 67, and for the youth, 37. It is understandable why the percentage for the seniors was minimal, since they have all passed retirement age; this was also the situation for many of the mid-age adult group. While a fairly large percentage of the teachers responded positively their decision was in terms of having a useful skill around their homes. Most of the youth aspired to university/professional careers, or to merely leaving the province and hoping for the best of what the future might bring. Of the two young adult groups, 96 per cent indicated that they would enrol in a trade/skills instructional program; these groups are of an employable age and would like some security in terms of future employment. The skills/trades in which they professed interest included:

carpentry	cooking
nursing	accounting
surveying	business
home decorating	crafts
secretarial	sewing
computer	electrical
plumbing	welding
draftsman	civil engineering
travel agent	medical/lab assistant
homecare worker	heavy equipment
cosmetology	service industry (hotels, etc.)

However, while such a vast majority aspired towards a trade and employment, some were not always sure that it would come after having attained the academic qualifications first (a school-leaving certificate). This was because even though they realized that the academic qualifications were a requirement, they found it difficult to apply themselves to schooling and study when they did not always see a direct relationship between what they learned in academic programs and what they would study for a trade/skill. As one said:

> Like today, we studied the movement of the planets. We had a guest speaker on AIDS last week and two weeks ago we went on a field trip to Pine Cove to see how they grew potatoes. We mess around with computers. I'd like to be a welder but I don't know why I must be doing what I am doing now to get there.

Figure 2: Traditional Adult Literacy/Education Programs and Work Relationships

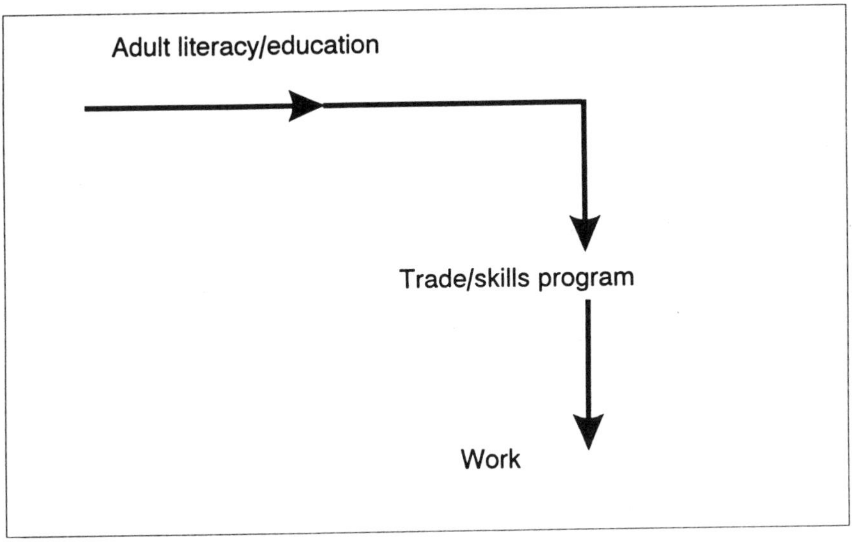

They would have liked to circumvent this route but were not aware of any other model. While alternative models are few, they do exist or can, in many instances, be put into place.

Adult Literacy-Education/Trade Instruction

Sticht (1987) emphasizes the key element in the success of any program (literacy, academic, technical) is its meaningfulness. When something is seen as *directly* meaningful to a person's life, he/she will become involved. What people decide to do on their own time is based on meaningfulness. This rationale has been used as an argument for a model of integrated adult literacy/education-trade/skills instructional programs. The form of this model, in contrast to the traditional model (Figure 2) is presented in Figure 3.

The integration of academic knowledge and trade/skill instruction is suggested by the wavy lines. Both sets of information are taught concurrently and interactively. If a person has difficulty recognizing certain words that pertain to welding, for example, the appropriate word study skills would be taught during the course on welding. How to use manuals, follow directions, assess a problem area and attain more information, complete appropriate forms, and contact proper authorities in regard to regulations would be taught interrelatedly with the technical aspects of welding. Fox and Powell (1990: 20) highlight the value of an integrated model: "If literacy is linked to vocational education, adults can learn to read and write at the same time as learning a skill they can use to make money." Sticht (1987) states that there is no reason why basic literacy/ education skills cannot be learned along with technical knowledge, rather than being prerequisites, while Reder (1987: 264) argues a much stronger point, "that literacy develops spontaneously among adults in response to preceived needs for new literacy capabilities."

Figure 3: An Integrated Model of Adult Literacy/Education-Trade/Skills Instructional Program

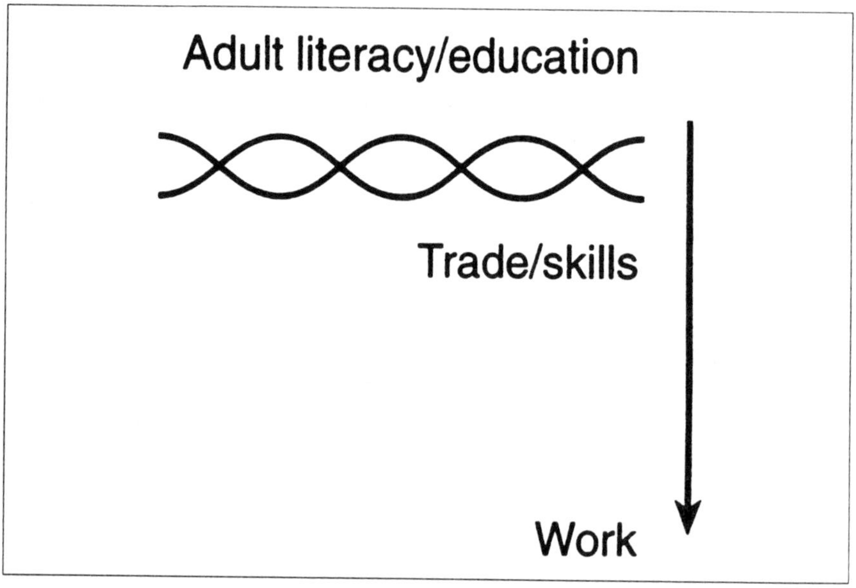

The notion of workplace/occupational literacy has been around for some time and is often based on an integrated model. Occupational literacy is generally defined as the ability to read and write required work-related materials. Research has shown that the kind of reading and reading materials in a job situation are different from those in academic programs. The kinds of reading in the workplace are generally of three types: *reading-to-do,* or following directions (Diehl, 1980; Siefert, 1979; Sticht *et al.*, 1977); *reading-to-learn,* or acquiring new information (Sticht *et al.*, 1977); and *reading to assess the need for more in-depth reading* (Diehl and Mikulecky, 1980). Each of these kinds of reading involves particular strategies. For example, Siefert (1979) points out that reading-to-do involves search and location strategies, while reading-to-learn requires storing information for later recall and involves such strategies as rereading, rehearsal, problem-solving, questioning, relating/associating, and focusing attention. Reading to assess the need for more in-depth reading includes the strategies of synthesizing, problem-formulating, and hypothesis-generating. In addition to reading /writing demands, there are also specific oral language needs (on-the-job speaking). In many work situations, talking between co-workers in regards to what is to be done is of great significance (Diehl and Mikulecky, 1980). With regard to work-related materials, Rush, Moe, and Storlie (1986) noted that such materials are usually expository in nature or are in descriptive prose. Also, considerable information is presented in chart and graph form. The implication is that different materials require the use of different visual and organizational strategies.

One approach that workplace literacy specialists have adopted is to conduct a task analysis of the required on-the-job reading and writing, the nature of this reading and writing, and the type of text material, and then to develop a program focused on helping the worker attain appropriate strategies to accomplish these tasks. A task analysis would include not only an analysis of tasks, of reading and writing demands, and of materials, but also would involve talking to supervisors and managers regarding the pertinency of such tasks. Work-related reading materials have often been analysed in terms of their level of difficulty on the basis of readability formulas. Rush, Moe, and Storlie (1986) mapped the literacy requirements of a number of occupations in terms of average daily reading time, type or form of material read, prose style, readability level, nature of reading required, and the frequency of the literacy demands. For example, they showed that an auto mechanic typically reads technical references, memos, and work orders for about sixty minutes a day, mainly to learn for future use and to do particular tasks; the difficulty of the reading materials ranges from grade 10 to college graduate. A machine tool operator, on the other hand, typically reads manuals, handbooks, checklists, and memos for an average of thirty-six minutes daily, mainly to carry on the job; the difficulty of the reading materials ranges from grade 9 to college graduate. This kind of knowledge should help program developers plan a meaningful experience for the participants.

A task analysis cannot narrowly focus on the trade or task. The importance of context has also been noted in trade/vocational programs. Sticht (1987), for example, noted that technical training may not always focus on the most productive aspects of the skill/occupation. He showed that in a course for electronics technicians an extensive amount of time was spent on circuit problems and that knowledge of circuits was a major factor leading to successful troubleshooting on the job. Yet, when the troubleshooting behaviour of highly capable versus less capable technicians was studied, a major problem for the less capable group was that they could not very well identify the basic components – the electronic parts or various pieces of equipment – and, therefore, had difficulty in isolating the fault. Furthermore, the less capable technicians had less well-developed problem-solving skills, did not always make complete or appropriate use of prior knowledge, were poor in generating hypotheses, and did not always know how to confirm or disconfirm hypotheses (hunches); they were less flexible in their approach and kept trying one way, not knowing when to switch to another plan. In essence, they lacked metacognitive knowledge.

Gowen (1992), who conducted an ethnographic study of employees in a large hospital, cautions that how supervisors and management conceptualize literacy work-related tasks does not necessarily correspond to how the workers understand them. The practicality of the workers must be weighed against the beliefs of management. A written document by management does not necessarily reflect how things actually are done. Therefore, how the workers perform tasks must also be understood. Prior knowledge must be taken into account, especially in interpreting the readability level of materials, for as Sticht (1988/89) showed, when *job-related knowledge* was taken into account the estimates of general reading skills needed to comprehend the job reading materials could be reduced by five grade levels, from the eleventh to the sixth grade.

The importance of job-related knowledge is usually underestimated in trade/skills instructional programs. Making allowances for such knowledge can enhance these programs, especially when based on an integrated model. Such a model was endorsed by UNESCO (Blaugh, 1966). Verne (1981: 293) believes that "adult education tends to disqualify people by devaluing experience and acquired knowledge." All entrants to a trades instructional program are often judged to be at the same level of knowledge with respect to the trade they have elected to study. The success of an integrated adult education/trades instructional program has been proven in the experiment in which 100,000 academically underqualified men were admitted to the U.S. military. Braddock (1967), in describing that program, indicated that the trade to be learned was broken down step by step in terms of procedural information and this knowledge *together with the necessary reading and writing skills* was taught in an integrated fashion. In this way what would have been a school or traditional type of program became functional in nature (Lytle, 1991); it was meaningful to the adults since they could see an immediate relationship between academic knowledge (general literacy skills) and the trade they had chosen to learn.

An integrated model would be appropriate for Newfoundland adults whose goal is to enrol in a trades instructional program. A survey of the respondents in Bridget's Harbour, for example, showed that 15 per cent of the young adults felt competent in plumbing and 12 per cent in electrical work. If these adults could enrol directly in a trades instructional program in these areas, and any necessary reading/writing skills were taught simultaneously and in direct relationship to the trade tasks, the program would be more motivational and the likelihood of success greater.

Work-Focused Model

The third model of academic-trade-related success may be termed the work-focused model and is represented in Figure 4.

Figure 4: The Work-Focused Model for Adult Education Programs

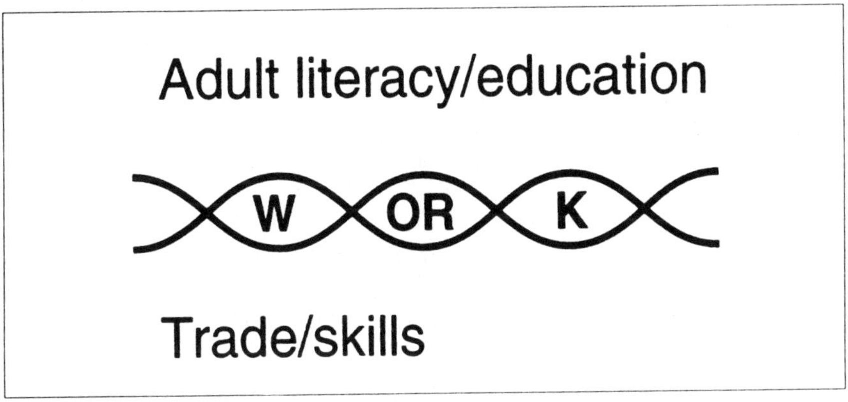

To a large extent this represents the kind of training/learning that existed in most of rural Newfoundland and in other rural regions of the country in years gone by. There was no "program" as such. Trade skills were learned in informal settings and without pay. While academic skills were not taught directly, a person usually learned a trade in "association with" or in the "company of" family, friends, or neighbours. The learner might be considered an apprentice. It was not uncommon for someone to be building a house or boat and for people to just drop by and begin to help. Through direction and observation they "picked up" the trade. It was in this manner that skills such as carpentry, plumbing, electrical work, small engine repair, cooking, baking, sewing, crocheting, knitting, etc. were learned. While academic (literacy) skills were not taught in this context, those necessary to understand the trade were often readily picked up.

Lave and Wenger (1991) pursue this concept of learning at great length and refer to it as "legitimate peripheral learning." They maintain that one reason why this model was so successful is that the learner had a sense of context in which the learning occurred. The learner was immediately aware of and worked alongside other practitioners, including the master practitioner, knew what the constructed object was going to look like when finished (boat, house, socks, etc.), and understood its function or use. The focus was not on changing the individual (which often reflects the orientation of most formal programs) but on inviting the learner to participate in a meaningful activity. There was also the motivation of participating with others and of benefiting not just from the "instruction" of the masters, but from peers who were also apprentices. This learning led to a sense of identity, for as Lave and Wenger (1991:115) state, "learning and a sense of identity are inseparable. They are aspects of the same phenomenon." The apprentices saw themselves growing into the roles of housebuilders, mechanics, or cooks. The context provided an immediate basis for self-evaluation. There were no tests, no praise or blame, but an acceptance into the identity of a role as determined by the actions and behaviours of the masters who decided when and how to allow the apprentices to share in the various tasks and responsibilities.

It is perhaps unfortunate that rather than promoting the learning of trades in informal situations when possible, the learning of such skills has been institutionalized and is often made less accessible to those interested. The tendency of government or government sponsored programs such as TAGS to institutionalize or over-institutionalize was greatly criticized by the Bridget's Harbour respondents. One such program involved discussions of the current situation and future prospects. Rather than shaping this program so the people could engage in these discussions in contexts within which they felt most comfortable – across back fences, during chance meetings on the road, in the kitchen, or in any of the many other meeting places (shopping, medical clinic, church functions, social functions) – the organizers rented a particular building and required the people to go there and talk. While institutionalizing skills programs often ensures their availability (learning as an apprentice in an informal context requires knowing someone who is using the skill and is willing to share), it takes away the responsibility of teaching and learning certain skills from a community-focused setting and puts the learning process into a less meaningful context. Furthermore, once the pattern of learning from one's mother, father, relative, or neighbour has been broken, it is difficult to return to that form of behaviour.

A limitation of an informal work preparation model is that it depends on a certain kind of activity occurring in the community. While people still build houses, including the carpentry, plumbing, electrical work, and masonry, and while they cook, hunt, and fix cars, some skills are becoming less common, whether through lack of need (such as boat-building, or even fishing) or through the availability of a competitive commercial product (such as bread-making). It would be possible for agencies to sponsor work preparation models for adult education programs. A good example of an opportunity for an appropriate context is that through the TAGS economic arrangement, a certain rate per hour was paid to employers if they hired displaced fisherpersons. It would be easy to co-ordinate such a work situation with the learning of a necessary trade and with the teaching of necessary academic skills for fisherpersons to qualify for a trades certificate.

If the relationship of education to job preparation and the economy is to be improved, then models for adult education/trade skills programs must be changed, as must the very nature of work in some instances, particularly the fishery. Verne (1981) maintains that in areas with unemployment and underemployment, there must be a restructuring of work, especially if this work is based on production such as the fishery. He advocates greater involvement of people in the industry and less control by central authorities. Jentoft describes at great length the fisheries crisis in Norway in 1989, from which Newfoundlanders can learn much. In a chapter titled "Working Smarter," Jentoft documents the nature of restructuring to meet such crises. He suggests that fisheries policy should be guided by "sustainable development," a concept introduced by the World Commission for Environment and Development in 1987. Jentoft points out that sustainable development is not just concerned with ecology and economy but also deals with democracy and culture. It advocates local involvement. Jentoft (1993:130) states, "One problem is that ecological crises invite centralization of power and control. This could lead to removing authority from those who make a living from harvesting the resources. Local knowledge could be pushed aside by scientific knowledge, people would find that their lives were subjected to forces over which they had no control."

The one major issue being constantly raised by fisherpeople but never satisfactorily answered by the government or the union, according to some respondents, is the role of draggers in the decline of the fish stocks and in a revived fishery. Fisherpersons fear that in a revived fishery, control will be more in the hands of companies and draggers, with fewer people employed. Some voiced their suspicions that schools for their upgrading are simply ploys to force them out of the fishery by pressuring them to obtain a school-leaving certificate and a trade. When questioned about the differentiation in the education upgrading program for those who chose to move out of the fishery and those who chose to return to a revived fishery, they could not see any difference. Because there was no perceived difference in the educational programs for those two groups of people, they did not see the relevance of what they were learning to a particular kind of future, and those who feared it may be a ploy to force them eventually to relocate approached these programs with an attitude of resistance, a force well documented in the literature (Giroux, 1983) as a statement of conviction, a means to empowerment at an individual level. One former fisheries worker explained:

> I go over to the [adult learning center] but I'm only there in body, not in mind. I believe the government is out to kill the inshore fishery and the union doesn't care. When the fishery comes back, it'll be in the hands of the big plant owners and the draggers. The government will hold out long enough to make sure all of us [inshore fishery workers] are gone.

IS LEAVING AN OPTION?

Leaving Newfoundland in search of a livelihood (out-migration) has been going on as long as Newfoundland has existed. Prior to Confederation with Canada, there were mass out-migrations to the United States, so much so that almost every family in Newfoundland has relatives in that country. After Confederation, this exodus to the U.S. slowed and Newfoundlanders began to move to parts of mainland Canada. House (1989) notes that Newfoundland differs from other provinces in that its level of immigration is lower but its level of net (but not gross) out-migration is higher. Herrick's (1974:178) contention is that as schools are currently constituted, they encourage migration. This belief arises from an analysis of the school curriculum, on the basis of which Herrick states: "virtually none of the textbooks or workbooks used by Newfoundland students reflect distinctive Newfoundland cultural patterns, especially the values, language, patterns of thought or patterns of social behaviour characteristic of rural Newfoundland." Little has changed in the content of textbooks in the past twenty years and, as will be discussed in a subsequent chapter, a course on Newfoundland culture that had been implemented has currently been dropped from the curriculum. The emphasis on urban values, beliefs, and skills provides a model and a goal for the graduating students – urban Canada is something to be attained, while rural Canada is something to leave behind (Herrick, 1974).

When the interview respondents in Bridget's Harbour were asked if they had relatives (defined as parents, children, siblings) working and living outside of Newfoundland, each group named a considerable number of people. The results are shown in Table 29.

Table 29

Number of Relatives Working/Living Outside Newfoundland

	Seniors	Mid-age Adults	Young Adults	Young Adults (high school)	Young Adults	Youth
With high school	28	32	15	32	23	92
Without high school	17	8	9	7	13	15
Total	45	40	24	39	36	107

Of course, there was overlap among people named as having left Newfoundland; for example, a son or daughter of one of the respondents may be a sibling of another. The point, however, is that a large percentage of each group had direct experience with family members having to leave home. One other interesting statistic is the large percentage of those who had left who had completed high school. Similar results were reported in the Port au Port study, which noted that of those youth who remained in the area, 59 per cent had completed between grade 10 and grade 12, compared to 73 per cent at a similar level who had left to seek employment elsewhere. These data support Norris, Phillips, and Bulcock's (1992) research on the loss of educated youth to the province and its implications for lower educational standards in this province compared to the rest of Canada.

Not only were many relatives working outside Newfoundland, but a considerable number of those interviewed had also worked outside Newfoundland at some point (see Table 30), with almost 50 per cent of the mid- and young adults who had not completed high school having been so employed.

Table 30

Did You Ever Work Outside Newfoundland? (Number of people responding)

	Seniors	Mid-age Adults	Young Adults	Young Adults (High school)	Teachers	Youth
Yes	8	11	11	7	2	—

Perhaps a more significant question was why they had returned. The results are shown in Table 31 and indicate that the main reason was that "home" and family were in Newfoundland (since only two teachers had worked outside the province, their data are not included here). The reasons given for returning home support a point made in Chapter 3 about the value placed on family. House (1989: 4) made a similar point about the strong attachment to the Newfoundland way of life, noting that "it is only by going away that a Newfoundlander learns to appreciate the economic benefits of staying home." For the three lower literate groups, job loss was also cited as a reason.

Table 31

Reasons for Returning (percentage of people responding)

	Seniors	Mid-age Adults	Young Adults	Young Adults (high school)	Teachers	Youth
"Home"/family	40.0	75.0	58.3	100	—	—
Job loss/employment down	26.7	25.0	41.7	—	—	—
Retire	20.0	—	—	—	—	—
Other	13.3	—	—	—	—	—

A final question was raised: "What advice would you give a nineteen-year-old with high school and a nineteen-year-old without high school planning to leave Newfoundland?" The results are tabulated in Tables 32 and 33.

Suggestions given to the youth with and without high school were in reverse; the youth with high school was advised to go while the youth without high school was advised to stay. However, responses were qualified. The suggestion for staying was most often coupled with the recommendation that the nineteen-year-old without high school obtain more education. Likewise, for the nineteen-year-old with high school, the two groups of young adults suggested going only if there was a job waiting, possibly on the basis of their own experiences.

Table 32

Advice to a 19-Year-Old (with high school) Planning to Leave Newfoundland (percentage of people responding)

	Seniors	Mid-age Adults	Young Adults	Young Adults (high school)	Teachers	Youth
Go	24.0	48.0	—	—	33.3	33.3
Go if can't get work here	36.0	8.0	16.0	36.0	3.7	33.3
Go if a job waiting	4.0	4.0	64.0	40.0	3.7	3.3
Total	64.0	60.0	80.0	76.0	40.7	69.9
Stay and hope for work	16.0	28.0	—	—	—	—
Stay and get more education	4.0	4.0	8.0	8.0	48.2	20.0
Stay	8.0	8.0	—	16.0	11.1	—
Total	28.0	40.0	8.0	24.0	59.3	20.0
Use own judgement	8.0	—	12.0	—	—	6.7

Newfoundlanders are not reticent to move in order to attain work. Their history is one of out-migration, as is their present. Yet they are quite realistic; they know that education is a necessary certificate for competition in the job market, but they are also aware that is it not a sufficient condition. Consequently, they express caution in sounding out the job situation before leaving home. Fortunately, this is often done through a network of family already living in mainland Canada. One of the best examples of such a network is taken from an editorial in the St. John's *Evening Telegram* (1 September 1995), which tells of one man who, after the decline of the cod fishery, moved from Savage Cove in northern Newfoundland to the Edmonton area to work in the oilfields. Not only did he establish himself in a good job and home, but he then helped others, who still helped others, until fifty residents – 15 per cent of the Savage Cove population – had moved to the Edmonton area. With respect to the success of the migration of these people, the editorial concludes that this solution to a lack of employment required "no government funding, no assistance, and no interference. All it did require was a little get up and go, and the willingness to help fellow Newfoundlanders when they arrived in a new city like Edmonton." However, there are cases of people moving to regions without a support system. As one woman said, "There's nothing sadder than a displaced Newfoundlander in downtown Toronto."

Table 33

Advice to a 19-Year-Old (without high school) Planning to Leave Newfoundland percentage of people responding)

	Seniors	Mid-age Adults	Young Adults	Young Adults (high school)	Teachers	Youth
Go	24.0	32.0	44.0	24.0	14.8	13.3
Go if can't get work here	8.0	4.0	4.0	20.0	3.7	6.6
Go if job waiting	4.0	4.0	—	—	—	—
Total	36.0	40.0	44.0	44.0	18.5	19.9
Stay and hope for work	—	20.0	8.0	—	—	3.3
Stay and get more education	56	32.0	36.0	40.0	74.1	63.3
Stay	8.0	8.0	—	16.0	3.7	6.6
Total	64.0	60.0	44.0	56.0	77.8	73.2
Use own judgement	—	—	12.0	—	3.7	6.6

In the meantime, many people are not prepared to move; they know that their ancestors have survived difficult times and they, too, are prepared to endure hardships to stay, or at least are prepared to verbalize this. This feeling of conviction of the people is best summarized in a popular song by a local group, Buddy Wasisname and the Other Fellers, "Saltwater Joys," one stanza of which reads:

This Island that we cling to
Has been handed down with pride
But folks who fought to live here
Take the hardships all in stride.
So, I'll compliment her beauty
Hold on to my goodbyes
And I'll stay and take my chances
With those saltwater joys.

(From the cassette, *Flatout*, by Buddy Wasisname and the Other Fellers); Wayne Chaulk, songwriter.

SUMMARY

The respondents were united in their perception that their community was existing on "soft money," such as the cod moratorium compensation and UI. They were likewise united in their belief that the most pressing need in the community and the province was employment. However, they were less certain about the relationship between literacy and work, and in this way their views were similar to the views of many writers on the topic. They responded with a sense of realism; they personally knew educated people who did not have jobs and uneducated or less educated ones who did. Therefore, they knew that education did not lead to work directly or even by way of acquiring a trade for obtaining work. They believed that education, while a necessary condition for work, was not sufficient. Other important factors included experience, connections, positive attitude, pleasant personality, energy, determination, and self-confidence.

Since education is not a direct link to work, then the nature of literacy/ABE programs must be considered. Three models were discussed. The current and common model – the traditional model – separates academic skills from trade skills. Individuals are first required to travel the academic road *and then* apply for permission to travel the trade/skills route.

Various educators support an integrated academic/trade acquisition model and such a notion would meet with the approval of the Bridget's Harbour respondents, who often possessed expertise in certain trades but were first required to complete an academic prerequisite – a prerequisite that had been questioned in terms of relevancy for the trade program to be enrolled in. Integrated academic and vocational training would ensure the presence of a key factor in any program – meaningfulness – and an accompanying condition, motivation. The third model, the informal work-focused model, is the one that the senior respondents were most familiar with as part of their community culture. While "learning on the job" could not continue as it was years ago because of changes in priorities and activities (e.g., boat-building), it is regrettable that instead of replacing the old with the new, there was not some plan by which some of the old (the informal apprenticeship model) could not have been maintained along with the new – "the institutionalization of expertise." As one respondent said, "Once it's gone, b'y, you can't get 'er back, you can't get 'er back."

Leaving the province in search of work has always been an option for Newfoundlanders. Practically every family in Bridget's

Harbour has a family member living and working outside the province. However, the respondents also shared two realities with regard to migration for work. They advised that potential learners ensure that work is available before they leave the province, an arrangement that was often possible because of the extended family network, especially in mainland Canada and the northeastern United States. The second reality was that the educated are mainly those leaving the province, a situation with implications for education and economic development that the government must face at some point.

Those Were the Times: Cultural Change and Continuity 5

Culture is both transmission and transition. Cultural transmission involves listening to tales of time gone by, gaining knowledge, and acquiring insight into how people conceptualized their lives in relation to others and how they formulated problems and proceeded towards a resolution. For some listeners, such tales foster an appreciation of their ancestors and admiration for their ingenuity and resourcefulness in times of adversity. For others, an awareness of their own culture provides a resolve to emulate these qualities as well as qualities of strength, endurance, independence, equanimity, and humour, all of which, Chantraine (1993) points out, contribute to survival even in the toughest of times.

But traits and values are not transmitted from the past to the present through a process of osmosis, of blind acquisition. Winterowd (1987) reminds us that the question is not whether we should work towards cultural literacy, for all literacy is cultural; the question is how we should achieve it. Worsham (1988) provides an answer when she says that culture cannot be acquired through memorization. The Newfoundland Department of Education removed a course on Newfoundland culture from the high school program because it was "unpopular." Communication with a number of students showed that the key method for "knowing" their culture was to memorize information from a text. Consequently, it became an arduous, meaningless task. Worsham (1988: 20) emphasizes that if we are to learn and benefit from our culture of the past, "We must empower students to analyse, compare, evaluate, communicate, defend, invent, and create. We must empower them to become not merely culturally literate, but culturally thoughtful." To do as Worsham recommends, a course on culture cannot be taught from a textbook or through memorization. An official from the Newfoundland Department of Education, in response to reaction against the cancellation of the course, stated that the course was not pertinent to students in Mount Pearl (a small city bordering St. John's) because it was not a fishing community. This begs the question of why it is not pertinent, why Mount Pearl would somehow be independent of the history of Newfoundland of which it is a part. Just as culture and history cannot be memorized, neither can they be compartmentalized. The significance of a course on local culture was voiced in a number of letters/articles in the *Evening Telegram* (4 February, 29 August, 5 September 1993). One writer pointed out that "whether you choose to ignore it or whether you live in urban or rural Newfoundland, our culture is rooted in the Newfoundland fishery." A union official pointed out that "Cultural heritage is universal. A Newfoundlander is a Newfoundlander whether he/she is from Trepassey or from St. John's. Furthermore, while Newfoundland culture is not synonymous with the fishery, the fishery is a significant factor in Newfoundland culture. It certainly has played a major role in shaping the way of life in this province." A similar point was made by a high school student who said, "Studying our own past explains why things are the way they are. Unaware of this past, what is a young person living in this province to do but form a false impression of a half-million hopeless, faceless people with the bad luck to be stuck on a 'bald rock', or in 'the land that God gave to Cain'. For we cannot truly understand our own society without some kind of historical context." Finally, a plea from a heritage group to reinstate the course emphasized that "it is vital students learn what it is that has made Newfoundlanders one of the few cultural groups in Canada with a distinct identity."

Chantraine (1993) expresses concern that the influence of culture/history through the qualities of survival and endurance, of growth and independence that may be acquired from one's ancestry, may be facing the biggest challenge in the absence of the cod fishery. Since one's culture is a mosaic rather than a fragmentation, the younger generation of Mount Pearl will be impacted by their past just as students in every other city, town, village, or community in the province. Are the younger generation being immersed in their culture, both past and present, in a way that will enable Newfoundland to have a future as well as a past? Certainly, cancelling a course on culture, whereby much of the problematizing can be done (the ability to frame and focus problems pertinent to one's life context), as advocated by Freire (1970), is not the way to go.

The older residents of Bridget's Harbour sensed there was a "move by the government" to devalue their culture and their past. While they had heard of dreams and visions and new societies, they felt that there was more superficiality creeping into their way of life. They felt that the campaigns for literacy were denigrating a way of life they looked upon with nostalgia and with realism. They felt that the ingenuity, adaptability, and creativity of former generations were not only not recognized, but the younger generations were becoming "soft," and rather than displaying independence and strength, it seemed they were becoming pawns of the government, dependent and complacent. The seniors tired of the constant cry that the government was to blame for all, that the government must pay for all, an attitude they felt the government had promoted and was now being "locked into." That this mentality had taken "such a strong hold" on the younger generations bothered them.

RESOURCEFULNESS

The mid-age adults and seniors, especially, liked to tell of the ingenuity of their generations and of the generations before them. They pondered the downturn of the economy and the effect on people of having to do with less. They wondered how those who were accustomed to much could do with less. They recounted many instances of the resourcefulness of their forebears. Some of these are noted below and show how former generations confronted problems and found solutions.

- Chimney brooms for cleaning chimneys were made from long poles with branches of trees fastened tightly to one end. Old fish nets with a small mesh were also used in place of branches.
- A birch broom was made to sweep snow or clean stables. This consisted of a short stick with fine branches (twigs of the alder or blueberry bushes) fastened tightly and trimmed for sweeping.
- A tar mop (for coating roofs) was made with a short stick and old rags fashioned into a ball and firmly attached.
- A variety of tools were made, such as band saws and hand planes.
- A weight attached to a piece of rope was used to keep a gate closed after someone went through. In the days when farm animals roamed freely, a closed gate was essential.

- A related invention was a fence stile consisting of a series of steps on both sides of a fence so that people could enter/exit easily but not animals. However, goats often defied stiles and crossed over. A light triangular frame was made and put around the goat's neck, which not only prevented the goat from going over the stile but also prevented it from going through holes in the fence.
- A bush harrow was made with several big trees with weights attached and pulled across a field to break up clumps of manure used for fertilizing vegetable and potato gardens.
- Paint brushes were made from hair cut from a horse's tail or from unravelled rope. A tobacco can was flattened and a handle fitted to one end and the hair/rope to the other.
- Unravelled rope was also used to fashion shaving brushes.
- Wooden "draw latches" were made for outside (storm) doors.
- Handles were made from local wood for shovels, axes, grubbers, etc.
- Part of an old motor boat was sawed off to make a hen house; old fish nets were used in place of chicken wire to make an enclosure.
- All kinds of transportation were constructed. For use with horses there were long cars, box cars that could be raised for dumping loads, sleds, and sleighs.
- Other means of carrying goods included wheelbarrows, handbarrows (barrel staves nailed over two long sticks), and tub barrows (half a barrel with handles attached to both sides.
- Fish nets were knit with needles carved out of wood.
- When fishermen went squid jigging (catching squid for bait) and it became very foggy, one man would light a small fire on a point of land at the entrance to the harbour to guide the boats back safely.
- Individual stories were told. One day when one man's boat motor broke down he realized that the trigger spring was broken. He cut a piece of elastic from the waist band of his underwear to fashion a spring to start the engine.
- Cut-off barrels with carved handles were used for wash (laundry) tubs.
- Soles of old rubber boots were used for door hinges on barns and small buildings.
- Old felt hats were used for strainers and for lamp wicks.
- Hand-held toasters were made from old coat hangers.

- When starch was not available for clothes, corn starch was mixed with cold water and hot water added for the proper consistency.
- Soap was made from rendered fat; the lye was made from boiled ashes.
- Making bread was a two-day affair. First, to make yeast, branches of the juniper and spruce were boiled to make barm and then molasses was added to make the sponge for yeast.
- Unleavened bread was used for poultices for infected wounds commonly received by fishermen after being pierced by old fishhooks, fishbones, etc. As indicated at the beginning of this text, in the strong religious customs of some residents, the bread was hung out on the fence during the night on the feast of St. Bridget (February 1) in the belief that she blessed it. Good Friday bread (bread baked on Good Friday) was used for the same purpose.
- All kinds of play equipment were made: metal hoops from barrels with a wire fashioned to roll them, hockey sticks, baseball bats, stilts, and wagons with wooden wheels that were greased with blubber. (If this occurred today, I wonder what bleach would be advertised on TV to get the blubber out of children's clothes!)
- Finally, inventions were made for special needs. One story was told of a man who had lost several fingers in an accident. He fashioned a hammer and knife he could effectively use.

While those who narrated these accounts did so with pride, an unspoken message often came through. The seniors spoke of such instances with nostalgia for a time when life was simple and nature predominated over modernity. The younger adult groups saw such actions as an example of the ingenuity and survival of a hardy people, at the same time being thankful that much of this had occurred in generations past.

The big question was how the younger generations were going to cope with less. The fisheries compensation income was seen as a temporary or stopgap measure. What would happen later was wondered aloud by many and pondered silently by all:

> I don't think they [younger people] know what they are in for. This money [TAGS income] cannot go on all the time; the government cannot stand it. I fear for the time when the younger people wake up and find out it is no longer there. I don't know. I just don't know.

LEADERSHIP

Leadership in times past was usually tied to the church and occasionally to a doctor/nurse or merchant. A "strong" priest usually meant "vision" and a "watchful eye" for the parish. The seniors, especially, narrated how much was often accomplished with so little. They could easily list achievements, especially parish buildings that were erected during the stay of a priest. Some now looked back on this communal activity as a necessity in those times when money was scarce – in order to get things done but sometimes in fear of the priest. Today, a common feeling was that the church was rich and any work should be paid for. Of course, the power and significance of the church had greatly declined in the lives of many of the respondents. As one said, "It's not the same now. Before we were all in it together; the priest was for the people and the people for the priest. Now they [the church] are taking in so much money it's an insult to expect people to do volunteer labour."

While the people of past generations felt competent in terms of providing for life's necessities, being inventive if necessary, they did not feel they possessed leadership traits. If a local person had assumed a leadership role, such as chairman of the local roads board, he (in times past, these were always male) was often accused of being partisan. "Outsiders" were viewed as being more competent in leadership roles even though the people from outside the community (nurses, welfare officers, or the occasional person married into the village) may not have had any more education than some of the locals. But, as one person explained, the outsiders had "travelled"; they understood how things could be and they were willing to get things done.

Some respondents pointed out that while leadership was much more diverse these days and there were more opportunities for leadership in various activities and projects, factions in the community were often split on the effectiveness of such leadership due to perceived favouritism. On the other hand, they resented "outsiders" being *appointed* to leadership roles, especially *if they felt that qualified people were available locally (provincially)*. One man pointed to an example of two people (not native-born Newfoundlanders) who had been recently appointed to promote Newfoundland culture. "You'd think they could find someone from Newfoundland who was qualified to do the job," said one woman. Another woman, referring to the same example, said, "It's hard to have faith in yourself when you're put down by outsiders taking over." An advertisement on radio for a local trade show by a person with a strong accent easily identified with another country resulted in various comments. As one person said, "It's hard to think it's a Newfoundland activity she's promoting. I can't believe they can't get someone we can relate to as being part of a local event."

One man felt that the greatest resource was leadership and that "in spite of all the schemes the government has put into place, they have done little to develop leadership skills." Leadership clearly was seen as the only hope for the future.

LANGUAGE: THEN AND NOW

Newfoundland's culture is predominantly oral, a fact often overlooked in literacy programs of today, whether for children or adults. In fact, people indicated they experienced a negativism about their language, that it was substandard to what the English language should be.

The nature of an oral culture and its implications for literacy development are controversial. Farrell (1977), for example, states that oral discourse is tied to the concrete, to describing the here and now; it is not conducive to abstract thought, to identifying causation, generating principles, categorizing, and formulating relationships. Such a conclusion denies the wit that has characterized Newfoundland culture and language. One anecdote from Bridget's Harbour concerns an old gentleman who was walking down the road near his home when an expensive car coming towards him stopped (there were very few cars in the village in those days), and the driver, a stranger, opening the car window, called out, "Excuse me, sir, but can you tell me where this road will take me?" The old gentleman paused for a few moments, then looking at the stranger said, "Well, I've been travelling this road for nigh seventy years and it has taken me nowhere yet." There is no need to spell out the level of abstraction in this remark – the weighing of the meanings of the words "take me," the comparison of the stranger's and his own experience, the noted relationships between the driver and himself, and the anticipated reaction of the driver.

Winterowd (1989) presents another common misperception of oral language versus print, that the former does not allow for objectivity, for scepticism. A distinction cannot be made that readily. Printed and written language can entail as much subjectivity as oral language, although there is no doubt that printed language can be put aside and returned to later for analysis and interpretation. But oral language can also be a medium to return to an issue for critical analysis. I recall one day an older lady who was annoyed about the content of a column in the newspaper some time before. She said she should have written her reaction to this and on at least three occasions she returned to this issue. She "recited" her response as if she were reading out from an imaginary screen. She also edited her "writing," displaying great objectivity, both of the situation (meaning) and of the language. This behaviour of "reciting/reading out" was fairly common among seniors in their relating oral language to written language, a behaviour that caused me to wonder why teachers/instructors often have difficulty in using a language experience approach with learners (basically, the transcription of oral to written language). This cultural pattern of mentally editing oral language to conform to more formal or written language norms, so common among seniors, seemed to have been broken at some point, or perhaps, more appropriately explained, not transmitted to younger generations.

With regard to the issue of scepticism and language, it should be pointed out that scepticism is not part of language, written or oral; rather, it is a matter of knowing the conditions, the context, within which language is used. Scepticism, in fact, was a pronounced trait of older Newfoundlanders; it was not uncommon in response to a repeated story to say of the originator, "Don't believe a word ____ tells you." Talk has been an integral part of Bridget's Harbour and surrounding communities and while some of its functions have largely disappeared, oral language (including song) still permeates the lives of the people. In the days prior to electricity and television in the Bridget's Harbour area (the 1960s), the frequent form of social entertainment was to "visit" after supper and share in "mulling over the news of the day," "telling yarns" and jokes, reciting, and singing songs. Almost all respondents reported hearing stories. The percentage of respondents who could relate stories of former days ranged from 50 per cent for the youth to 50-60 per cent for the teachers and young adult groups, to 80 per cent for the mid-age adults and seniors.

Similar percentages of the groups also recalled "unique" sayings, such as:

come hell or high water
sick as a crow
so hungry I could eat a horse
the moon is up (reference to a bald-headed person)
big galoot
stund as a bat
saucy as a crackie

old as Buckley's goat
dark as pitch
like a birch broom in the fits
'pon my word (upon my word)
busy as a nailer
black as soot
dry as a bone
crazy as a loon
deaf as a haddock
foolish as a caplin
flat as a pancake
lonesome as a gull on a rock
thick as tar
rough as a dogfish's back

People had a knack for using figurative language – an abstraction in the sense that a situation was represented by a few words of comparison often drawn from the local environment – dogfish, gull, tar, birch broom, loon, soot.

Comparison was also a linguistic device for emphasizing a particular incident or for description. An example of the former from earlier years takes place in a boarding house in Bridget's Harbour, the mistress of which was known to be extremely stingy with food. From the window of the dining room, one could look across the bay to Caplin Bight (about seven miles away). One day after the boarding mistress cut bread and put it on the table, one boarder took a slice and, placing it before his eyes, exclaimed, "Good God, you can see Caplin Bight through it!"

An example of comparison in description also comes from an anecdote about describing an illness. Sally was known to suffer from head pains, which varied in degree and which she reported felt like a "rush of wind in her head." She described the degree of severity in wind terms: breeze, squall, hurricane. One day as she walked down the road past Ellen's house, Ellen, who was outdoors, greeted her, "Well, Sally, how is your head today?" "Don't be talking girl," said Sally, "There's a real hurricane today, a real hurricane."

The respondents generally agreed that oral language as a form of entertainment was less common today, as were the types of yarns and sayings that formed part of the oral language behaviour. All groups except the youth felt that the key reason for this was that other forms of entertainment, especially TV, had taken over. The youth, too young to remember a time without TV and electricity, believed that people had simply changed. A significant minority, except the seniors, believed that this was the domain of the older people, who, inevitably, were "dying out."

The seniors, who represented past generations, thought that modern architecture had a part to play in the demise of oral language. The kitchen, as pointed out in Chapter 1, was the focal part of the rural Newfoundland house. Today, modern houses are being built and the main room is the living room, usually with a rug or carpet, and it is customary for visitors to remove their footwear when entering. For some seniors, this seemed to constrict the freedom of "dropping in." As one man said, "When you have to take off your boots, it's just not the same." An additional reason given was that people were away from home more and therefore it was not convenient to drop in. As well, the telephone made dropping in unnecessary in many cases. Over 75 per cent of all groups also believed that the custom of families sitting around and chatting was dying out. Reasons for the decline of this custom were similar to those for the decline in the value of oral language for socializing in general.

The Potency of Language Terms

The relationship of language and knowledge has long been debated. Is language the naming of knowledge, or is language, itself, knowledge? There is no doubt that one can know something without naming it. Likewise, the significance of language in directing a person to know something also has merit, as was pointed out by Benjamin Whorf, a linguist in the early twentieth century. This is certainly a thrust of the women's rights movement. What is perhaps even more significant is that knowing also entails forming values, attitudes, and inclination for involvement/non-involvement. The potency (a psychological concept) of certain words in various cultures is well documented (Goody, 1968). There are many examples of potent words in Newfoundland culture. For example, Faris (1973), in his landmark ethnographic study of Cat Harbour, points out that "fish," "fishing," "fisherman," or "fisherperson" have one and only one meaning – they are understood as being preceded by the word "cod." Therefore, a fisherman is one who catches codfish; if a person catches salmon, herring, mackerel. or lobster, he is just that – one who catches salmon, herring, mackerel, or lobster. When the fishery closed down, its psychological effects were as great as the physical effects; it meant the closing of not just a chapter in one's history, but a closing of history itself. Common expressions using the word "fish" in response to this situation were, "Your poor father would turn over in his grave if he knew he couldn't catch a fish to eat" or "Would [name of someone who fished in the 1950s or earlier] ever think there'd come a day when there wasn't a fish in the ocean?" However, language is always in a state of change, and "fish" is now being expanded to include many species other than cod, although it is still quite common to hear about the fishery being shut down even though a fairly prosperous crab fishery, lump fishery, and flounder fishery may be in progress.

Other words of great potency are "crowd" (as identified by Faris) and "auld" (a pronunciation of "old"). The meaning of "crowd," as analysed by Faris, depends on its context. When someone speaks of "our crowd" it may mean a reference to a family; a "crowd" gathered at the dockside simply means a gathering of people, while "Tommy Smith's crowd" or "that crowd" entails a negative connotation from the speaker's point of view and characterizes a group, particularly a family, and transcends generations. An unexpressed meaning of "Tommy Smith's crowd" is that Tommy Smith's family never amounted to anything and never will. This latter meaning serves to segregate and disempower people – "Surely, you are not going to listen to Tommy Smith's crowd," in response to a suggestion by some of Tommy Smith's kin regarding an ongoing project or issue, or "Tommy Smith's crowd are at it again," in reference to an objection by some of the Smith family regarding some proposed activity or project, even though the objection may be most meaningful and appropriate. In this way, Tommy Smith's family does not get to make an impact on the community.

The bias against certain families, and its conveyance through words such as "that crowd," is one of the key factors impacting on effective leadership. It is a tremendous challenge for a leader to accept all families as equally significant to the community, to mobilize their talents for the betterment of the community, and to appreciate the contribution they make. While comments on instances of partisan behaviour rarely occur in public (largely because it won't do any good), it is frequently the subject of kitchen talk and is always conscious in the minds of those who feel they are part of the wrong crowd.

The word "auld" is used in much the same way as "crowd." "That auld Tommy Smith, who's going to listen to him?" or "Auld Mary Brown always wants things her way." It can even be used to disparage politicians, church officials, or even an object: "Who'd ever vote for that auld Robert Jones?"; "Who'd vote for that auld thing?"; "That auld [name of church official], he's only interested in money"; or "It's time to get rid of that auld car." Once the word "auld" is used, there is no redemption, no place for raising a positive or constructive comment; there is no analysis. It represents a hardened attitude, an ingrained bias. This is an example when cultural thoughtfulness shuts down, when no alternatives, no history, no rationale, or no possibilities are entertained. Imagine the impact on a school child if a parent qualified her/his teacher as "auld"?

Words, of course, are part of literacy and culture and, as such, signify relationships. Words such as "ducky," "dearie," and "love" are commonly used by women. These words may be used in a home context in response to a neighbour giving the woman of the household a jar of berries or some other commodity. "My, aren't you a ducky to do that." It occurs frequently in commercial situations, such as stores and restaurants. "Can I help you find anything, my ducky?" or "No, my ducky, we're all out; the last one went yesterday." In developing an overall understanding of the context, such words have great significance. For example, when I am shopping for something I discover is out of stock, and if the saleslady, in response to my request for the item, says, "I'm sorry, my ducky; there's no more left," I somehow do not feel so badly. It seems as if the salesperson has a genuine understanding of my situation. A friend of mine from western Canada who was in Newfoundland on business was quite taken by these forms of address. She said she would often go to stores to shop just to hear these expressions because they made her feel good. What a pleasant change from the current "robotization" of business-customer communication today. What a welcome change from such interactions as the following, when a customer seeks a service by phone.

Customer: Dials the number
Response: If you wish to speak to someone in general sales, press 1.
If you wish to speak to someone in the parts department, press 2.
If you wish to speak to someone in customer service, press 3.
If you would like to hold and speak to a receptionist, press 4.
If you would like to leave a message, press 5.
If you would like to hear your recorded message, press 6.
If you don't have a touch-tone telephone, please stay on the line.
Customer: Presses 4.
Response: Thank you for calling. Please stay on the line and someone will be right with you.
(Recorded music).

While businesses may claim that this is more cost-effective, it certainly lacks humanness; furthermore, it is quite likely the customer gets turned off and does not bother to pursue her/his inquiry. In such cases, the business never knows how many customers decide to go elsewhere. It does not provide for a feeling of warmth and caring. It is computerized, not personalized.

Language as a Communal Act

Language, like any other aspect of culture, cannot be viewed in isolation from the overall cultural context. In Bridget's Harbour, language was integral to socializing and personal interaction (wit). Many of the words and expressions were based on the local environment/events and so had an immediate reference, while being used metaphorically. The use and form of the language in Bridget's Harbour provide a sense of community, a sense of collegiality marking the locals from outsiders, who would not understand or fully understand the references many of the expressions were based on. In addition to references to natural and person-made landmarks and to local events, particular people in the community were also used as the basis of comparisons. "You're the real Bridget Jones" made sense only if one knew the attributes for which Bridget Jones was best known. Oral language shaped much of the communal behaviour of the area. In earlier times when the main form of communication with the world beyond Bridget's Harbour was the battery-operated radio, owned by a few families, it was not unusual for people to gather at the house of a radio owner and listen to the nightly news or a favourite entertainment program of Irish songs, such as the "Big Six Program."

The telling of yarns and tales about historical events provided a sense of identity with the community. Older people who were renowned storytellers would only engage in this activity in the presence of trusted friends and neighbours. Their role seemed to be a sharing of community events of the past. In more recent times when these older people were approached to relate these stories for recording and transcription, they refused, for they felt this was an encroachment on something communal, even personal, since a person's historical legacy and personal style were part of the yarn. They felt that converting such yarns to print was demeaning because they would be catalogued among millions of other texts only to be stumbled over by the occasional reader who would not appreciate its context, or sought after by a researcher only for analysis and dissection. Their contention was that you can't change culture and still give it authenticity.

Part of the authenticity of the oral tradition lay in the medium through which oral language operated – memorization. Those with great memories were marvelled at and found themselves socially desired and at times needed, such as when landownership was in dispute. Transcription could not preserve the uniqueness of oral language. Written language, as far as they were concerned, had its place, but when it came to cultural history and folklore, the written word reduced local culture to the commonplace. "I'd rather take it to my grave," said one man, "rather than have it bandied about among strangers."

If oral language is a form of literacy, and there is no reason to believe otherwise, the mid-age and senior adults were very literate. They narrated meaningful episodes of times past through unique, personal, and captivating styles, while displaying the capacity and power of memorization. One wonders why there was not a smooth evolution from oral to written language competence, why these two forms of language were often perceived as divisive rather than compatible. Jennings and Purves (1991) suggest that education (including competency in written language) actually leads people away from their families (and from their culture). As pointed out in Chapter 3, the literacy of schooling tends to be oriented to the individual. Not only was oral language of the past, community-oriented in terms of its occurrence and use, but the tales and yarns were usually set in a communal/family context. The loss of communal identity and allegiance obviously affects how people relate to each other and to values commonly held. This is especially so for the younger generations. Williams (1987) maintains that such alienation (loss of support) from family and community plays a more critical role in determining whether or not students are successful in school than does the socio-economic level of the parents.

Oral to Written Language

Problems in becoming literate in written language arise when the relationship between oral and written language is considered divisive, rather than as a transition from one language mode to the other. One example of how transition could easily be achieved was illustrated by the example given earlier of the older people who "read out" from their thoughts what they would convey in a written text. Another example of the interrelatedness of oral language and visual images (not necessarily print) comes from watching TV, after which people sometimes give a running commentary on programs. These people are attempting to come to grips with a situation where TV has usurped the oral language interaction of socializing that always occurred on visits to neighbours and relatives. Since they cannot (or should not) talk to their family and friends when watching TV, they talk about what is happening on TV. Their commenting is a way of "connecting with those present," yet is not as distracting from their focus on the TV as it would be if they engaged in conversation.

While written language fosters changes (Topping, 1992), such changes are even more marked when written language abruptly usurps the role of oral language and sets apart the user from others. A good example of this is the manner of communication of some community and town councils. While the community is still oriented to oral language in daily transactions and those elected to the council are often friends and/or neighbours of everyone else and may interact orally in many situations over the course of a year, yet when a matter relates to council business it is conveyed by written language. This usually has a formal and alienating effect. One person told of receiving a letter from the council that the collection of his property taxes (about $100) was turned over to a collection agency. The person, who was still waiting for an assessment notice from the council, felt he was being harassed by the agency to pay his bill. Needless to say he was upset and frustrated, and wondered why the council, whose members knew everyone in the community, would resort to such high-handed tactics. Another example concerns a person who was served a notice to have debris removed from his property, something he had already arranged to have taken care of, although it had not been done. These and similar situations could have been dealt with more easily and cordially through a house visit, in a phone call, or through a chance meeting of the parties involved. Using written language as power, as alienation, served only to destroy the communal spirit of an oral language culture and caused people to "get their backs up."

Interestingly, in recent days a council in another community in the province decided to take this alternative (talking directly to people) in its efforts to collect back taxes. It was having so much success that other community councils not only indicated their intention to follow suit, but one wished to hire the "communicator" from the community that initiated this project. It is difficult to understand why it took a council so long to realize that direct oral communication, which shows personableness and respect for others, is more effective than the coldness and formality of written language! Sadly this instance also illustrates the low self-image in many Newfoundland communities. Why would any council think it does not have qualified people with excellent personal interaction and oral language skills but would have to hire a person from another community to talk to the people of their own community? This may signify a false image of competency, a problem that occurs when regulation and structure replace the naturalness of social interaction. It may reflect a lack of appreciation for "simple" solutions, or a belief that "outsiders" are more competent than people from within the community.

Schools, too, are focused on written language in the sense that learning is usually from books. A contradiction here is that while written language supposedly lends itself to analysis, synthesis, evaluation, and objectivity, the method commonly used in learning from written language in schools is memorization (Bourdieu, 1991). Students are expected to remember answers to questions, recite passages, etc. Memorization, it may be remembered, was the basis for being able to use oral language in transmitting cultural history and folklore. If children are to appreciate fully oral and written language differences, then the methodologies for analysing and understanding written language must be pertinent to the particular language mode. Understanding when oral language is unique, when written language is unique, and when there is a smooth transition from one to the other is a challenge for teachers and instructors. This understanding is necessary, however, if one is to capitalize on the power of language, especially the richness of an oral culture.

Overall, the Bridget's Harbour respondents expressed regret over the decline of the uniqueness of oral language in terms of knowing and using words, expressions, and yarns and tales. The percentages of people in the adult groups expressing regret at the decline in use ranged in the mid-60s; however, almost 90 per cent of the teachers and youth thought it was a pity that the oral language legacy of the area was in serious decline. One wonders why a course on Newfoundland culture could not devote a section to local language, once again understanding its use through problematizing the context in which it was used and analysing today's happenings in terms of its current applicability. Knowing the oral language of the community would be essential in understanding the past as a backdrop for the present and in understanding the possibilities for the future against both present and past behaviour.

One form of oral language that is alive and well in the Bridget's Harbour area is the composition and rendition of song. The number of local songs named ranged from twenty to thirty-eight per interviewed group, and the number of local singers named ranged from thirteen to twenty-one per group. Song was not just a means for socializing; it presented an avenue for expression. Through song, the people found occasions to laugh, to cry, to raise issues, and even sometimes to suggest solutions.

CHANGES IN THE COMMUNITY

Perhaps the most stable characteristic of culture is change; change is inevitable. Goody (1968) tells us that when one generation hands on its cultural heritage to the next, three fairly separate elements are involved: material assets, including natural resources; ways of acting and of doing things – i.e., behaviours; and the language itself, with its meaning, emotions, and attitude.

However, Szwed (1987) reminds us that cultural change is not an overnight event but represents a gradual process. Winterowd (1987) helps us better understand this process of acculturation and cultural change by distinguishing "kultur" from "culture." "Kultur" is what people and institutions pass on in the form of canons, collections, societal norms; it is considered of value and is unquestioned. "Culture," on the other hand, is always in the process of becoming. There is no ownership of it by earlier generations; it represents a temporary set of circumstances enacted by current generations for their use and convenience. It is an "interruption" in past cultural experiences, yet it is not so much a rejection of the past expressed by some seniors as "the young crowd got away from us" as it is a succumbing to the present. For example, the seniors believed that the style of present-day houses was not conducive to dropping in while the homeowners viewed modern houses as more functional, especially with the number of modern conveniences necessitating kitchen space and with central heating making the kitchen no longer the heating source of the house.

What is confusing and was not resolved in this study was that seemingly contradictory values were held concurrently by younger generations. For example, a person would take great pains to put in a landscaped lawn and maintain it, yet deface the environment by dumping all kinds of garbage in a nearby wooded area. Materialism seemed to be the basis for many changes: crops were no longer grown because it was easier to buy vegetables, or the wake for a deceased was no longer held at home because it was such a "tear up" on the house. Money as a solution to problems was being widely accepted.

The respondents were asked to talk about how the community had changed over the years (Table 34). All groups except the youth

Table 34

How the Community Has Changed (percentage of people responding)

	Seniors	Mid-age Adults	Young Adults	Young Adults (high school)	Teachers	Youth
More material comforts	40.0	68.0	72.0	64.0	48.1	10.0
Population increase	20.0	20.0	16.0	40.0	18.5	10.0
Community council	—	40.0	20.0	12.0	8.0	6.6
More community interaction	—	4.0	20.0	12.0	29.6	—
Better schools/ education	16.0	—	16.0	8.0	14.8	—
Better transporta- tion/ mobility	12.0	8.0	—	—	3.7	10.0
Employment: fishplant/business	4.0	4.0	4.0	12.0	—	3.3
People changed	4.0	20.0	8.0	12.0	44.0	—
Church changed	4.0	—	4.0	4.0	7.4	—
Better recreation facilities	—	4.0	—	—	—	23.3
Better medical facilities	—	8.0	—	—	—	—
More social prob- lems/young people	—	—	—	—	3.7	—
Less isolated	—	—	—	—	7.4	—
Cod moratorium	—	—	—	—	—	26.6

believed that most changes occurred in terms of more material comforts. This supports the point about materialism being a catalyst for cultural change. No single factor was cited by a large percentage of the youth, perhaps because they had grown up in an age of materialism and therefore would not have experienced a time with few material benefits. About one-quarter of them named the cod moratorium, a fairly recent change, and the increase in recreational facilities in the area, a factor that would have directly affected them. The mention of the cod moratorium by the high school students and not by any of the other groups may be explained by the fact that the high school students were interviewed later than the other groups, at a time when the moratorium had been announced. Other instances of changes noted by fairly significant percentages of people included: an increase in population in the area, the municipal incorporation of the community, changes in people, and an increase in interaction among people from different communities in St. Bridget's parish. The latter change was no doubt influenced by the centralization of schools and the busing of students; two schools have now replaced five former schools.

A second question dealt with perceived differences between young people during the youth of each group and young people of today. This question was not asked the high school students as they would have no referent point for comparison. The results are given in Table 35.

Table 35

Differences Between Young People Then and Now (percentage of people responding)

	Seniors	Mid-age Adults	Young Adults	Young Adults (high school)	Teachers
More material possessions/ entertainment	48.0	44.0	50.0	52.0	44.4
Less respect for elders/ tradition	32.0	28.0	60.0	44.0	37.0
Better educational opportunities	24.0	36.0	28.0	20.0	22.2
More mature /independence	12.0	16.0	16.0	8.0	74.1
Irresponsible/reckless	8.0	24.0	44.0	36.0	11.1
More free time/don't work as young	8.0	16.0	—	16.0	14.8
More peer/social pressures	—	—	—	12.0	24.8
Other	—	8.0	—	—	11.1

Once again, material possessions head the list. The other frequently mentioned differences were that there is less respect for the elderly and for tradition today and that youth of today have better educational opportunities. It was interesting that the "lack of respect" difference was noted more by the younger than by the older respondents. The two young adult groups believed that youth of today were more irresponsible and reckless, while the teachers were more aware of the peer and social pressures that young people today face.

Cultural change was obvious to all groups, with three-quarters of the high school students, approximately four-fifths of the teachers and young adults who completed high school, and almost all of the mid-age and senior adults noting such change. The main reason cited for cultural change was materialism, especially technology, with television and the telephone being most frequently mentioned. Fairly large percentages (more than 50 per cent) of all groups except the seniors believed that times change and people change with them. The seniors, having the greatest vision of experience, questioned why people had to change so much so quickly; they longed for simpler times. Twenty-six per cent of the high school students felt that one aspect of change was merely a lack of interest in past customs and traditions. The seniors, mid-age adults, and teachers believed that changes in the church had made a big difference to the community. The church had been seen as a stabilizing force, a focus of community activity, the basis of many customs and traditions, and the source of interesting anecdotes. Many felt that the church, too, had succumbed to materialism and had drifted away from its original mission – the care of souls. One woman, still agonizing from the changes of Vatican II and Pope John XXIII in the 1960s, bemoaned the decline in saying the rosary as a family activity and believed that the church had actually discouraged this practice. Another person regretted the removal of the altar rail, which she had thought symbolized the table at which Christ sat at the Last Supper; she said the church's reason for its removal was that it symbolized a barrier between the priest and people. Still others felt that the nuns had been a significant part of their culture and by their very dress (habits) and behaviour emphasized cultural values. They stood out as models against the encroaching materialism. One man said, "Now you can't tell them from any other woman. I know clothes don't make the person, but a uniform [habit] represents a statement of conviction, an external sign that 'I am not afraid to show what I stand for.'" The general impression was that the nuns, like other aspects of the culture, were "fading into the woodwork"; "there's no model to encourage young girls to join." Many church customs relating to birth, marriage, and death had disappeared so that there was a sort of neutralization, a dullness to church events – they all seemed the same.

> I don't know what the world is coming to. One time we all seemed to know what to do. Now it's damned if you do and damned if you

> don't. You'd think the church of all things would remain the same. It makes you wonder who knows what they're talking about.

The significance of changes in the church was as great spiritually and socially as the cod moratorium was materially.

When asked which cultural custom they would reinstate, the most popular choice was house visiting with its storytelling and card-playing. About one-third of the two older adult groups would have liked to see the return of the traditional observance of religious holidays, which required people to attend Mass and participate in processions and other religious activities. Other customs, named by at least 10 per cent of the respondents of the two older groups, included old-time dances, neighbourliness/helping, respect for elders, and the traditional work ethic. The respondents were unable to name any contemporary customs they would like discontinued. As one man said, "There's not very much special today, is there?" Instead, in response to that question, they named various behaviours they wished were not part of current times: drugs, alcohol, violence, war, racism, child abuse, sexual abuse, indifference, disrespect, and arrogance.

SUMMARY

There is no doubt that Newfoundlanders have a great pride in their history and in the deeds of their forebears. The respondents were very much aware of the resourcefulness of their ancestors, a source of pride and nostalgia for the seniors and of admiration by the younger groups, who were thankful that times were "easier for them." There was considerable knowledge of the yarns and tales, expressions, and terminology of former days.

But the culture of Bridget's Harbour, as of all Newfoundland communities, was in a state of change. The stories of the resourcefulness of former generations were just that – stories. They provided glimpses of a life now past. Written language seemed to be usurping the role of oral language as a form of communication rather than being used in a co-equal, transitional, and interactive manner. Oral language terms such as "ducky," "crowd," and "auld," while very potent in the current lives of the Bridget's Harbour residents, were not usually analysed in terms of their meaning and impact by the younger generations in either the school or adult education programs. Written language, in its usurpation of oral language, at times leads to alienation among community members.

"We're caught up in it!" That characterized many of the responses of the Bridget's Harbour residents with respect to change.

There were hardships in the past to which people did not want to return. But many would opt for the personableness and neighbourliness of former days. They would readily trade the complexity of the present, with its drugs and violence and crime, for this simplicity. But change is inevitable. The church, their pillar of stability, changed more than some were prepared to accept. One wonders, however, whether some changes were necessary. Oral language, for example, still plays a key role today in Bridget's Harbour, not only in socializing, but also in formulating problems and in resolving them. There is no reason why the oral language of the community cannot be integrated into the language of the school curriculum.

Even when change is necessary, such change can only be fully understood when past events are understood. In this way, plans can be mapped for the future and the wheel need not always be reinvented. Removing a course on Newfoundland and Labrador culture from the high school curriculum deprives the students of access to a significant body of knowledge. With the seniors declining in numbers, with oral language as a medium of socialization through yarns and tales and wit becoming less important, the youth of today will have a "present and a future without a past." While culture changes, knowledge of traditions provides a stability and a context within and against which to understand current happenings and events. One wonders if the materialism cited by so many respondents as the potent force in the community, and in the lives of young people, will be the only basis for future decisions.

Now You Have a Better Chance 6

> In the most general sense, schooling is about the regulation of time, space, textuality, experience, knowledge, and power amidst conflicting interests and histories that simply cannot be pinned down in simple theories of reproduction and resistance. (Giroux, 1988: 68)

A major question is: who regulates the time, space, textuality, and knowledge of schooling – who wields the power of decision-making? Depending on which ideology prevails, schools may be made adjuncts of the workplace, the church, or the local museum (Giroux, 1988). Schools, one would expect, like the culture they reflect, are constantly in a state of change, in a state of becoming, for as Duke (1983) reminds us, values, purposes, and ideologies of a people are the call to action. The Newfoundland education system, at the time of this study, was unique in Canada and in the Western world.

While Newfoundland's education system was publicly funded, it was denominational in nature. This meant that the responsibility for education was shared between the provincial Department of Education and the major Christian churches through three Denominational Education Councils (DECs): the Integrated Education Council (representing Anglican, United Church, Salvation Army, Presbyterian, and Moravian churches), the Roman Catholic Education Council, and the Pentecostal Assemblies Education Council. While the Seventh Day Adventists operated a school system, there were few students and it was not part of the Denominational Education Council structure.

The province oversaw the general education welfare of the students through the enactment of laws and regulations governing the operations of schools, the development and prescription of basic courses of study (excluding courses of study in religious education and family life education), the establishment and maintenance of minimum standards, the financing of education by making payments to school boards and, in the case of school construction, to the Denominational Education Councils.

The role of the DECs included determining the need for new school buildings, extensions, and equipment, and developing and prescribing courses in the areas of religious and family life education. The DECs also made recommendations to the government regarding the establishment and alteration of school district boundaries, the appointment of school board members, and the initial certification of teachers.

A Royal Commission of Inquiry on the delivery of educational programs and services (1992) proposed changing this denominational system. The commission considered four options for a provincial school system and endorsed one, a modified form of the current denominational system. Under this plan, churches would:

> have educational input at the highest level of government and a continuing role in the spiritual development of students in their denominational persuasion through the development of religious education programs and pastoral care initiatives. It envisions a system which would involve the formal integration of all faiths and the development of policies and practices which would involve all citizens in schooling and governance. (p. 221)

The churches would lose all other rights they had in the education system. There was considerable opposition to the proposed changes,* especially from the Roman Catholic and Pentecostal Assemblies churches.

The purposes, content, and product of the school are reflected in the school curriculum, which generally reflects what school is about. Purves (1991) points out three major functions of school curriculum, and especially of the language curriculum: (1) to develop cultural loyalty, that is, to know the expectations of the culture; (2) to move beyond the local structure and learn how to interact with a wider range of people in terms of appropriateness of language and content; and (3) to actualize oneself as an individual to formulate goals and plans peculiar to oneself, i.e., to map out a course of action. While this seems to provide a nice summary of the role of a language curriculum, it is not that simple, for the key term

---

*The proposed changes with some modification were eventually adopted by the Federal Parliament and the Newfoundland House of Assembly.

"culture" in terms of *whose* culture is not defined. As indicated in Chapter 3, the people of Bridget's Harbour saw school literacy as something valued by their culture, yet in a sense removed from it, since the expectation was that it would enable the graduates to "do something else" away from their culture. Culture, in other words, operated at two levels here, the local culture, the folk culture of the people, and the culture of the educational power structure (Department of Education, Denominational Educational Committees, school boards). The role of the church was often confusing, at least for the residents of Bridget's Harbour. In times gone by there was no doubt about the role of the church in education; church and school were integral and the church program (including services) was intertwined with the school program. Now the church role was often identified with that of the government, in spite of the stand by the Catholic Church on the Royal Commission report. The scarcity of priests, the closure of convents, and the amalgamation of school boards often made church and government control in education distant and impersonal. One woman described it: "They're all alike; you only hear from them when they want something."

CHANGE IN EDUCATION

The respondents were asked to indicate changes they had noticed with regard to schools/education. The results are given in Table 36. It must be remembered that the younger generation of adults, and especially the youth, had a much shorter reference time frame than the older adults in answering this question.

Positive Changes

A greater number of people in each group indicated more positive than negative changes. The responses of the senior adults reflected a material/external control philosophy. They believed that conditions dictate the kind of educational system, and in reference to school in the days of their youth they believed that there was no reason why the youth of today could not get an education; after all, there were these beautiful buildings, large and bright classrooms, a steady source of heat, books and writing materials, gym and play areas, buses to take them to the door, warm clothes to wear, good food, more teachers and with better credentials, and, in addition, it was mandatory that they go to school. One senior best summarized the comparison in this way:

> I minds when we were going. You had to walk, that's for sure and some youngsters walked two or three miles and all you carried was

> a slate under your arm and a junk of wood. There you were crowded into a classroom, bundled up until the stove got going and then the ones near the stove roasted and those of us by the windows were still freezing. By the time you reached [age] ten or eleven, you had to stay home and work.

"If we only had the chances they have today, we'd do something" was a common remark by the seniors. The favourable conditions were now there; youth had only to take advantage. Because of the seniors' view of material and external control, they were more accepting of regulations from government, church, and school boards distant from the parish. The mid-age adults, like the seniors, reflected the importance of the material and human resource conditions of schooling; however, as a group, they also focused on internal factors – the nature of curriculum and grading. Curriculum was generally discussed in terms of the range of course choices available. They were not so much concerned with the specific content of courses or its immediate relevance, for as indicated in Chapter 3, schooling was not meant to have immediate benefits in terms of its use; rather, their views portrayed an emphasis on the rights and role of the individual – the right to choose. Curriculum choice was pertinent only at the high school level, and the mid-age adults were judging change in terms of the reactions of their children, who in many cases were still in high school or had just finished. The satisfaction of the students was an important criterion for them in determining what was positive about schooling.

The two younger adult groups were like the mid-age adults in their emphasis on an internal aspect of school – curriculum and grading. This comparison was more pronounced in that they placed less emphasis on material conditions (buildings, number of teachers, and teacher qualifications). Also, the rationale for focusing on curriculum/grading by the younger adults differed. While the mid-age adults interpreted this change largely through the views of their children, the young adults, in many cases, "just missed" the changes, which would have made school so much easier for them. The young adults remembered that being successful in grades 9, 10, and 11 (grade 11 being the highest when they were in school) meant passing exams set by the provincial Department of Education, which accounted for 100 per cent of their final mark. One woman said of the final exams:

> It was such a solemn occasion. Students from Caplin Bight, Wild Cove, and Long Beach all came to Bridget's Harbour to sit for the exams. The supervisor was a teacher from another village. The exams were held in the parish hall. We'd go in and the first thing we had to

Table 36

Changes in Schools/Education (percentage of people responding)

	Seniors	Mid-age Adults	Young Adults	Young Adults (high school)	Teachers	Youth
Positive						
More opportunities/ conveniences	84.0	52.0	64.0	52.0	48.1	16.6
Mandatory education	26.0	—	—	—	—	—
Better buildings	64.0	68.0	16.0	8.0	11.1	—
More/better qualified teachers	64.0	56.0	30.0	32.0	33.3	13.3
Low teacher-student ratio	—	—	16.0	12.0	—	—
Improved curriculum/ grading	16.0	40.0	40.0	36.0	100	40.0
Improved teaching methodology	4.0	—	—	4.0	18.5	3.3
High standards/ expectations	4.0	6.0	4.0	16.0	40.7	53.3
Management/organization	—	4.0	8.0	4.0	55.6	—
Extracurricular activities	—	—	8.0	16.0	7.4	3.3
Negative						
Lack of discipline	24.0	18.2	12.0	16.0	—	—
Less emphasis on religion	24.0	20.0	—	—	—	—
Too little time in school	4.0	14.0	24.0	28.0	—	—
Lower expectations/non-challenging curriculum	—	8.0	20.0	32.0	29.6	3.3
Required courses	—	—	—	—	—	22.0
Stress/demands	—	—	—	—	22.2	—
Teaching: job vs. profession	—	4.0	14.0	16.0	—	6.6
Higher teacher-student ratio	—	4.0	—	—	3.7	—
School distance/early hours	—	—	4.0	4.0	—	—
Increased costs	—	—	—	—	—	26.5

> do was to find our desk which had our name on it and there were chalk marks drawn on the floor and you had to keep your desk within those lines. I can still remember my heart pumping when the exam was given out. There was always an objective part for thirty minutes and then the main questions. You'd panic when you knew it was about time to hand in the exam and you weren't finished. Sure, now they have it so great. Now up to grade 11 if they get a certain mark in their school work they don't even have to write the finals, and even for the grade 12s, the final is only worth 50 per cent. (Final exams have since been discontinued.)

Not only did they have to write an external final exam valued at 100 per cent to pass, they also had to pass all required subjects at a particular grade level to be promoted. If seven subjects were required, for example, they could have passed six and fail the grade, having to repeat all subjects again the following year. Now, with course credits arranged across levels, each course passed becomes a credit, and if a required course is failed, only that course must be repeated. One adult who had not passed grade 9 (repeated it twice) made the following comment: "You know, we [his age group] might look like we were stupid or something, that we couldn't pass. But when I look back at it, I had something like ten of what are now three credit courses in grade 9 [some of these were repeated passes but with different exams, as he pointed out]. If the situation then was as it is today, I'd have no trouble getting my grade 12. It makes you wonder what grade 12 means, doesn't it?"

The teachers differed from the young adult groups in their stress on outcome (need for higher standards/expectations) and on organization. Being more "integral" to the school system, they were understandably more aware of how schools were administered, of the resources available to teachers through in-service or workshops, and of the organization of school boards in relation to the functioning of schools. While 40 per cent of the teachers believed there were higher standards and greater expectations for the students, almost 30 per cent of them believed otherwise.

Finally, the high school students without the experience of another generation focused on internal matters that directly affected them; they believed there were improved curriculum and grading practices, high standards, and expectations.

Negative Changes

The number of changes of a negative nature were few. The four factors of any significance were lack of discipline, less emphasis on religious instruction, lower expectations/non-challenging curriculum, and too little time in school. The two latter concerns were mainly expressed by the young adult groups (teachers also expressed concern about lower expectations/standards) and were related since some believed that the closure of school on so many occasions indicated lower expectations. These respondents viewed schooling from a "service" ideology and felt that the taxpayers and the students themselves were cheated when school was not in session. It makes sense why these two groups would voice this concern since they were the parents of children of school age. They cited many instances when school was closed for such reasons as weather, concerts, spirit days (supposedly to foster a spirit of school pride and involvement). One person said: "I never saw the likes of it. If the children can't get out of Caplin Bight because the roads are slippery, the whole school is closed." Another commented: "You should listen to (radio station); the broadcaster almost gets on a high announcing school closings. As every new announcement is made he reaches a higher pitch of excitement. It's like an auction; he builds up this level of excitement as different closures come in and it's almost like he's looking for more takers of more closure announcements."

However, all respondents had adopted a fatalistic attitude towards the many occasions of school closure and lost instructional time. They felt that the power was in the hands of the school board and the teachers and there was nothing they could do about it, except raise the issue as kitchen talk. It was a "cross" they felt they had to bear.

If curriculum is viewed in terms of knowing the community culture, knowing the context beyond the community, and attaining individual goals (Purves, 1991), the two major concerns, one expressed by teachers and the other by the high school students, focus on the larger context beyond the community. The teachers were concerned that some students would not be successful in an academic stream and that this focus would not always assist them in getting jobs; consequently, they advocated courses of a more practical or functional nature, courses that could transfer to the job market (electronics, welding, cosmetology, etc.) and courses that would be useful in everyday life (home safety, health-related practices, parenting, etc.). The youth were also concerned about life beyond the community – the larger world of sexually transmitted diseases, drugs, and crime – and felt that they needed more knowledge to be able to cope with the realities of the world approaching the twenty-first century.

The other two issues that merit mention deal with knowing the culture of the community and relating to it. Some of the respondents from the four adult groups (excluding teachers) thought that there needed to be more emphasis on discipline and/or religious instruction, both of which were related and reflected their cultural values. Some of the seniors felt that discipline was too lax and that limits and conditions had to be set for children. In times past, the school was considered the epitome of discipline and the quality of teachers was judged by their ability to keep discipline. Respondents felt that this made discipline in the home easier. Now, with discipline in school seeming to be more lax, parents felt that it was more difficult to instil discipline at home. Those who advocated more focus on religion believed that one main outcome of religion was its impact on behaviour – discipline. One woman reminisced about her days in school when there were regular choir practices, tasks such as cleaning and dusting the church getting ready for feast days (days of special celebration), hours assigned to visit the church on special occasions (exposition of the Blessed Sacrament), First Friday devotions, and May processions with hymn singing and the recitation of the rosary. "It really made you grow up [be responsible]," she said.

In terms of curriculum changes that did not meet with the approval of the respondents, the only one of any significance was voiced by the high school students and related to the required study of specific subjects such as biology, math, history. They did not see the study of such subjects as pertinent to attaining economic or work-related goals. They believed that such subjects should only be taken as a matter of personal like or interest; such courses would serve the purpose of self-actualization, the third function of curriculum indicated by Purves. It seems that a *laissez-faire* philosophy was held by many students with regard to curriculum planning, a philosophy they felt was best actualized in a curriculum with a wide variety of choices – and choices that did not demand rigour. The concern expressed by 30 per cent of the teachers regarding changes in expectations and standards was also tied to this attitude of the students and to the differential standards in attaining credits.

SCHOOL, COMMUNITY, AND PARENTS

How school is understood obviously impacts on its meaning and effectiveness. Street (1984) maintains there are two major ideologies with respect to conceptualizing literacy. One is the "autonomous model," which considers literacy and education as a body of knowledge that in and of itself is good for something else. This is the general understanding the respondents had for school-related literacy as discussed in Chapter 2. This notion separates the "haves" from the "have nots," since a certificate of some sort is usually seen as a passport to further opportunities. Street's second model is "ideological." Within this model, literacy/education does not entail an endorsement of a person to a special status; instead, its significance can only be understood among a host of other factors: political, economic, social, religious, and community.

The significant role of the community and of the family in enhancing literacy and education today is reflected in the current emphasis in the literature on family literacy programs, programs that bring together adults and children, parents and children, with all stakeholders benefiting from the program offered. Connell *et al.* (1982: 186) remind us that "families are very powerful institutions, and their influence over their young members registers in every part of their lives, including schooling. No sound educational setting can ignore it."

Favourable Conditions

While the literature is replete with support for school/community/parental involvement in education, this, of course, cannot be generalized to all communities. The ideologies of particular communities can only be determined by the talk and actions of the people involved. The respondents in Bridget's Harbour were asked which conditions fostered educational success. The results are given in Table 37.

All adult groups (excluding the high school students) believed in the impact of the home on schooling. Home influence took three forms: giving encouragement to the children to stay in school, to study, and do well; providing a supportive environment in which children were cared for and their basic needs were met; and parents, very early in their children's lives, taking the role of teacher. The need for a supportive home environment was most strongly held by the two older groups and is consistent with their emphasis on the importance of material conditions for school success. About one-quarter of the young adult groups and the high school students and over 40 per cent of the teachers believed that parents had a role as "teachers," and it was essential that that role begin early in the child's life, a belief commonly promoted by educators and researchers today. A small group of teachers also believed in the need for parent-teacher collaboration. Resources for schools, including money (for fees, field trips, special equipment), clothing, school supplies, were more likely to be mentioned by the young adult groups (the parents of children currently in school) and the teachers, groups that would more likely be aware of such costs.

Table 37

Factors Enhancing Success in Reading and Writing (percentage of people responding)

	Seniors	Mid-age Adults	Young Adults	Young Adults (high school)	Teachers	Youth
Encouragement (stay in school/do well)	36.0	32.0	32.0	32.0	25.9	17.2
Supportive home environment	64.0	56.0	28.0	26.0	48.1	17.2
Begin early/parents as teachers	4.0	8.0	24.0	28.0	44.4	23.3
Teacher/school influence	24.0	40.0	40.0	48.0	51.9	60.0
Student involvement/ application	34.0	34.0	10.0	12.0	47.4	—
Within child factors	—	—	—	—	22.2	10.0
Resources (including money)	12.0	20.0	36.0	48.0	51.9	23.3
Return to old methodology	4.0	4.0	8.0	4.0	7.4	—
TV/educational programs	—	4.0	8.0	—	—	6.0
Parent-teacher collaboration	—	—	—	—	18.5	10.0

All groups were convinced of the importance of the school and the teachers in fostering success in school. Several respondents readily named specific teachers to exemplify this statement (see Table 38). The role of the teacher was the factor most strongly identified by the youth. This reflects a rather narrow perspective of the youth on the basis for their achievement. To them, the teacher and the school "make or break" their success; they attribute their success or failure to external factors. Specific characteristics of teachers best remembered are shown in Table 38.

The youth believed that an effective teacher was one who was kind, nice, and sincere, who provided good teaching, and who was pleasant and displayed a sense of humour. Stories were told of teachers of earlier days and the criteria on which they were judged. Said one man, "You knew if a teacher was good when the results of the CHE (Council of Higher Education public exams) came." A woman commented, "I minds this one teacher; the youngsters took over. No wonder we learned nothing." A third person noted the changes in teacher qualifications: "One time there was no teacher for Wild Cove, and the priest just took ____ out of grade 10 and put her in teaching."

Table 38

Kind of Teacher Best Remembered (percentage of people responding)

	Seniors	Mid-age Adults	Young Adults	Young Adults (high school)	Teachers	Youth
Kind/nice/sincere	20.0	20.0	64.0	48.0	100	53.3
Good teaching	42.0	42.0	46.0	60.0	44.4	50.0
High qualifications	—	12.0	—	—	—	—
Strict	30.0	32.0	28.0	24.0	18.5	3.3
Specific teachers	24.0	24.0	20.0	12.0	—	13.3
No fond memories	—	12.0	—	—	—	—
Casual/pleasant/ humorous	—	—	—	—	—	23.3
Openness/easy to talk to	—	—	—	—	—	13.3

It is interesting that while the high school students held a relatively narrow or constrained view of what factors enhanced success in literacy, the teachers presented a very broad perspective on influencing factors. They believed strongly in the home and community playing significant roles. They believed in the importance of promoting education from a child's early years through reading to children and by engaging the child in language activities. In addition to the home playing a supportive role, not just for young children but throughout a child's school career, they also believed in encouragement for education at a community level and for adequate resources, some of which would be based in the community. While the teachers possessed a broad vision with respect to factors enhancing success in school, they were not always clear on the most effective way of achieving this collaborative support – only 18 per cent suggested parent-teacher collaboration. One teacher remarked:

> Education is very complex today; there are so many factors affecting why students are or are not successful. Certainly, the home and school play major roles but the community with its sociocultural mores and peer pressure is a strong force in young people's lives. Society changes; roles of teachers change. The students are no longer isolated from what is happening in the world. Their community is not just Bridget's Harbour any more; it is much broader than that.

Just after study data were collected, a referendum was held on whether or not to reduce church influence within the educational system of the province. Approximately 57 per cent of the eligible voters in St. Bridget's Parish voted (this was consistent with the provincial turnout), with 81 per cent of these voting to maintain the current religious denominational system. The 43 per cent who did not vote, according to reports, seemed to be distributed across age groups. One would expect the mid-age adults and seniors to vote "no" (not to change the system), since they expressed a concern over lack of religious instruction in the schools. But religious instruction was a low priority with the younger age groups and one might have anticipated that they would vote for change. The referendum results may be understood in terms of the immediacy of the issue and the fact that "culture" is not a rejection of tradition, but a change influenced by present conditions. One respondent perhaps summarized the reason why so many voted "no" when he said, "When you're pressed, it's a different matter." Further discussion revealed that this meant that when something becomes a pressing issue, all other issues are put aside and one's attention is devoted to this one issue. There was a strong "no" campaign in the area with teachers and the elected government member supporting the "no" side. Since the younger generations had not really rejected traditional values, when they, too, were pressed with the issue, they supported what they had known and were familiar with from their early years. It appears that "When the chips are down, you fall back on tradition." It wasn't so much a support of the church that was expressed in the vote as an opportunity to maintain a cultural identity.

A second referendum was held in September 1997 to abolish church influence within the education system. This time 57 per cent voted against change. However, there were 25 per cent fewer voters than in the previous referendum. One person who did not vote this time explained: "Why be bothered? They (the Government) are going to get their way anyhow?"

Parent Involvement

A supportive home environment was generally endorsed by all adult groups, although less so by the two groups of young adults. Certainly, a key question is the nature of this support. The respondents who were parents were asked how they best supported their children's education/literacy development, while the youth were asked about the nature of the support they had received. The responses are tabulated in Table 39.

Table 39

How Did You Best Support Your Child's Literacy Development? (percentage of people responding)*

	Seniors	Mid-age Adults	Young Adults	Young Adults (high school)	Teachers	Youth
	(20)*	(24)*	(20)*	(21)*	(21)*	(30)
Encourage to stay in school/work hard	30.0	41.7	50.0	42.9	73.7	80.0
Helped with homework	45.0	50.0	65.0	61.9	36.8	90.0
Supervise homework	20.0	29.2	30.0	33.3	26.3	—
Provide basic needs/good environment	55.0	25.0	5.0	4.8	21.0	10.0
Helped with reading/ provided books	10.0	4.2	15.0	—	47.4	10.0
Showed interest in school work	—	16.7	10.0	50.0	21.0	3.0
Told them to obey teacher	35.0	—	—	—	21.0	16.6
Supportive/ non-critical/ just being there	—	—	20.8	22.4	15.8	16.6

* Numbers of respondents with children are given in brackets.

There was general agreement on the importance of encouraging children to become involved in education, stay in school, and work hard. As might be expected, the teachers as a group were more inclined as parents to provide this kind of encouragement. Also, 80 per cent of the high school students remembered being encouraged to attain an education. Home support was generally of two kinds: helping with homework and supervising homework. Ninety per cent of the students indicated they remembered being helped with homework; while they did not mention supervision, more than likely they considered supervision as a form of help. The young adults who completed high school also mentioned that parents show an interest in school work by simply asking questions about "What went on in school today?" Only the teachers as parents were inclined to help their children with reading at home and to read to them. The two older groups of adults indicated that they had provided for their children's basic needs and welfare. It must be remembered that the children of the seniors were in school prior to the entry of Newfoundland into Confederation with Canada, when resources were scarce. As one senior said, "I made sure they had enough to eat, good boots and warm clothes – what else could I do?" When one considers the difficulty in providing these basic needs in the late 1930s and early 1940s, that indeed was an achievement. The changes in parent-child relationships were reflected in the comments by the mid-age and younger adults that by "just being there" they provided support and encouragement for their children.

School, community, and parents working together provide the best context for literacy/education. How these three stakeholder groups interact is crucial. In order to pursue the nature of school-parent involvement, parents were asked for what reasons they would visit their child's school. The results are shown in Table 40.

There was clear agreement by all adult groups (teachers excepted) that the main reason for parents going to a child's school was to check on the child's progress and, to a lesser extent, to check on problem behaviour or the child's welfare or to attend school activities - concerts, open house, PTA meetings. The teachers perceived the situation somewhat differently and all believed that school activities were the main reason for parents being at a child's school. Over one-third of the teachers believed that parents assisted teachers in volunteer activities and this was confirmed by 12 per cent of the young adults who completed high school, the group most involved in volunteer activities for young children.

These reasons did not differ much from those given by respondents of an earlier generation. In the earlier generation, parents supported school activities. However, the concept of parent-teacher interviews was not as popular then and report cards were mostly delivered to parents via the children. Volunteer classroom work was minimal or non-existent in earlier days. Also, many older respondents remembered that when parents went to schools it was mostly to challenge the teacher in support of the child who, the parent insisted, had not been treated fairly. A parent or grandparent coming to the school usually "spelled trouble" and certain families (_____'s crowd) were noted for "taking on" teachers.

> I minds the time when ___ challenged the nuns. No one challenged the nuns then. But ___ wasn't afraid of them. ___ was her granddaughter and she felt the nuns picked on her so this day she marched up to the school and into the classroom. The nuns tried to get her out but she was determined. She faced the nun and read her the riot act about how she treated ___ and then told her that the next time she had to come back it would be in "full force."

Table 40

Reasons for a Parent Going to a Child's School Today (percentage of people responding)

	Seniors	Mid-age Adults	Young Adults	Young Adults (high school)	Teachers	Youth
Check on progress	84.0	92.0	100	80.0	74.1	93.3
Check on problem behaviour/welfare	16.0	28.0	20.0	28.0	33.3	50.0
School activities (including PTA)	36.0	32.0	36.0	32.0	100	30.0
Question curriculum/learning	4.0	—	—	12.0	14.8	26.6
If requested by teacher	4.0	—	12.0	—	—	16.6
Assist teachers/volunteer	—	—	—	12.0	37.0	3.3
Collaborate effort	—	—	—	—	11.1	10.0
Child injury /sickness	—	—	—	—	—	20.0

Home-School Interaction

Epstein (1986) discusses various school-family connections, two of which are applicable to Bridget's Harbour. In past generations the school and family had "separate responsibilities" for the children. The teachers did what they believed was in the best interests of the children and the parents operated in a similar manner. When teachers and parents were on the "same wavelength" there was strong support for teachers, but clashes occurred when there was disagreement over what the child's best interests were. In earlier days, teachers were often seen as antagonists, as challenges for students, especially for older students who had been "held back," and many students told stories about how they "outsmarted" a teacher. The "separate responsibility" relationship gave way to a current "shared -assigned" relationship. The role of parents in helping their children was more openly expressed, whether in the expectation for parents to check on a child's progress, to attend school functions, or to become a classroom volunteer. The home role was "assigned" by the school, perhaps the most common home-school relationship today. Reading to children at an early age at home is being strongly advocated by schools today, but this, too, reflects a school-assigned task. Hannon (1993) cautions that while reading to young children and other such tasks may be quite beneficial for literacy development, if the task does not "come naturally" to the parents, and parents view it as an interruption in their lives, it may not lead to the intended outcome.

There were individual stories of parents communicating with teachers regarding their children's learning. However, no examples were given of a truly collaborative model in which parent and teacher sat down, each describing the problem as he/she saw it, each proposing a solution, and then both working towards a common plan of action. Teachers were still regarded as the "authority," a concept unchanged from times past, and their decisions usually prevailed. Examples of attempted parent influence included one parent who was concerned about her child's spelling and the fact that spelling was not formally taught. The parent was told that everything would be all right. The parent worked with the child at home and eventually the problem disappeared. This child seemed to be very bright. A second example concerned a parent whose young child wanted to write at home, was interested in writing, and asked questions about spelling, etc. The parent raised this with the teacher, who indicated that reading must be taught first and writing was to be left until later. Even though the parent was aware of the child's interest in and readiness for writing, she acquiesced to the teacher's directive. A third parent was concerned over her child who had been given special class assistance but was now being moved back to the regular classroom even though the parent felt he was not ready for whole-class instruction. After visiting the teacher, the teacher agreed to leave the child in the special class. Finally, a parent of a junior high student was asked to come to the school (along with the other parents of students in that class) to see a film and give reaction to a proposed course on family life education. This, perhaps, was the best example of a collaborative relationship between school and home. However, very few parents showed up and the parent respondent said that she was not sure how to react to the proposed course. There was no prior preparation for the parents on course evaluation and no criteria/guidelines were available, according to the parent. All examples of parents approaching teachers involved mothers.

Research by Graue (1991) showed how parents differentially interact with teachers. She studied parents from two communities: Fulton and Norwood, the former being mainly a working-class rural community, the latter, a middle- and upper-class suburb. The Fulton parents accepted their children's going to school as a necessary milestone in life and they trusted the school to do its job. A major criterion for their children's success in school was that their children liked school. They participated in school functions and honoured school requests, such as attending teacher-parent interviews. They believed that the role of the teacher as authority was to inform, to tell, to explain; their role was to attend and listen. They felt that as long as there were no complaints from the school, everything was all right. Many of them lowered their expectations for their children the longer the children were in school.

The parents of Norwood, on the other hand, talked to each other about their children's developmental levels and readiness before they entered school, often sought other opinions, obtained psychological assessments, and may even have delayed their children's entry into kindergarten. These parents had no hesitation about going to school and voicing their opinion; they did not wait for an invitation. As parents, they assumed they were active partners in their children's education, and when they attended parent-teacher interviews they had their own agendas. They were not simply interested in how their child was doing but asked for specific information about alternate programs, gave information about their child's activities at home, sought suggestions of what they might do at home, and suggested what might be done in school.

The parents in Bridget's Harbour were similar to both groups but much more like the Fulton parents in their relationship with the school. While some had no hesitation in approaching the school regarding a child's learning, the teacher's agenda usually dominated. Like most parents in rural areas and similar to working-class areas of cities, they had not attained independence in deciding their own agenda, even though they had developed keen insights based on experience, such as the parent who had noted the child's early involvement in writing.

A Royal Commission of Inquiry (1992) on the delivery of educational programs and services in Newfoundland has recommended that school councils be established. These are perceived to be part of a collaborative model, with parents having the right to "make decisions on matters that directly affect the school and to advise other levels on issues which concern them" (p. 231). To be truly a collaborative (and democratic) model, parents must understand the nature of their contribution (usually based on experience with their children) and must understand the criteria behind school decisions, participate in developing criteria, and become involved in using them. They must be seen as equal partners, as true collaborators, sharing similar goals, yet often advocating different means of achieving them. They must understand the organization of the schools and the educational system and how changes can be effected. The manner in which parents are chosen for school councils is also important, considering how the respondents viewed leadership and how some felt excluded from the democratic process of the community because they belonged to the "wrong crowd." Representatives on school councils must include people from all segments in the community, and especially the currently disenfranchised. This may be a problem, for these parents will not be identified by those currently in power positions. Without this representation the councils will be a form of oligarchic rule that was criticized by the respondents as the form of rule now governing their parish church.

There is no doubt about the importance of the family in the education of children. This point is aptly made by Darling (1993: 2), who states that "the family [is] the most powerful educational institution" and must be included if education is to be effectively provided. As Darling says, education cannot be confined to schoolhouse walls. Connell *et al.* (1982) remind us that the power of families is not only confined to the middle and upper classes but is the domain of working-class families. ("Working class" is defined by Darling as including people who have common interests because they are dependent for their living on a wage or wage substitute, including pensions or the moratorium income, and who don't have means of gaining larger shares of the social product through ownership of capital, power in organization, or professional monopolies.) A major question is how families understand and relate to schools. When one thinks of the family role, one immediately thinks of school-based activities such as helping with homework, a common activity of the parents in Bridget's Harbour. The older generation talked about "hearing their children's lessons," that is, having the children recite their catechism, poetry, times tables, etc. at a time when the mode of teaching was strictly memorization. One senior gentleman summarized school in his day: "I really never understood what school was all about, but as long as we had our lessons off by heart we were all right."

Home Values

Beyond language, the value system of the home and its impact on the child's educational development is often not understood by teachers and administrators. Becker (1991: 68) elaborates: "While a significant body of literature has focused on the parents' role in the development of their child's early literacy skills, little is known about the impact of non-literate aspects of the home environment on success in beginning reading." The manner in which the home is organized, the roles played by family members, including grandparents, and the expectations for the children provide the first structured (or unstructured) environment for the child's learning. Due to a lack of research on home factors that are not language-specific, values of this nature that affect a child's learning have not been adequately identified. Educators are sometimes too likely to be blinded by the assumption that homes fostering "school-like tasks" provide the best model for school support. While no one would deny the importance of school-like language activities in the home, research such as the ethnographic study by Heath (1980: 127) has shown that while parents in one community did not read to their children and did not model reading and writing behaviours at home, "yet preschoolers could read many types of information in their environment." In fact, none of the mid-age or senior adults and very few of the young adults of Bridget's Harbour remembered anyone reading to them as young children. The myth of the children of working-class parents not making it in school is refuted by Ogbu (1981: 416), who says that "given the opportunity, one does not have to be born and raised in a white middle class home or receive supplementary childhood care to become a doctor or lawyer or professor in the Western social economic system."

The situation that is more supportive is a mutual understanding by teachers and parents of what goes on in homes, of what goes on in schools, and of how both can best collaborate and synchronize their efforts for the good of the child's educational welfare. A follow-up study with working-class families in the northeastern United States by Snow *et al.* (1991) identified a number of family variables that contributed to the later school success of their children. These included providing literacy materials in the home, having high expectations for the child's success, especially by the mother, and the structure of the family in terms of providing organization and stability.

More attention must be paid to the overall home environment, not just the reading of books to children. Studies (Becker, 1991; Connell *et al.*, 1982) on non-linguistic factors have shown that such values as responsibility, respect, pride in accomplishment, if also supported by the school, can be very significant in fostering a child's learning. The child who has respect for others, for the possessions of others, who takes responsibility for completing assigned chores and for putting away toys, who can work independently on tasks (puzzles, building blocks) and proudly show the results to a parent or other family member is very likely to transfer these qualities to learning in school. Such qualities were often an expected part of growing up when the children of the seniors in Bridget's Harbour were in school. The discrepancy between the emphasis on discipline-related values by the seniors versus the lack of such emphasis by the younger adults reflected their value system.

In addition to promoting qualities as indicated above, the seniors mentioned other non-linguistic behaviours. As pointed out earlier, providing for the basics of food and clothing was a challenge for them, yet they met this challenge not as an obligation but as a support so that the children could attend school. One parent spoke of the significance of the public exams in the past and how she tried to have most of the chores done (water brought, wood chopped and brought in) so that her son could devote his time to study in the couple of months prior to the exams. The priority his mother placed on his studying must have been obvious to the son. Parents of today may have occasion to do similar things. If they keep informed of the child's schoolwork, then it might be that the child has a special assignment and the parent may help out with one of the child's chores or responsibilities so that the child can devote more time to the assignment. Parents and teachers must be aware of the overall home environment and of how parents support learning. It is assumed, of course, that teachers will reinforce these forms of support.

One may question why, if the seniors as parents provided so much non-linguistic support for their children, so many of them did not graduate from high school. While the answer may not be known specifically, there are many hypotheses. Firstly, classroom conditions were not conducive to learning. Facilities such as heat, light, plumbing, and transportation were either sparse or non-existent in those days. Classrooms were overcrowded, with over forty students to a classroom being not uncommon and with several grades being taught by a single teacher, who in most cases had six weeks of "teacher preparation" after grade 11, and some less. There were very few materials and resources. Secondly, a high school certificate was not a requirement for the various jobs as it is today and many who did not finish high school could be successful in a career. Thirdly, the grading system was based on a final exam worth 100 per cent and unless all required subjects in grades 9, 10, and 11 were passed, the grade was failed and no credits were given. Finally, students were different. Connell *et al.* (1982) remind us that the "teenager" is actually a fairly recent category in history, as are adolescent peer groups and a youth culture with its own music, clothing, and amusements. Connell *et al.* give the post-war years and the 1950s as the time of change. However, respondents in Bridget's Harbour say that the distinction there was not evident until the late 1950s and early 1960s. Prior to that time there was almost an immediate transition from childhood to adulthood so that by the age of fourteen, the individual was considered an adult, and if he/she was not doing well in school, then that person, as an adult, did not belong and so it was almost natural that one moved to the adult world by withdrawing from school. Often overlooked in analysing the educational system of the past is that it was also not uncommon for individuals to graduate from school at the age of fourteen or fifteen and then enrol in university or, more commonly, enrol in a six-week teacher preparation course and take a teaching job. A newspaper article (*The Express*, 20 July 1994: A5, A14) about Rex Murphy, a well-known Newfoundland news commentator who had recently received a one-year appointment at CBC television's *Prime Time News* and CBC radio's *Cross-Country Checkup* in Toronto, noted he entered university at the age of fifteen. I, myself, was a school principal at the age of seventeen, and certainly was not alone in that category at the time.

Language, Dialect, and Schooling

One final issue regarding school support that merits comment is the matter of language dialect. Newfoundland is well known for having a range of dialects, some almost unchanged from those of the eighteenth-century English and Irish. While the relationship of dialect to the language of texts and school learning has not been established, there are pros and cons regarding the nature of this relationship.

One of the Bridget's Harbour respondents told of his childhood days when a certain teacher mocked his dialect and in a derogatory tone of voice called him an "old Irishman." He, like his peers, did not use the "th" sounds, instead substituting a "t" or "d" as in "thin" ("tin") or "then" ("den"), nor did he use the "ng" sounds at the ends of words, "runnin(g)," "walkin(g)." Another told of being called "old-fashioned" and like her grandmother when she sounded "a" as "ah," and a third told how the teacher laughed at the answer to a catechism question – while the answer was correct, the pronunciation ("divil") was not accepted. In the mid-1950s when students enrolled at Memorial University in St. John's there were special speech classes for students from rural areas, classes in which sounds were practised in drill form. Some interesting dialect changes in the Bridget's Harbour area have been noted in recent years, particularly the pronunciation of such words as "calm" and "palm," which were pronounced as "cam" and "pam."

One study on the relationship of the Newfoundland dialect to spelling (Walker, 1979) showed that the misspelling of certain words was due to dialect interference; however, the ability to distinguish different sounds (phonological categories) was based on the subject's responding to an auditory discrimination test of simple words – thick/tick, moor/more. One wonders about the relevance of such a task. "Thick" versus "tick" in isolation does not make much sense, whereas "a thick head" versus a "tick on a sheep" would allow a person to clearly distinguish one word from another and perhaps to spell it correctly. In another paper Walker (1978: 221) states, "There is no convincing evidence, in spite of a large body of research, that for the beginning reader who speaks a nonstandard dialect, a written code which does not conform closely to his own dialect speech is a significant handicap."

Factors mentioned earlier have a greater relationship to doing well in school than does dialect. However, a key factor could be the pride or, unfortunately, the embarrassment that may be engendered by one's dialect. A recent visitor to the province, enthralled by the local dialects, wondered about the absence of these dialects in radio broadcasters. This is not to suggest that there is an attempt to hire non-noticeable dialect speakers, but as the visitor said, it also does not portray local dialects as a model for evaluation and pride.

Unfortunately, dialects are usually understood and judged on the basis of phonology – the sounds of the language. As was pointed out in Chapter 5, the Newfoundland dialect is rich in meaning conveyed through unique expressions and potent words. Capitalizing on this aspect of the dialect in the analysis and use of language and in understanding the relationship of oral and written language may do much towards fostering literacy development.

LITERACY RESOURCES

While the school and the home may be considered as prime sources of resources for learning, the third stakeholder in education – the community – should not be overlooked. When respondents were asked if it was important that reading material (other than school-related material) be available for children and adults, over 90 per cent of the respondents in all groups answered in the positive. The reasons suggested for the importance of children reading are listed in Table 41.

Table 41

Why Reading Materials are Important for Children (percentage of people responding)

	Seniors	Mid-age Adults	Young Adults	Young Adults (high school)	Teachers	Youth
Provide information/ knowledge	76.0	36.0	60.0	68.0	25.9	53.3
Help reading/spelling/ writing	12.0	28.0	48.0	40.0	29.6	53.3
Broadens their outlook/ experience	12.0	48.0	—	24.0	44.4	23.3
Fosters interest/imagination	—	8.0	20.0	—	11.1	10.0
Occupies leisure time	4.0	—	4.0	8.0	11.1	—
Learn values	—	—	—	—	—	3.3

The main reasons cited by all groups are related to academic achievement. Children are expected and encouraged to read to obtain information and knowledge, broaden their experience, and increase their reading, spelling, and writing abilities. This emphasis is consistent with the respondents' belief in a school/traditional model of literacy discussed in Chapter 3. Reading for leisure – i.e., as a pleasant pastime for children – was not an expressed value of the respondents. Purves (1991) points out that reading involves two approaches: reading competence and reading preference. The former is oriented to academic achievement, the latter is for personal enjoyment. Clearly, the value on reading for children proposed by the respondents is reading competence.

The sources of reading materials for children as perceived by the respondents are given in Table 42. The main source is obviously the school library, with the younger age groups also mentioning local general stores. The reasons why reading materials are important for adults are shown in Table 43 and the expressed sources of materials for the grown-ups are indicated in Table 44.

Table 42

Sources of Reading Materials for Children (percentage of people responding)

	Seniors	Mid-age Adults	Young Adults	Young Adults (high school)	Teachers	Youth
School library	44.0	72.0	76.0	76.0	96.3	83.3
Local general stores	8.0	12.0	28.0	20.0	22.2	46.6
Local pharmacy	4.0	4.0	—	8.0	—	—
Mail order/book clubs	—	16.0	16.0	16.0	22.2	6.0
Borrow from friends	—	8.0	—	8.0	11.1	3.0
Home/gifts from relatives	4.0	4.0	4.0	4.0	7.4	6.0
Stores in nearby city	—	—	—	4.0	—	6.0
Library in nearby city	—	—	—	—	7.4	—

Table 43

Why Reading Materials Are Important for Adults (percentage of people responding)

	Seniors	Mid-age Adults	Young Adults	Young Adults (high school)	Teachers	Youth
Leisure time	60.0	52.0	12.0	24.0	22.2	16.6
Information/knowledge	44.0	52.0	84.0	64.0	18.5	43.3
Educational	4.0	—	—	4.0	44.4	30.0
Provides practice/ improvement	4.0	24.0	8.0	20.0	18.5	23.3
Role model for children	—	—	4.0	—	22.2	—
Other	—	—	4.0	4.0	14.8	3.3

Table 44

Sources of Reading Materials for Adults (percentage of people responding)

	Seniors	Mid-age Adults	Young Adults	Young Adults (high school)	Teachers	Youth
Borrow from others	24.0	28.0	36.0	48.0	22.2	10.0
Subscriptiion/book club	32.0	20.0	16.0	8.0	29.7	13.3
Local general stores	40.0	36.0	56.0	40.0	52.0	56.6
Local pharmacy	16.0	16.0	20.0	8.0	—	—
Bookstores (nearby city)	8.0	12.0	8.0	20.0	40.7	20.0
School	—	8.0	4.0	4.0	7.4	10.0
Nowhere	4.0	16.0	12.0	16.0	—	16.6

While reading for educational purposes is a priority for the adults as it was for the children, leisure-time reading was endorsed by the mid-age and senior adult groups. In spite of the current emphasis in the literature and the media on literacy in the home, only about one-fifth of the teachers and no other groups indicated that reading at home as a role model for children was a viable reading task for adults.

The main source of books for adults is the local general store, followed by borrowing from others and book club subscription. While the community provides some reading material for children and adults through local stores, there is no public library in the Bridget's Harbour area. A number of adults felt deprived over the lack of books to read and spoke of the high cost of books in bookstores, especially if "best seller" books were purchased in St. John's.

When all groups except the high school students were asked which reading material they most remembered from their youth, there was a wide range of responses (Table 45). The seniors clearly remembered the availability of religious material, particularly religious magazines, which carried secular as well as spiritual articles. One respondent thought that the *Sacred Heart Messenger*, which came directly from Ireland and was distributed by one of the sisters, was the most commonly read material at the time. The respondent added that the magazine always contained a serial story, "the start of the soaps." One woman produced a copy she had recently obtained from a home for seniors in St. John's as she wanted to subscribe again. She pointed out how the format had changed (cover design, paper quality, etc.) but still marvelled at the quality of the contents and referred to one article, "If You See What I Mean" by E.J. Keane, SJ. The article was about how the ancient Greek colony of Sybaris had been associated with corruption and laziness, a description with which Keane disagreed; the respondent quoted from the article, "Those who control the media have power to create the image, and in ancient times they were mainly the writers of history" (*Sacred Heart Messenger*, May 1992: 10). "How true," she said, "how true! Don't you think that very same thing is happening to us here today?"

The respondents from younger generations were more likely to have read storybooks and novels. Only within the past few years has a daily paper been available in the area. In former years a number of people subscribed to a newspaper, notably the *Family Herald* and *Weekly Star* from Ontario and the *Winnipeg Free Press*.

Table 45

Reading Material Remembered from Youth (percentage of people responding)

	Seniors	Mid-age Adults	Young Adults	Young Adults (high school)	Teachers
Religious material	60.0	16.0	12.0	52.0	22.2
Newspaper	24.0	12.0	8.0	16.0	18.5
Storybooks/novels	20.0	32.0	56.0	64.0	70.3
Western/mystery	4.0	8.0	—	—	11.1
Comics/children's magazines	12.0	40.0	8.0	16.0	33.3
Nursery rhymes	4.0	—	24.0	—	—
Readers' Digest/magazines	12.0	8.0	8.0	28.0	25.9
Almanacs	12.0	8.0	8.0	—	3.7
Catalogues	—	—	16.0	—	14.8
How-to books	4.0	—	4.0	—	—
Encyclopedia/dictionary	—	—	4.0	4.0	4.0

The absence of a library in the Bridget's Harbour area reflects the value placed on reading non-school material, especially leisure-type material. What is perhaps ironic, as one person pointed out, was that for several years the provincial Minister of Education was the elected government representative for the area. People also felt that the local council did not support a public library. One person said that a few years earlier a former resident of Bridget's Harbour offered the now deserted family house as a public library, but the general understanding of the respondents was that the council did not accept the offer because it could not afford the cost to repair and renovate for this purpose. Yet it is not uncommon for baby showers to take in as much as $1,000 in cash, again emphasizing the priority of values, the value of literacy pitted against family.

EXPECTATIONS

While various factors, both language and non-language, provide a supportive context for children's learning, Fine (1987) states that the single most important influence on reading performance and academic development is expectation. Expectation crosses many spheres – home, school, community. With regard to parental expectation, Fine suggests that it be studied in three major areas: (1) expectation for the execution of home responsibilities, (2) expectation for school performance, and (3) expectation for future education. She believes it is important that expectations be present in all three areas and that there be parental recognition when expectations are met.

A major difference between the time when the children of seniors were going to school and children of today is that the first set of expectations was the focus – carrying out household chores. Children and youth had many responsibilities, some of which took them out of school – drying salted cod, helping with the hay, weeding vegetable gardens, picking berries, getting wood and water, milking cows, tending to horses, sheep, and poultry, sewing, ironing, cooking, baking, cleaning, and looking after younger children. Today, the emphasis has shifted. Granted, many of the above chores are no longer applicable, but there seem to be fewer expectations for children to have home responsibilities. While academic success is valued (verbally) and expected, without similar expectations in regard to home responsibilities, one wonders about the mixed messages that children are receiving. Also, with regard to expectation for future education, a note of realism often clashes with expectation. While Mrs. Jones may expect her daughter Mary to enrol in trades college, Mary can point to students who graduated from high school one, two, or three years earlier and are still waiting to be accepted at college. This was especially frustrating for those high school graduates and their parents. To add to this frustration, they perceived the cause to be the priority given to displaced fishery workers at regional colleges.

Within school there are also expectations. While changes in the curriculum in terms of a greater variety of offerings have been viewed positively, they have also changed the expectation for a school-leaving certificate and future education. As noted earlier, students did not like the rigour of subjects such as math and the sciences, and hoped (expected) that there would be an easier route to graduation. A study by O'Sullivan (1992) of grade 3, 6, and 9 students of low-income families in Newfoundland showed that reading comprehension was influenced by expectations, which in turn were influenced by one's self-concept and beliefs about the difficulty of reading. While grade 3 student expectations were more influenced by their parents, grade 6 and grade 9 students were influenced more by parents and teachers; in addition, grade 9 student expectations were influenced by prior achievement standards.

Finally, the community has a role to play in expectation. One man believed that there were greater expectations for achievement in sports than in academics in terms of community financial help. The significance of language in categorizing people ("crowd") also surfaced with regard to its influence on expectation. Bridget's Harbour has still not changed that much over the years with respect to expectation for the children of "this crowd" or "that crowd"; "no one expects _____'s crowd to do well."

The Bridget's Harbour respondents were asked two questions about expectations—whether they expected that all students would graduate from high school and whether they believed that all students were taking full advantage of educational opportunities. The responses are tabulated in Tables 46 and 47.

Table 46

Expectation that All Students Will Graduate from High School (percentage of people responding)

	Seniors	Mid-age Adults	Young Adults	Young Adults (High school)	Teachers	Youth
Agree	84.0	92.0	80.0	84.0	51.9	76.6
Disagree	16.0	8.0	20.0	16.0	48.1	23.4

The senior adults, young adults without high school, and the youth overwhelmingly believed that young people were taking advantage of the educational opportunities. The percentages were more modest for the mid-age adults and the young adults with high school, with fewer than 75 per cent of either of these groups indicating this belief. Only 18 per cent of the teachers believed that young people were making the most of what was offered educationally. This suggests a major division in the beliefs of parents who know children best from their home environments and the beliefs of teachers who are witnesses to the involvement and success of the students in school.

Table 47

Belief that all Young People are Taking Advantage of Educational Opportunities (percentage of people responding)

	Seniors	Mid-age Adults	Young Adults	Young Adults (high school)	Teachers	Youth
Agree	80.0	68.0	84.0	72.0	18.5	80.0
Disagree	12.0	24.0	16.0	28.0	71.5	20.0
Partly	8.0	—	—	—	—	—
No response	—	8.0	—	—	—	—

The expectations of the respondents that all students will graduate from high school roughly parallel the patterns of their beliefs about student involvement. Just over one-half of the teachers expected that all students would graduate. There was a discrepancy in the beliefs of the mid-age adult group in that 92 per cent expected students to graduate, while only 68 per cent believed that they were taking advantage of current educational opportunities. This may be best explained by one person's remark that "students can get away [get by] with less and less." In other words, you don't need to take advantage of what education has to offer; you don't need to apply yourself with rigour and commitment to obtain a high school certificate. It is possible that the teachers' expectations also reflected this thinking.

From the discussion on expectations above, it must be noted that the data from Tables 46 and 47 refer to expectations on one level only – doing well in school. To understand the overall picture, expectations for students carrying out their responsibilities at home and for success in future education must also be considered. Certainly, the disagreement between teachers and parents on the extent to which students are applying themselves in school suggests a need for more collaborative interaction. Issues of this nature would be of great importance for the proposed school councils to pursue.

SUMMARY

There is no doubt that all respondents believed that youth of today have a better chance of getting an education, of becoming literate. Many changes have occurred across the generations represented by the respondents and the majority of these changes were perceived as positive.

The nature of the perceived changes is related to the generation of the respondent. For the seniors and, to a lesser extent, the mid-age adults, material improvements represented a major change, while the younger groups were more likely to perceive change in curriculum and grading policies. Some felt cheated by having attended school in a generation when grading (final exams in high school worth 100 per cent and a required pass in all subjects) worked against them. The teachers were more likely to note changes in standards and expectations and in organization. There was an interesting contrast between teachers and the other adult groups over organizational matters, which, at the time of the study, were making headline news as state and church battled for educational control. The teachers, being integral to the system, were very aware of the issues and of other organizational changes. The other adult groups felt that organization (church, government, school boards) was both impersonal and distant compared to former times, when the priest in the parish was the school board. They saw any conflict between institutions, including government and church, as removed from them. They felt that, as in most cases of educational decision, they "would be informed."

Teachers and high school students were concerned about education for a context beyond the community. Teachers felt that current courses did not always meet individual needs and relate to life beyond school from a work-related aspect, while students felt that they were not prepared to deal with a number of personal and societal issues. Students also felt that studying such subjects as math and the sciences did not lead to job opportunity and should be taken only by those who had a keen interest in them.

The older age groups believed strongly in the influence of the home on educational success, while younger groups, especially the high school students, thought that school and teacher factors were more significant. Only a very few teachers advocated home-school collaboration as a means to enhance school success. When asked specifically about home support, encouragement to stay in school and supervision/assistance with homework were most frequently mentioned. When parents attended school it was usually to check on a child's progress or to attend a school function. A collaborative model did not yet characterize the home-school relationships in Bridget's Harbour, yet there were many anecdotes of such need.

The importance of reading materials was noted by high percentages of each group. For children, materials were generally seen as adjuncts to school success, as sources of information and knowledge. On the other hand, significant numbers believed that reading material was not only important for adults in terms of providing information but also as a way to occupy leisure time. While children could obtain reading materials at the school library, there was no one source where adults could get such materials. There is no public library in the Bridget's Harbour area.

The significance of expectation for school success has been pointed out in the literature. Expectation encompasses three aspects: expectation for home responsibility, for school performance, and for future education. The children of the seniors had mainly been expected to take responsibility for home tasks, providing one of several explanations as to why their children did not progress well in school. While parents of today's students generally expected students to do well in school, the lack of similar expectations for home-related tasks may have led to a situation of non-congruency between home and school expectations. A large percentage of teachers did not believe that today's students were taking advantage of the educational opportunities available.

Proposed school councils may provide avenues whereby teachers, parents, and students can share experiences, perceptions, and expectations, provide suggestions for a collaborative effort, and take action in fostering education/literacy development.

Life Beyond Literacy 7

The title of this chapter may be turned into a question: is there life beyond literacy? Of course, the answer depends on whom you are talking to. Some, like Delattre (1983: 53), would have us believe that life beyond literacy is a meaningless form of existence. He maintains that those who are literate are the insiders and have access to vital information, the wherewithal to discover what is possible for them. As he says, "It makes us the heirs and beneficiaries of civilization." But this statement suggests another question: what civilization? Those who are literate, especially educators and literacy promoters, seem to believe that the only real civilization is the civilization of the literate, the world of books. I authored a book on activities for teaching adults and children how to improve their reading and writing (Fagan, 1992) based on a program called the L-I-T-E-R-A-T-E program, L-I-T-E-R-A-T-E being an acronym for Literacy Independence Towards Enabling, Responsibility, Attainment, Trust, and Excellence. When I had written a draft of this book, I asked some colleagues to read it and give me feedback. When I discussed the concept of excellence in the text, I suggested that it may come in many forms – it could be the enjoyment of an exciting novel, the feeling of power in writing a persuasive letter, or even the excitement of walking along a seashore at sunset. One colleague could not accept the seashore example as a way of contributing to the excellence of a person's life. My learned colleague could only see excellence as the result of involvement in literacy and books. This also indicates a narrow or biased form of thinking. My colleague did not see life beyond literacy.

Hunter and Harman (1979) remind us that the expected level or standard of literacy is often an artifact of the times. They say that increasing everyone's level of literacy only leads to a situation of "inflated credentials," a situation that in fact could cause a breakdown in the whole educational system since the more "qualified" would take jobs from the relatively less literate and less educated, forcing the latter down or out of the economy. There will always be a range of education, skills, and workers. Educators in their naïvety often encourage young people to pursue further education by saying something like, "What do you want to be – a waiter for the rest of your life?" One of my friends who is a waiter asked, "What is wrong with this? Is being a waiter something to be ashamed of?" If there were no waiters there would be no restaurants and if there were no restaurants, the élite would not enjoy their business lunches or after-hours cocktails. Being a waiter is a very respectable job, and a good (skilled) waiter can make a lot of money on tips. While these same educators value literacy, they do not seem to realize that one of their own characteristics is tunnel vision or narrow-mindedness.

Scribner (1984) maintains that literacy is not necessary for personal survival, that a person with low literacy skills is not excluded from full participation in economic and social activities – of course, these economic and social activities, while quite fulfilling for the particular person (such as being a waiter), may not be the choice of others, and vice versa. Hunter and Harman (1979) caution about viewing the world of literacy (or illiteracy or non-literacy) through middle-class assumptions about what constitutes quality in life. Kozol (1975) makes a poignant point when he says that those who believe that people with low literacy skills are the victims, the oppressed, also believe in victimization and oppression. When we pursue where victimization and oppression comes from, it often stops at the very doorstep of these same believers.

COMMUNITY INVOLVEMENT

Quality of life can only be understood from the perspective of the person whose life is being evaluated, not from the evaluator's life with its biases as to what life is supposed to mean. One aspect of the quality of life includes social relations and social or community involvement. Szwed (1987) notes that social relations may be understood as possessing three dynamics: the dynamics of communication (addressed to some extent in Chapter 5), the dynamics of the economy (addressed in Chapter 4), and the dynamics of occasion. The latter refers to times or opportunities for people to get together. Bourdieu (1991) indicates that in social relationships and community involvement, cultural patterns are evident not just in customs that reflect a group consensus but in activities that are idiosyncratic to particular community members.

There are many community organizations in Bridget's Harbour: church, social, health, charitable, seniors, and crafts. When the interview respondents were asked whether they participated in any of the community organizations, the results reflected a high degree of involvement (Table 48).

Table 48

Do You Take Part in Community Organizations? (percentage of people responding)

	Seniors	Mid-age Adults	Young Adults	Young Adults (high school)	Teachers	Youth
Yes	72.0	48.0	40.0	40.0	48.1	56.6
No	28.0	52.0	60.0	60.0	51.9	43.4

Involvement was particularly high for the older adults, which is not unexpected since there is an active seniors' club in the community. Although a significant number of people (the majority of all the adult groups except the seniors) did not belong to a community organization, the number of people who supported these organizations, that is, attended functions, was very high. The percentages of involvement ranged from 75 per cent of the youth to 80 per cent for seniors, except for the teachers, of whom 63 per cent said they attended functions sponsored by the various community organizations. The most common social activity at community functions was card-playing, and all who indicated attending the functions also indicated they played cards. The two most popular card games are auction (120s) and 45s. These games have been the most traditional in the area and have been popular as long as any of the seniors could remember.

There were some people in the community who reflected Bourdieu's (1991) observation on the idiosyncrasies as well as the commonalities of culture. While some people of Bridget's Harbour did not belong to or support organizations because of lack of interest, health reasons, or other commitments or priorities, others were critical, especially of church and church-related social organizations. They felt that such organizations were solely for the purpose of making money and it was not always clear how this money was spent. They felt that while the church's role and practices (ceremonies) had changed considerably over the years, the one way it had not changed was in its zest to make money.

The commonality and the individuality of a community culture are also evident in how the respondents described the characteristics of a good community member. Over 75 per cent of the seniors, mid-age adults, teachers, and youth believed that a good community member is judged by his/her degree of involvement in community activities. Eighty-five per cent of the young adults without high school and 96 per cent of the young adults with high school believed that a good community member was one who is helpful, caring, and unselfish, regardless of whether or not he/she becomes involved in community organizations or community-sponsored events. Twenty per cent and 16 per cent of these two groups, respectively, also maintained that a community exists beyond specific events, and people should be valued for their contributions to this larger community in their own individual ways. One person quoted a man of a past generation from Bridget's Harbour who in response to any comment such as "Times are tough" or "Times are not like they used to be" would respond, "Yes, and we're all in it together." You can't judge a book by its cover, nor a person by his/her involvement in community organizations and practices; the silent, non-participatory type may be making a unique and positive contribution.

DOING FOR OURSELVES

Ogbu (1981) reminds us that subsistence or making a living is one environmental demand that has a powerful influence on human competence and is faced by all human groups. Competence, therefore, should not be assessed in terms of how long people went to school or the level of education they received, but by their degree of competence in making a living. Making a living does not merely include work for pay, but also involvement in activities that contribute to their welfare and the economy of the household. This form of subsistence is very important in Newfoundland, which, as Szwed (1987) tells us, has a household-based economy where such activities contribute to the welfare of all members of the household, including parents-in-law and grandparents. House (1989) points out that while some who migrate to other parts of Canada may have a higher gross income than their Newfoundland counterparts, they are sometimes less well off because they lack the advantages of being part of a household economy where household repairs, babysitting, and other tasks are supplied "free" by being part of a household or extended family.

Evaluation of one's competency within one's culture cannot be done by objective means by outsiders (or even insiders), but by subjective means, whereby an attempt is made to view one's environment and one's existence within it and contribution to it from the perspective of the person involved (Verne, 1981). Verne states that we may be so utterly dazed with a handful of individual success stories, testimonials that are frequently the display of literacy/ education conferences, that we forget there are many kinds of success stories (competencies) that may be told. Unfortunately, the literacy success testimonial is often used as a model that if these few can make it in literacy, so can the others; there is also the corollary that those who don't make it, in terms of literacy, are failures. This is rather unfortunate and reflects another bias of the "educated." We are making the wrong comparisons, says Ogbu, when we compare the success of some with the lack of measured literacy success of others and when we infer certain causal factors to this lack of success. Ogbu (1990: 522) emphasizes that "not genetic differences, nor institutional deficiencies, nor social class differences . . . explain low-literacy, but the social reality of the people, their notions about literacy or schooling, and their interpretations of their social reality."

In another Newfoundland ethnographic study (Faris, 1973), the importance of one's social reality was pointed out. The social reality of many Newfoundlanders, especially rural Newfoundlanders, involves control over many aspects of their environment and perceptions of competence that often are not shared with the more literate citizens. In other words, these people have learned *their* culture and have learned it well. Characteristic of this competence is a generalized or non-specialized ability – the multiskilled individual who can cut wood, build boats and houses, mend fish nets, install and fix plumbing, repair cars, etc.

The demonstration of multiple skills was also obvious in Bridget's Harbour. When a person could not complete a task, such as building a brick chimney or making cabinets, there were always others in the community who could do so. In order to gather more specific information on the involvement in subsistence activities, those interviewed were asked about the nature of their involvement, and those who did participate were asked if they felt that such activities were on the increase, that is, if more members of the community were engaging in them. The results are given in Table 49.

There was a high degree of participation in all subsistence activities, with house repairs and renovations and berry picking and making preserves leading in degree of involvement. Over 50 per cent of at least three groups were involved in each of the other listed activities. The nature of involvement varies by generation and level of education. The seniors, for example, were less inclined to participate in car and truck repairs or trapping, hunting, and fishing, and the teachers were less involved in gardening and trapping, hunting, and fishing. It is interesting that the youth are very much a part of their cultural heritage and must, therefore, evaluate their role in society and their overall competence within a similar framework to older members of the community. What is unfortunate, of course, is that success in these activities is not generally promoted as a criterion of success by the educated élite, especially those from outside the area.

Table 49

Subsistence Activities and Perceived Trend (Increase*) (percentage of people responding)

	Seniors	Mid-age Adults	Young Adults	Young Adults (high school)	Teachers	Youth
Cutting firewood	56.0	68.0	68.0	68.0	55.6	73.3
Increase	50.0	76.4	55.0	65.0	63.6	30.0
House repairs/renovation	76.0	92.0	100	100	59.2	90.0
Increase	54.5	87.5	83.3	73.9	47.6	80.0
Car/truck repairs	28.0	44.0	64.0	72.0	44.4	76.6
Increase	35.7	61.5	73.3	52.6	68.4	53.3
Gardening	44.0	56.0	36.0	56.0	44.0	76.6
Increase	41.1	46.6	36.3	50.0	35.3	40.0
Trapping/hunting	16.0	50.0	48.0	52.0	33.3	60.0
Increase	36.4	57.1	56.2	30.8	33.3	20.0
Fishing for own use	16.0	48.0	64.0	56.0	33.3	50.0
Increase	25.0	50.0	44.4	38.1	22.2	23.3
Berry picking/preserves	84.0	92.0	76.0	60.0	74.1	80.0
Increase	60.9	54.5	57.1	52.3	42.8	36.6
Sewing/making clothes	60.0	44.0	52.0	60.0	51.9	46.6
Increase	40.0	46.7	57.9	52.4	35.0	16.6

* This represents the percentage of people involved in the activity who indicated there was an increase in the activity.

In general, large percentages of those respondents in each group who participated in the various activities perceived that participation was on the increase. It is not clear why the seniors who were involved in car and truck repairs thought that participation in this activity was on the decline in comparison to the perception of other groups. It could be that they were thinking in terms of their own generation. There was considerable variation among groups as to whether trapping and hunting were on the increase, with over 50 per cent of the mid-age adults and young adults without high school believing they were while the consensus of the other groups was generally the opposite. Likewise, teachers and high school students believed that sewing and making clothes were on the decrease. Fishing for one's own use was also considered to be on the decrease, which may be explained by the fact that respondents were interviewed at the time when a moratorium on commercial cod fishing had been implemented and fishing for one's own use was restricted to full-time fisherpersons. Since then it has been forbidden outright.

The importance of engaging in subsistence activities has also been documented in other Newfoundland research studies (Hill, 1983; House, 1989). The results of both of these studies were similar to the data reported here, with the repair and renovation of homes being the most common activity. According to the Hill study, in which the respondents were asked to estimate the savings by engaging in various subsistence activities, repair and renovation were perceived as resulting in the greatest savings among all subsistence tasks. Hill also showed that participation in these tasks was not differentiated by the level of family income, a finding also noted for the Bridget's Harbour area. Participation in such tasks is not family-based but is centred on the community culture.

COMPETENCY IN SPECIFIC TASKS AND ACTIVITIES

Gaining access to one's culture involves acquiring competencies practised by that culture. Hunter and Harman (1979) state that low-literate individuals do not perceive literacy as being the solution to problems in their daily lives. Instead, their lives are usually constructed around activities necessitating other solutions. Ong (1982) says that as individuals learn the skills and activities of their culture, they use them to mediate or operate on their culture. Such skills and activities are usually learned in an apprenticeship manner by watching and helping others. Eventually, the individuals incorporate these skills into their own competency system and use them not only to solve problems of a type that confronted an earlier generation, but also they improve on them to solve new problems, thereby bringing about change in the culture. Smith (1988:119) tells us that "both education and experimental psychology have overlooked the social nature of learning." Learning that takes place through social interaction and cultural tradition is also often overlooked by educators. Verne (1981) indicates that as a result of this oversight those with educational credentials obtained in an institutional setting are given preference for jobs or further training while competencies acquired in a social apprenticeship setting in which one learned from the family or from a neighbour are not as highly recognized.

The interview respondents were asked about their competencies in a number of skill areas and activities. The results are given in Table 50. The interview respondents in Bridget's Harbour indicate a range of competencies. There were approximately equal numbers of males and females in each group (except for the teachers), a fact that is important in interpreting the table data. A very large number within all groups felt competent in cooking, as well as a substantial number in baking. The teachers as a group generally indicated less competency in the skills and activities indicated, except for cooking and baking. This raises the issue of whether increased education/literacy takes a person away from the culture and from the acquisition of various skills and competencies. Perhaps, as Hunter and Harman (1979:108) point out, "literacy is an accompaniment to, rather than a prime cause of social progress." Except for sewing and knitting/crocheting, the youth seemed to have learned well from their culture, yet they also have successfully pursued formal education, at least to a high school level.

The issue, then, is to recognize and acknowledge that adults possess a variety of skills and competencies regardless of their literacy level. Currently, adults planning to enrol in a trades instructional program must first obtain a school-leaving certificate. It is also a practice that the criteria for a high school certificate include a number of credits for maturity, which is based on age and assumes that all of the same or similar ages have had similar experiences contributing to maturity. As one respondent remarked sardonically:

> When you go back to school they give you so many credits because you are older. It doesn't matter whether you have worked hard all your life, [are] skilled in a trade, won awards for bravery, or been in jail for the past ten years. As long as you're twenty-five or thirty you get the same number of credits.

It would make much more sense to allow adults to bypass the school-leaving certificate program and enrol directly in a trades instructional program (this model was discussed in Chapter 4 as an example of an integrated model). Individuals already having some skill or experience in the trade could be assessed in terms of the level of this competency and issued so many credits depending on their expertise. A similar practice has also been recommended by the Secretary's Commission on Achieving Necessary Skills (1990) in the United States. Unfortunately, under current practice a person who might be skilled as a carpenter, for example, and who enrolled in a carpentry program after having completed the high school certificate program has to take the same courses as the novice who never drove a nail. For the person with competency credits, those academic skills (usually reading and writing) essential to learning additional skills of the trade should be taught in conjunction with the job-related learning. At the end of the program, the person could be given the regular certificate for passing the carpentry course and, if necessary, a school-leaving certificate for having mastered the academic skills necessary for the successful completion of the trade skills.

Table 50

Competency in Activities/Tasks (percentage of people responding)

	Seniors	Mid-age Adults	Young Adults	Young Adults (high school)	Teachers	Youth
Cooking	88.0	80.0	84.0	84.0	100	83.3
Sewing	52.0	36.0	36.0	40.0	25.9	10.0
Baking	72.0	56.0	52.0	60.0	66.7	63.3
Knitting/crocheting	40.0	52.0	24.0	32.0	11.1	6.6
Crafts	32.0	24.0	20.0	40.0	22.2	20.0
Carpentry	36.0	36.0	44.0	40.0	11.1	43.3
Plumbing	20.0	22.0	25.0	32.0	3.7	20.0
Electrical work	16.0	4.0	12.0	15.0	—	20.0
Fishing	44.0	56.0	40.0	36.0	11.1	33.3
Singing	28.0	44.0	12.0	16.0	14.8	30.0
Playing musical instrument	8.0	28.0	16.0	18.0	7.4	23.3
Other	20.0	36.0	12.0	28.0	28.1	26.6

"YOU CAN STILL KNOW WHAT'S GOING ON"

According to Gearing (1979), every man, woman, boy, and girl moves daily in and out of at least two different worlds. One represents the life in the community with family, relatives, friends, social interaction, subsistence tasks, and skill competencies. The other transcends the community and brings them into contact with the world outside the community, the world of international news, bureaucratically organized business, and government. People move into this second world through the media and especially through television, where powerful visual images bring them face to face with the realities of conflict, strife, and war. As one senior said, "I have to turn off the TV now when the pictures of the Rwanda refugees are shown. It is totally mind-boggling that people can do this to one another. I just sit and pray for them; that's all I know how to do." Communication (usually by telephone or visits) with family members living outside the province often acquaints the respondents with conditions not likely to be experienced locally – earthquakes, tornadoes, various laws regarding firearms, smoking, etc. Contact with the world external to the community may also be personal and direct, such as in regard to UI claims, hospital admission procedures, obtaining licences or certificates from government departments, or involvement through the courts.

Since literacy has often been equated with empowerment, then should not empowerment be equated with a form of literacy? Furthermore, there is need to question that literacy as competence in printed language is the only way to empowerment. In order for the individual to make any impact on the world of conflict or bureaucracy, that person must have knowledge, which may be acquired in a variety of ways. To pursue the nature of knowledge, the interview respondents in Bridget's Harbour were asked if they watch and listen to television news and radio talk shows. The results are reported in Table 51.

Table 51

Participation in Information Networks (percentage of people responding)

	Seniors	Mid-age Adults	Young Adults	Young Adults (high school)	Teachers	Youth
TV news	100	100	100	100	100	90.0
Radio talk shows	76.0	68.0	56.0	68.0	29.6	73.3

Almost all of the respondents indicated that they watched the TV news. As a check on the reliability of their reports, they were asked to indicate current news stories. There was considerably high agreement among all groups, with a large number of people from each group listing the same news items: fisheries closure, economic cutbacks, the Hibernia offshore oilfield being developed off the Newfoundland coast, the Canadian constitution issue, the U.S. election, wars and famine in various parts of the world, major crimes, and hardship stories of individuals or communities within the province.

A fairly large percentage also indicated they listened to radio talk shows. Since these shows are usually on during mid-morning or late at night, it is understandable why the percentage for teachers is lower than for the other groups; however, it is interesting that the percentage for the high school students is so high. Respondents' reasons for listening to talk shows fell into three major categories: interest in current topics, to hear the pros and cons of complaints, and to pass the time or for entertainment. A smaller percentage said they listened because the radio just happened to be on. The "pros and cons" rationale needs some elaboration. Public figures, including the Premier, are frequent guests on talk shows and in this way are readily available to the people. These guest appearances usually coincide with a major issue in which they play a significant role. Since many of the callers present an opposing viewpoint from the guest, there is opportunity to lay out the pros and cons of the issues. This is especially true for government-related issues, since the major newspaper in the area is perceived as being anti-government in its stance and the columnists generally present an anti-government perspective.

Talk shows also provide an opportunity for the listeners to evaluate the information from and arguments of the callers. For example, a teachers' strike at the time of the study seemed to have very clear-cut issues, one being that the teachers opposed the government's removal of a clause guaranteeing the retention of a certain number of teachers in spite of declining enrolments while the government indicated it could not afford to pay extra teachers, usually in small schools. Furthermore, it was constrained from moving teachers to larger centres where the teacher-student ratio was higher. A resident of Bridget's Harbour noted that one teacher called in one day on a radio talk show and insisted that the strike was due to adding grade 12, an action that had taken place within the past decade or so. As the resident said, "How can she [the teacher] vote on the proposals?" (meaning, on what basis can she make a decision when she seems to have missed the key issues in the strike). While many people listened to talk shows, very few indicated that they phoned in or would phone in. The key reasons for not phoning in included: not feeling directly involved with the issues raised; nervousness; unsure of their ability to state, elaborate, or argue a point; and when they had tried, it took too long to get through.

Although few respondents availed themselves of radio talk shows to make their views known on current issues, there were other avenues of expression through which these people sought such empowerment. Not unlike people throughout Newfoundland and Labrador, the people of Bridget's Harbour resorted to song, drama, and even demonstrations and picketing to address key issues. Local issues that may have easily been "swept under the rug" were immortalized in song – songs that were heard at family gatherings, as public entertainment, and occasionally recorded by a local studio. Drama surfaced at times of public entertainment (local concerts). Both song and drama constitute an expression of individual consciousness, that necessitates familiarity not only with issues but with the social conditions, both of the present and the past. Demonstration and picketing were used selectively either when a group felt all other avenues for redress of a grievance (such as suitable road access) had been pursued and failed, or when an issue was considered of more general and vital concern (such as the privatization of Newfoundland Hydro).

Song and demonstration depended solely on the power of oral language. While drama was always played out via oral language, at times when "a play was made up" it may have been written down to foster the ease of memorization for the actors; however, it was not uncommon to "sketch out" the sequence of a play, memorize this, and then choose the appropriate language, which may undergo slight variations each time the play was rehearsed or staged. Song was rarely committed to print, and the "older people generally balked" at any such suggestion, maintaining that song was not meant to be written down or narrated for dictation; songs were for singing.

"SURE I CAN ALWAYS GET___!"

While people without a high level of literacy can tune into local and world events on the TV news, catch the innuendo of local issues on radio talk shows, express feelings, concerns, and issues through song and drama, and make a point via demonstration, what do they do when they must *write* to deal with issues and concerns? One woman responded as follows: "Sure I can always get [first name of the local MHA, the elected government representative]." And she was not alone in expressing this solution. When respondents were questioned as to whom they would ask if they needed help with a literacy task, high percentages still named the MHA. Percentages are shown in Table 52. The youth, because of their age, were not questioned about times past.

Table 52

People Who Would Assist with Literacy Tasks (percentage of people responding)

	Seniors	Mid-age Adults	Young Adults	Young Adults (high school)	Teachers	Youth
Past						
Priest	80.0	60.0	52.0	48.0	85.1	—
MHA	84.0	80.0	92.0	84.0	81.4	—
Doctor/nurse	84.0	92.0	80.0	80.0	70.3	—
Other	—	8.0	—	12.0	48.1	—
Present						
Priest	68.0	44.0	44.0	32.0	18.5	10.0
MHA	100	84.0	96.0	88.0	100	86.6
Doctor/nurse	84.0	84.0	76.0	64.0	33.3	46.6
Other	—	4.0	—	8.0	51.9	56.6

While the role of the MHA as a mediator/scribe was perceived as popular in the past, it was even more popular in the present. The notion of the MHA as a scribe may sound unusual, but it is very similar to uses of scribes by literate people in other aspects of society. Purves (1990: 12) states that "while literacy may be the province of the many, scribalism will be the province of the few." Scribes include secretaries, lawyers, lobbyists, and even public relations personnel for large institutions. One would never think that a manager or executive officer was illiterate because he/she used a secretary to shape requests, commands, and concerns into acceptable written language; why, then, should anyone think differently of a person engaging the services of an MHA as scribe? Purves (1990: 2) explains that scribes are not simply people with the ability to read and write, but in addition to this ability, they must understand the culture of the person initiating the correspondence and "have a goodly amount of knowledge about what is to be written, to whom, under what circumstances, and what is intended by the writer of a text that has been written." As one woman respondent said, "He knows it much better than I do."

The importance of using an MHA as a scribe is explained by Street (1984), who points out that different forms of writing require different skills of the writer and the reader that are best understood as different social practices. Darville (1989) elaborates on this point. He distinguishes narrative literacy from organizational literacy. Narrative literacy originates from personal experiences and represents past memories. Organizational literacy, on the other hand, refers to events that are relevant to their being acted on organizationally. Trying to cope with organizational literacy may render a person illiterate if that person does not understand how the form or organization of the text may be used within an organizational process – the role and status of the person receiving it, the relationship of this text to others of a similar nature, etc. Using an MHA as a scribe is an ingenious act on the part of the people because MHAs have "inside" information, especially on the workings of government bureaucracy, and therefore are in an ideal position to capitalize on that information in their correspondence. And if correspondence is directed to agencies other than government departments, the MHA also has an advantage, because as Street (1984:90) notes, writers often belong to a "known social role: academic, journalist, newspaper editor, lawyer" or politician; the writer in an MHA role is more likely to have greater impact on the reader/agency than would an ordinary citizen. Rather than exhibiting a dependency, the use of the MHA as a scribe shows instead, the intelligence of the people. This is actually a form of collective literacy – a striving for empowerment by dealing with a common concern, with the expert (MHA) taking the role of explicating this concern via print.

In comparison to eliciting the services of the MHA, other sources of literacy help sought by the interview respondents are also given in Table 52. The role of the priest in assisting the people through written transaction decreased considerably, while the role of the doctor/nurse decreased to a lesser degree. The still fairly high involvement of the latter, however, was due to their mediation in medical concerns, again exemplifying the significance of choosing a scribe who understood the intention of the writer and the audience to whom it is directed. Other sources of assistance with literacy tasks include teachers, social workers, and business people.

SUMMARY

Certainly, there is life beyond literacy. In fact, it is ironic that the so-called "literates" tend to be most narrow in their view of a fulfilling life. Life beyond literacy takes many forms. The respondents of

Bridget's Harbour were very involved in community organizations, either directly (directing, planning, executing) or indirectly (attending functions). Attendance at community functions, regardless of the intended purpose, was basically an opportunity for social interaction. However, involvement in the community, while considered a characteristic of a good community member by most of the respondent groups, was not so considered by the two young adult groups, who believed that a good community member is best characterized as helpful, caring, and unselfish.

The respondents were also very much involved in subsistence activities, from house repairs to berry picking, and these activities contributed to the economy of the household. Likewise, the respondents expressed competencies in a range of other skills and tasks, from cooking and baking to plumbing and electrical work to playing a musical instrument. The people of Bridget's Harbour displayed a high level of competence in many skills and subsistence activities. They had learned well from their culture and had developed a self-image of independence and self-sufficiency.

The respondents were not shut out from local and world news events. All respondents in all groups listened to the six o'clock news and were aware of major news stories. Considerable numbers also tuned in to a radio talk show, mainly to keep abreast of local concerns and to hear the pros and cons of major local (provincial) issues. The respondents made their voice heard in song, dance, and demonstration.

Finally, when it was necessary to use writing as a medium for intervention, for empowerment, the respondents chose the MHA as a scribe, usually when the issue was government-based or government-related; when the issue concerned medical help they were more likely to turn to a doctor/nurse. Their use of appropriate scribes in "getting the job done" is a testimonial to their intelligence and insights. Regardless of the literacy levels of the Bridget's Harbour respondents, they functioned very well in their community and in their lives. Literacy attainment was not the only criterion for quality in life.

What It Boils Down To Is Me! 8

The point has been made in previous chapters that what a person is depends on his/her self-perception within the sociocultural context. Regardless of what others believe, if we have unshaken faith in our own beliefs we will have a fairly intact self-image. Some literacy experts and educators tend to promote a negative image of low-literates or illiterates, as they define these terms. The following chart reflects that image (Cairns, 1988:16); it portrays those characteristics often associated with illiteracy.

Canada's Illiteracy Bill

[ ] Unnecessary UIC payments
[ ] Inflated consumer prices to cover mistakes
[ ] Extra medical and worker compensation charges
[ ] Tuition fees lost by illiterate students
[ ] Dwindling revenue for publishers
[ ] Subsidies for industry retraining
[ ] Wages lowered by illiteracy
[ ] Jail for frustrated illiterates
[ ] Lost taxes
[ ] Reduced international competitiveness
[ ] Blighted, unhappy lives for millions
GRAND TOTAL $BILLIONS

One Bridget's Harbour resident, responding to a discussion on factors that facilitate literacy development, said, "What it boils down to is me!" This certainly has a ring of truth to it and is actually a more colloquial version of the old saying, "You can lead a horse to water but you can't make it drink." While opportunities may be held out for individuals, only the individual can decide if he/she wishes to take advantage. Learning is a personal matter; no one else can learn for you – you can only learn for yourself. From another perspective, some people may be termed illiterate or low-literate by criteria external to the particular sociocultural context, yet these people lead very productive lives, have positive images of themselves, and are unlikely to check any of the characteristics on "Canada's Illiteracy Bill" as pertaining to them. Unfortunately, positive images are not always accepted as a criterion of literacy by those who measure literacy narrowly and without reference to the sociocultural context.

To obtain information about the self-image, the "me" of the Bridget's Harbour interview respondents, they were asked to rate themselves on a number of statements. These statements are taken from a study of socio-economic conditions in Newfoundland and Labrador (Hill, 1983); however, the manner of administration was altered. The statements and results are given in Tables 53 and 54.

Table 53

Which Statements Best Describe Your Competency? (percentage of people responding)

	Seniors	Mid-age Adults	Young Adults	Young Adults (high school)	Teachers	Youth
Can put my hand to almost anything	68.0	72.0	52.0	68.0	22.2	66.6
I work harder than most	72.0	76.0	64.0	40.0	40.7	46.6
I can do a good job in my line of work	72.0	92.0	96.0	92.0	70.3	60.0
I can do a good job when given the chance	94.0	100	100	84.0	70.7	90.0

With respect to belief in one's competencies, there is no doubt that the respondents hold a very positive image. The image described is that of being versatile, hard-working, and efficient. Interestingly, the self-competencies displayed by the more literate groups tended to be less strong than those displayed by the others. Is it possible that literacy makes one more prone to question one's competencies? It has often been said that the more you know, the more you realize you don't know. While this attitude is healthy in terms of motivating one to further learning, it may have negative impacts if one does not fully believe in his/her capabilities.

Table 54

Which Statements Best Describe You as a Person? (percentage of people responding)

	Seniors	Mid-age Adults	Young Adults	Young Adults (high school)	Teachers	Youth
I am closer to my family than most	100	100	96.0	96.0	74.0	60.0
I get along well with other people	100	96.0	100	96.0	100	96.6
I have lots of friends	96.0	88.0	76.0	52.0	29.6	63.3
I am kind and considerate	100	100	100	60.0	88.0	93.3

The respondents also provided a very positive self-image. They are kind, considerate, get along with others, are close to family, and have lots of friends. This profile is vastly different from that presented in the chart at the beginning of this chapter. Once again, it is interesting to note that some of those at the more literate end of the scale do not indicate as many close family ties, do not have lots of friends, and do not rate themselves as kind and considerate to the same degree as the less literate groups. Perhaps understanding literacy does boil down to "me"; certainly, anyone considering literacy policy and literacy programs must consider the "me" of the participants or potential participants.

The findings from the Hill (1983) study from which the statements in Tables 53 and 54 were chosen resulted in similar conclusions. In spite of unemployment, people generally had confidence in themselves and felt good about themselves. Hill's findings, however, showed that more sobering thoughts about unemployment were expressed: boredom, mental depression, and feelings of uselessness. One problem with gathering data on people's reactions to events and issues is that they try to give the response they feel the interviewer expects and these responses are often influenced by what they hear and read in the media. In fact, the media may be a significant factor in developing poor self-images and lack of confidence in people. After all, if the people continually hear how badly off they are, how they sit around and do nothing, "some of it is bound to rub off."

ME AND THEM

Since a person takes on an identity only in the context of others, it is important to understand participants in the social context from which they take their identity. The Bridget's Harbour informants were asked which groups of people they felt most comfortable with. The results are shown in Table 55.

Table 55

Groups I Feel Most Comfortable With (percentage of people responding)

	Seniors	Mid-age Adults	Young Adults	Young Adults (high school)	Teachers	Youth
Family	88.0	84.0	96.0	96.0	59.2	53.5
Friends	36.0	40.0	20.0	28.0	70.3	90.0
Teachers	—	12.0	—	12.0	40.7	23.3
Clergy	8.0	12.0	—	12.0	7.4	6.6
Merchants	—	12.0	—	8.0	11.1	10.0
Politicians	—	12.0	—	8.0	11.1	3.3

There is no doubt that family ranks high, a verification of the professed values discussed in Chapter 3. However, teachers and high school students indicated they felt more comfortable with friends than with family. While this characteristic of the youth may be interpreted in terms of cultural change, it is not clear why teachers ranked friends higher than family. As might be expected, teachers ranked teachers higher than did any of the other groups. Clergy, merchants, and politicians as general categories of people do not rank high in terms of the respondents' zone of social comfortability. When asked why they felt uncomfortable with certain groups of people, their main reason was that some groups were in a different class from them and they were not always sure what to talk about. The second reason was a lack of trust in others; this was especially true in terms of clergy and politicians in general, whom they did not know very well (though, of course, many respondents would consider that they *did* know the local priest and the local MHA).

"WHAT IS IMPORTANT TO ME"

Importance, like values (one actually reflects the other), is not an either/or matter of something being important or not; rather, importance is ranked on a scale so that things are of greater or lesser importance. When asked to indicate the three things most important to them, the interviewees responded as shown in Table 56.

Table 56

Three Most Important Things in My Life (percentage of people responding)

	Seniors	Mid-age Adults	Young Adults	Young Adults (high school)	Teachers	Youth
Family	76.0	84.0	88.0	100	66.7	63.3
Friends	70.0	75.0	72.0	80.0	50.0	50.0
Health	68.0	64.0	60.0	48.0	29.6	3.3
Financial security	40.0	40.0	24.0	32.0	11.1	16.6
Work	—	40.0	60.0	52.0	77.8	16.6
Education	—	—	28.0	20.0	3.7	100
Social interests/sports	—	—	—	—	—	30.0

Consistent with the ranking of value priorities discussed in Chapter 3, family and friends were very important. These were followed closely by health for all groups except the young adults with a high school education, teachers, and high school students. It is understandable that the older adults would be more conscious of health, especially in light of cutbacks to health services. Financial security was of great importance to the seniors and the mid-age adults, but work or future employment was of greater importance to the younger adult groups and the teachers. The difference between financial security and work/future employment represents a passive /active distinction: financial security was generally understood in the form of pension and any supplementary income (money from sons and daughters, many of whom had left the province to work), and savings ("putting a bit away"), while work and future employment, although contributing to financial security, also involved filling an important role in a person's life – the notion of breadwinner – as well as the enjoyment of the task and the social interaction with the other workers. The attitude towards a successful situation is reflected in the title of this chapter – "What it boils down to is me!" – and was often expressed in other sayings, such as "It's what you put into it that counts"; "Work is what you make it"; and, in response to how to handle difficult work situations, "You've got to make the best of it" or "You can't spend your time bickering with others; you have to get along."

Education was ranked low by all, except by the high school students, all of whom ranked it as important. It needs to be emphasized once more that this does not mean that education is unimportant. If the respondents are asked if education is important, they will always emphatically say "yes"; what it means is that other priorities "spring to the forefront" and must be dealt with before energy is invested in education. In actual fact, the respondents do not see a direct cause-effect link between education and the other issues (family, friends, health, financial security, work), a relationship that is usually promoted in the literature. They view education in a traditional/school sense as having potential pay-off but not always being essential for other things to happen, for other benefits to be attained. The high school students, without the benefit of hindsight, see education as their salvation, as their ticket to the important things that the other respondents named. One has to question whether ranking education as the most important issue in one's life reflects a naïvety of youth (a naïvety lost through experience) or a hope that it will constitute a bridge to the "good life." It would be interesting to discuss this with the high school respondents in ten years.

When questioned about the major accomplishments in their lives (see Table 57) marriage and raising a family were most important for all groups except teachers and of course, the youth. In interpreting the percentages for the different groups it must be remembered that not all respondents were married and had families, and so this would not represent an accomplishment for them. Related to marriage and raising a family was owning one's home, indicated by between one-fifth and one-quarter of the young adult groups. Education was mentioned by the three most literate groups, in descending order from the high school students to the teachers to the young adults who had completed high school. The fact that the three lower literate groups did not mention education as a major accomplishment reflects a realism in their assessment of themselves within their sociocultural context. They have no illusions of what they are not, yet at the same time they do not see this as a limitation but instead readily name accomplishments that have contributed to a fulfilling life. Teachers mentioned employment and promotion as accomplishments; other responses consisted of having served in the military (seen war action), competency in skills /crafts, being able to visit a much desired place (often the home of a son or daughter now living outside of Newfoundland, or a religious shrine), and in the case of the youth, sports achievements.

"THERE'S NO BETTER PLACE THAN HERE"

At least one aspect of quality of life must deal with being contented, with a sense of satisfaction and relaxation in being where one is. The responses of the interviewees, shown in Table 58, indicate that for the majority there is satisfaction in living in the Bridget's Harbour area.

Table 57

Major Accomplishments in Life (percentage of people responding)

	Seniors	Mid-age Adults	Young Adults	Young Adults (high school)	Teachers	Youth
Marriage/raising a family	72.0	68.0	40.0	52.0	25.9	—
Owning home	—	—	27.0	20.0	3.7	—
Education	—	—	—	40.0	74.0	83.3
Employment/ promotion	—	—	—	—	40.7	3.3
Other	28.0	32.0	33.0	—	—	13.3

Table 58

There's No Better Place Than Here (percentage of people responding)

	Seniors	Mid-age Adults	Young Adults	Young Adults (high school)	Teachers	Youth
Agree	100	92.0	92.0	88.0	70.3	66.6
Disagree	—	8.0	8.0	12.0	11.1	33.4
Maybe	—	—	—	—	18.6	—

The group with the greatest variation in response was the high school students. One-third of these disagreed that the Bridget's Harbour area was the best place to be. This is understandable since these students are just beginning their adult lives, and with the cod moratorium and practically no work outside the fishery, their responses are certainly not unexpected. Perhaps what is more remarkable is that in spite of these conditions, two-thirds of the student group thought that there was no better place than Bridget's Harbour.

When asked the reasons for their decision that Bridget's Harbour was a great place to be (Table 59), the respondents cited their belief that they actually had a good life there. In spite of the cod moratorium and high unemployment they felt financially secure and had access to many conveniences, including good health facilities. Part of feeling financially secure was that they owned their own homes, a point made by many. One other aspect to this opinion was based on a sense of realism pervading many of their responses. As one woman said, "If everyone put their troubles on a table and you could go around and take your pick, you'd end up taking back your own." Other reasons included having family and good friends and neighbours, feeling happy and contented, and feeling safe.

Table 59

Why There's No Better Place Than Here (percentage of people responding)

	Seniors	Mid-age Adults	Young Adults	Young Adults (high school)	Teachers	Youth
Good living conveniences, health, financial security	36.0	44.0	32.0	44.0	70.0	20.0
Family	16.0	48.0	32.0	44.0	22.2	45.0
Friends/neighbours	12.0	16.0	8.0	20.0	22.2	55.0
Own home	20.0	36.0	24.0	24.0	14.8	—
Happy/contented	16.0	8.0	4.0	24.0	22.2	—
Relaxing lifestyle	40.0	28.0	32.0	20.0	14.8	10.0
Always lived here (home)	12.0	4.0	—	—	—	—

Table 60

How Would You Like Things Changed? (percentage of people responding)

	Seniors	Mid-age Adults	Young Adults	Young Adults (high School)	Teachers	Youth
Better financial security	—	8.0	8.0	8.0	14.8	40.0
More activities for children/adults	—	4.0	—	—	22.2	80.0
More free time	—	—	—	—	7.4	—
More friends	—	—	—	—	7.4	—

The feelings of contentment were further emphasized when the respondents were asked how they would like things changed (Table 60). Only a significant number of the teachers and the youth suggested change. The youth, just about to start work careers and develop financial independence, would like to see greater financial security, while 80 per cent of the youth and a smaller percentage of the teachers would like more recreational activities for children and adults. All other groups were basically happy with present conditions.

This feeling of contentment and satisfaction is not unique to the people of Bridget's Harbour. Similar feelings were documented in a book by sociologist Ralph Matthews (1976), the title of which is used as the heading for this section. Likewise, House (1989) found that when respondents in his study were questioned about what they disliked about living in rural Newfoundland, one-fifth answered "nothing," and any complaints were about the weather or unemployment. Also, in the Port au Port study (1983: 20), the authors noted that 74.8 per cent of the youth preferred to continue living in the area because they considered it "a good place to be." Only lack of employment forced them to leave. The feeling of belonging, of security and contentment, helps to explain the positive attitudes people have about themselves, as discussed in previous sections. Unemployment (absence of paid work) is not seen as a social stigma, the result of being lazy, but as another of the tribulations characteristic of Newfoundland history.

"TAKE MY ADVICE"

The respondents of Bridget's Harbour represent a fairly homogeneous group with respect to their views on literacy and education, their relationship with their culture, their involvement in the community, their views on the relationship of education and work, their major accomplishments, and the degree of satisfaction with their place of residence. Occasionally, differences did surface between the older and younger generations, the more literate and the less literate, and between the teachers and high school students, on one hand, and the remaining groups, on the other.

In light of what has been presented and discussed about each of the groups, it is interesting to take a look at the advice they offer to others, namely: parents, young people, schools, and leaders. While "take my advice" is a common expression among Bridget's Harbour residents, acting on advice may not be as common. An old Irish priest who was once located in a parish near Bridget's Harbour is reported to have said, "The only vice that Newfoundlanders don't take kindly to is ad-vice." This was mentioned by several people, one of whom recalled that within the past few years local leaders had asked for input about the future of the community. While many excellent suggestions had been made, according to this man, none had been acted on. Another resident explained that advice was often taken as criticism and therefore rejected, with the attitude that the advice-giver should mind his/her own business. Perhaps, as one person suggested, Newfoundland has been the brunt of criticism and solution for so long, and in light of the many great qualities Newfoundlanders possess, they see criticism and advice as another attack on them. What would make most sense, however, would be to promote the many strengths that exist, and at the same time examine and evaluate advice and criticism as a possible means to improvement. This would entail critical reflection, an often cited characteristic of literacy.

Whether or not the people are inclined to heed advice, there is no doubt that the respondents were ready to share it, as indicated by the responses displayed in Tables 61 to 64.

Table 61

Advice to Parents (percentage of people responding)

	Seniors	Mid-age Adults	Young Adults	Young Adults (high school)	Teachers	Youth
Understand children/ treat fairly/be there	24.0	92.0	100	100	100	100
Encourage children and keep them in school	48.0	36.0	48.0	24.0	74.1	79.8
Set standards/expect good behaviour	76.0	44.0	32.0	40.0	55.6	31.8
Look after the general welfare of children	24.0	16.0	20.0	4.0	3.7	17.2
Avoid family conflict	12.0	—	—	—	—	3.4
Take parenting course	—	—	—	—	12.4	8.4

The *advice to parents* was as follows: (1) Understand children, treat them fairly, give positive feedback, and just be there for them. Only the seniors did not give this the same priority as the other groups. This reflects a generational difference and current philosophy in terms of child-raising. The emphasis on love, friendship, and time together was important for the younger adult groups, a perspective of family relationships being promoted today, especially in light of the disclosure of many incidences of child abuse. (2) Parents were urged to stress education and encourage children to stay in school. This advice was most likely to be given by teachers and high school students. (3) Parents as role models for standards and expectations for good behaviour was also suggested, significantly so by the seniors, for whom this was a strong cultural trait of former times, and by teachers, who were more aware of changes in this area. (4) Looking after the general welfare of the children and providing for their basic needs were also advised. (5) A few of the seniors spoke of family conflict today and advised parents to try to avoid conflict, especially in front of children, to try to resolve problems that may lead to family breakups. One senior, expressing the value system of her day, recalled that in her day you married for life: "You were forced to work out your differences." "Is life always a piece of cake?" asked another. "You can't have all icing, there's likely to be a bit of soggy dough someplace." All the advice given to parents was generally aimed at how they treat the children. Only a few teachers and youth suggested that parents take a parenting course or other self-education activity as a way of actualizing their own needs.

Table 62

Advice to Young People (percentage of people responding)

	Seniors	Mid-age Adults	Young Adults	Young Adults (high school)	Teachers	Youth
Stay in school/get an education	92.0	96.0	92.0	84.0	92.6	100
Strive for responsible behaviour/avoid drugs	44.0	12.0	4.0	16.0	25.9	13.7
Know yourself/set goals	8.0	8.0	4.0	8.0	33.3	13.7
Seek personal fulfil-ment/ be optimistic	—	36.0	8.0	16.0	22.2	31.0
Listen to/respect family/ elderly	40.0	16.0	4.0	12.0	7.4	3.4
Seek employment/meet challenges	—	—	16.0	12.0	18.5	—
Other	8.0	12.0	—	—	11.1	6.8

Although other priorities sometimes get in the way of "doing" education, there is no doubt that the major piece of *advice to young people* is to stay in school and get an education. While almost all of the respondents emphasized the importance of education, perhaps what is missing is an effective plan of action as to how this can be best accomplished, a plan of action with a role for all members of the community. The remaining pieces of advice vary somewhat from group to group and sometimes reflect the attitudes of a particular group based on age or education. For example, seniors and, to a lesser degree, teachers advised young people to stay away from drugs and to demonstrate responsible behaviour. The seniors were also more inclined to advise having respect for family and the elderly, to listen to stories of their experiences, and to heed their advice. One-third of the teachers suggested that young people get to know themselves and set realistic goals. The high school students advised their peers and those younger than them to seek personal fulfilment and to be optimistic in light of current economic circumstances. This advice was conveyed in such expressions as "Reach for your dream"; "Try your best"; "Never give up"; "Enjoy youth" - powerful words from the present generation.

Table 63

Advice to Schools (percentage of people responding)

	Seniors	Mid-age Adults	Young Adults	Young Adults (high school)	Teachers	Youth
Provide good and meaningful teaching	40.0	24.0	28.0	60.0	88.9	75.8
Encourage students to value education	32.0	20.0	28.0	56.0	18.5	20.6
Be sensitive to and help with individual needs	24.0	16.0	12.0	8.0	33.3	37.9
Be kind/considerate/develop mutual respect	20.0	8.0	44.0	12.0	44.4	20.6
Spend more time in school	4.0	8.0	32.0	16.0	—	—
Establish better discipline	4.0	8.0	—	4.0	11.1	3.4
Understand children's life outside school	8.0	8.0	8.0	—	—	—
Continue doing a good job	—	20.0	8.0	8.0	3.7	6.8
Other	4.0	8.0	8.0	12.0	7.4	—

Table 64

Advice to Leaders (percentage of people responding)

	Seniors	Mid-age Adults	Young Adults	Young Adults (high school)	Teachers	Youth
Promote job opportunities	40.0	44.0	40.0	44.0	48.2	32.8
Listen to the people/show interest	8.0	16.0	44.0	48.0	18.5	60.7
Invest in leadership development	—	4.0	22.8	38.6	38.4	32.8
Invest in young people/ education	12.0	20.0	—	16.0	33.3	32.1
Show direction/initiative	—	4.0	—	8.0	18.5	17.8
Promote fairness and justice	8.0	8.0	4.0	—	14.8	10.7
Promote unity/harmony	—	8.0	4.0	8.0	18.5	3.5
Avoid reducing services	4.0	—	8.0	—	—	—
Be open/learn from the past	—	—	4.0	4.0	7.4	—
Keep up the good work	8.0	4.0	—	—	—	—
Other	4.0	—	8.0	4.0	11.1	21.4

No one major piece of *advice for schools and teachers* was consistent across groups. (1) The teachers themselves, the youth, and, to a lesser degree, the young adults who had completed high school advised teachers to provide good and meaningful teaching. Other suggestions to teachers included the following. (2) Encourage students to value education. This marks a consistency between advice to parents and teachers and perhaps could provide a common point of discussion for these two groups in collaborating on their children's education. (3) Be sensitive to children and help with individual needs. (4) Be kind and considerate and develop mutual respect in dealing with individual differences and in promoting a good classroom environment. To a lesser extent, teachers were advised to (5) establish better discipline, and (6) understand children's lives outside of school. The latter is interesting in that it is related to the discussion on prioritizing values. Since family is a major priority, some adults felt that school work not completed or the socialization behaviour of students was sometimes due to family functions and demands, and it was important for teachers to understand this, such as understanding a student not getting homework done if that student had been attending a family celebration over the weekend. A small number of individuals also expressed appreciation for the teachers and advised that they continue doing the good job they are doing.

Finally, we consider the *advice given to leaders*. Since leaders included those at the local, provincial, and federal levels, the nature of the advice varies; nevertheless, the advice from the various groups is appropriate for all leaders.

The main concern was employment and the most common advice for the leaders was to activate the job market. Several people talked about the need for diversification and of finding opportunities unique to Newfoundland. Although the advice to show direction and initiative and to be action-oriented was cited less often, this advice was intertwined with the need to promote employment. Some respondents felt it was necessary to break out of a "traditional model" in job creation; it was suggested that think-tanks be created and ideas brainstormed for consideration. However, as one man pointed out, this was not new so what had to be added was to structure committees or other mechanisms to study the feasibility of these ideas and to take action rather than "just allowing them to be a lot of talk."

A second fairly strong piece of advice to leaders was to listen to the people, to show interest in what they said. All respondents were critical of leaders who had constantly ignored the warnings of local fisherpersons about the depletion of the cod and other fish stocks. One older woman said that she remembered her husband and other men, at the time the draggers and factory trawlers were introduced to Newfoundland, saying that "nothing could stand all that dredging off the bottom."

Another example of not listening to people came from respondents who had successfully initiated a small industry. They said that as soon as the government officials "got wind of its success," they financed other expansions of this kind of endeavour in other areas of the province, yet as the respondents pointed out, they had told the officials that "There just wasn't a market there for expansion." Consequently, faced with too much competition, they saw their initiative fail.

The younger adults, teachers, and youth believed that leadership should invest in leadership. Are leaders born and not made? "We used to say that about teachers," said one woman, "but if teachers spend five years in university, it can't be true, can it?" While no one advised leaders to attend leadership programs similar to teacher education programs, many believed that the municipal government was a fairly new concept to much of Newfoundland and that many issues could be addressed in seminars/workshops based on the advice shown in Table 64. One man felt that budgeting was a crucial item "that you just didn't come into"; this was not in reference to balancing books, etc., but to spending money where it would have its greatest impact and to having long-term plans. As he said, "You get confused with all the organizations on the go that are supposed to be creating jobs, but I can't see any difference year after year." One man felt that leadership was too often "removed from the people . . . it was becoming too much on paper and not enough face-to-face." It was changing the personal interaction of cultural tradition, and, according to some respondents, not effectively.

Some respondents felt that leaders should always provide time for reflection and planning. "Not only would they learn from themselves," said one man, "but others could also learn from them." One man, in particular, pointed to the eyesores of two dilapidated swimming pools as reminders of a waste of taxpayers' money. "If we could show this to others," said the man, "perhaps they could avoid similar useless projects."

The teachers and high school students advised leaders to invest in the education of youth, advice that ranged from federal policy providing financial assistance, to a meaningful and stimulating provincial curriculum, to local community support such as scholarships recognizing academic achievement.

The other areas of advice to leaders, while not promoted strongly by any one group, are worth noting: promoting fairness and justice; promoting unity and harmony; avoiding reducing services; being open and learning from the past; recognizing their own limitations; and setting examples of restraint. A small percentage of the two older groups commended leaders for their current actions.

SUMMARY

Literacy cannot be a matter of legislation or proselytization. It is basically an individual decision within a sociocultural context. The respondents of Bridget's Harbour, in evaluating themselves in terms of their competencies and their personal traits, were not differentiated according to levels of literacy. In general, they felt they worked extremely hard and could be successful at whatever they tried. They believed they were kind, considerate, got along with others, were close to family, and had lots of friends. If there was any discrepancy in ratings it was that those with lower literacy standards gave themselves higher ratings. The respondents tended to feel most comfortable socially with family and friends and were inclined to shy away from clergy, politicians, and merchants, with whom they felt they did not have a lot in common. Their major accomplishments in life dealt with family; this priority of family is consistent with their expressed values, which were discussed in Chapter 3. There was general agreement that the Bridget's Harbour area was a great place to be, a place where they had family and friends, felt secure, and were happy and contented.

The respondents had lots of advice to give. For parents, the significant advice was to understand children, take care of them, treat them fairly, set appropriate standards, and encourage them to stay in school. Young people were advised to stay in school and to study hard in order to succeed. They were also cautioned about the dangers of drugs and irresponsible behaviour. While schools and teachers received a potpourri of advice, all was focused on their providing the best learning context for the students. Advice to leaders was more focused. The two main bits of advice dealt with promoting job opportunities and listening to people's advice and acting on it. A significant number of the younger generations also felt that there was a need for provision for leadership development. "After all," as one young adult said, "without good leaders we have no direction, no movement, we're all over the place."

Undercurrents (Undertow) 9

An undertow or undercurrent is a strong current below the surface; undertow sometimes flows in a different direction from that of the surface current. This chapter examines the undertow of what has been presented in the previous chapter.*

AM I LITERATE OR NOT?

Perhaps this is not the right question to ask. The thrust of this book has been that literacy cannot be separated from sociocultural context and people's conceptualization of themselves. Those who function effectively within their sociocultural contexts may be considered culturally thoughtful and culturally literate. They are not subservient to the context; they are not passive participants. Rather, they interpret the context in the process of shaping their own roles. They situate themselves within their environment by formulating their goals or problems, by examining the wisdom of past cultural acts and beliefs, and by analysing current conditions in terms of support and challenges. The direction they eventually take is based on what is meaningful for them in their particular situation and not on pressures from external officials, educators, or bureaucrats.

In trying to decide whether a person is "literate" one cannot base the decision narrowly on the results of a school or literacy program or curriculum; a valid answer can only come from a life curriculum. Purves (1991) provides a framework for understanding such a curriculum (this was discussed for another purpose in Chapter 6). To

*Since Bridget's Harbour in many ways is a microcosm of rural Newfoundland, data from other sources are used in this chapter to discuss the notion of "undertow" and the issue of change.

recap, curriculum must entail three functions: (1) to develop cultural loyalty, that is, to know the expectations of one's culture; (2) to move beyond the structure of the local culture and learn how to interact with a wide range of people in terms of appropriateness of language and content; and (3) to actualize oneself as an individual, to formulate goals and plans peculiar to oneself, to map out a course of action. This framework might be represented diagrammatically as in Figure 5.

Figure 5: A Culture Curriculum

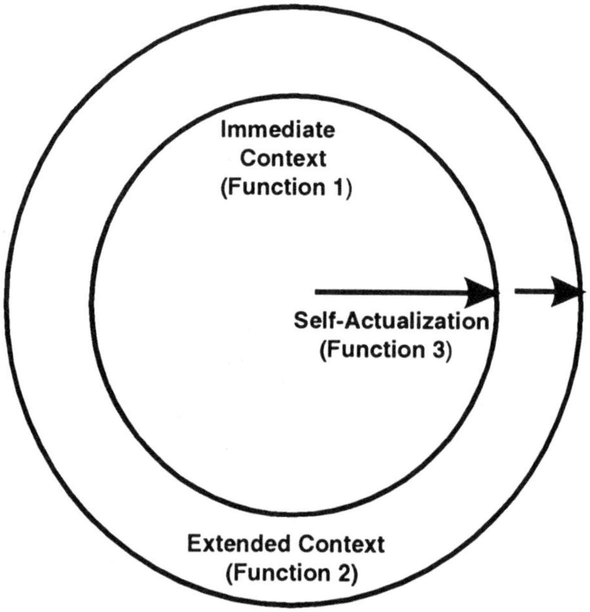

Immediate context refers to the socio-environmental context or culture within which a child is born and raised. In Gee's (1991: 3) terminology, this is one's primary (culture) discourse, which Gee defines as "a socially accepted association among ways of using language, of thinking, and of acting that can be used to identify oneself as a member of a 'social network.'" Within this cultural context, each person has goals or plans that vary in terms of the degree to which the person wishes to become involved in cultural activities. *Extended context* represents the culture of a broader society that includes officials, business, institutions, the media, etc. It is represented in Figure 5 as a larger circle encompassing the immediate context because there are more people in this extended cultural domain than are found in one's primary culture; furthermore, the direction of impact or encroachment is usually from extended to immediate context.

In order to answer the question of whether a person is "literate," one must consider the cultural domain (immediate or extended context) in which the person functions. Levine (1982) maintains that to be literate means more than possessing reading and writing skills; it also involves knowing one's culture – its norms, attitudes, and behaviours – and being able to operate thoughtfully within that culture.

There is no doubt that the respondents of Bridget's Harbour were both literate and culturally thoughtful within their primary culture and functioned adequately within that context. While there were some changes across generations, such as the youth being less immersed in the language of the culture and being less inclined to place a high priority on religion than were the seniors, overall, regardless of age and literacy levels, respondents seemed to have learned their culture well. They knew the social mores, were involved in subsistence activities, had acquired various skills, engaged in a variety of literacy tasks, were aware of the enfranchised and disenfranchised in the community, were sceptical of church and government authorities over various decisions, had noted similar changes in their community and education, were knowledgeable of the economic bases of the community, were clear on their main goals (economic security) and on how they might have a better future (investment in jobs, effective leadership, and less administration or bureaucracy). They were generally active in the life of the community, had strong family ties and good friends and neighbours, had positive and strong self-images, and were generally satisfied with their way of life and with Bridget's Harbour as their place of residence.

They valued life experiences. As one informant noted, "There's only so much you can learn from books." Book learning without having learned the lessons of experience from culture was viewed sceptically. This was reflected in a comment about one individual who had achieved highly in education (book learning) but lacked in cultural experience: "Poor thing, she can't boil a cup of water for herself." Learning from books was respected but learning from experience was often more significant. One senior told of a ship's captain of years gone by who could not read his name in print but who continuously took "his boat across" (to European ports). She continued that he often told her that he would lie awake at night thinking about all the information in navigation manuals and wondering how he could get access to it. Yet, he learned well from experience, and, as she added, "He never had a mishap in all the trips he made."

While the various groups of respondents could be identified with respect to literacy levels, this was not a factor in distinguishing their identity with their culture and their ability to function well within it. Comparisons of data between the more literate and less literate (based on grade level achievement) showed insignificant differences in terms of how they perceived literacy, professed certain beliefs and values, engaged in cultural tasks, or entertained images of self-competency and self-satisfaction. Except for the youth (whose identity was as much based in an extended as in an immediate context), the residents of Bridget's Harbour were relatively homogeneous in their perceptions of the relationship of cultural values and literacy development and in their use of literacy within their lives.

To return to the question "Am I literate?" you may indeed ask, "Am I poor?" If I tell you that I only have a grade 8 or a grade 4 education, am I illiterate? If I tell you I have only $20 to my name, am I poor? But in the case of the latter, if I add that I own my home, do not have any mortgage, pay low property taxes, can do my own house maintenance and can help others in this regard, have enough meat (game), fish, and berries in the freezer to last the winter, enough wood in the shed to supply heat for two years, that the wife's father is living with us (husband, wife, and two children) and he gets his Canada pension, the old age pension, and a war pension, then with $20 in my pocket, am I poor?

Likewise, if I have grade 4 but am financially secure, have no problems in having reading and writing needs met, am independent, have a loving and supportive family, own my home, have an active and enjoyable social life, am happy and contented, then am I illiterate?

If by illiteracy or low-literacy is meant deprivation, ignorance, despair, and lack of opportunity, then the respondents of Bridget's Harbour are far from being illiterate or low-literate. If the respondents were to remain within their primary culture there would not be the least concern with respect to their functioning, their literacy, or their future.

TRANSCENDING CULTURAL DOMAINS

It would be a misrepresentation to suggest that the residents of Bridget's Harbour were contained within their primary culture.

They had frequent contact with rules, regulations, business, law, health care, and other institutions from outside their immediate context. But as long as these regulations and activities could be understood within their immediate context and integrated into their lives, they developed control over them. For example, UI formed a significant part of the community's income structure and those who received this income were brilliant in their display of knowledge of the procedural aspects for accessing it easily and quickly. They were astute in using as scribes such people as the MHAs and medical personnel, who were knowledgeable of matters within an extended context, to resolve problems and attain requests. They tuned into the provincial and national news and listened to radio talk shows and so understood what was going on outside their immediate culture and whether factors raised at a provincial or national level would affect them. While they were critical or sceptical of the decisions of officialdom, they knew that if they were to benefit from these decisions they did not raise any questions (at least, not publicly), for as they said, "You don't look a gift horse in the mouth."

The manner in which the people of Bridget's Harbour coped with the literacy/language demands of an extended culture is aptly described by Gowen (1992). One analogous context she describes involves the slave days of the Old South in the U.S. The master of the plantation usually considered the slaves (the workers) to be ignorant and helpless with no control over their lives. Yet, many of them had learned very effective coping strategies (often involving literacy) and in many cases could "out best" the master's authority. Gowen indicates that in the slave quarters, this was referred to as "puttin' on ole massah." As a second analogous context in which the astuteness of people was also evident, she describes a hospital setting of the 1990s, in which many of the entry-level laundry and kitchen workers were perceived as illiterate and helpless. They were issued handbooks by their supervisors on how to complete various tasks. Yet the workers realized that following these printed directions was not always meaningful. They had their own techniques that were much more effective. Rather than confronting the system with its consequences, they worked around it. Like the slaves, they were more alert and knowledgeable than the supervisor recognized and so they succeeded in "puttin' on the supervisor."

The people of Bridget's Harbour showed similar astuteness and competence. They capitalized on the system to their advantage. They were sometimes accused of "using" or even "abusing" the system. What they were actually doing was being culturally thoughtful and ingenious in their understanding of the system and in the selection of strategies for their effective functioning.

Interestingly, the youth, a literate group and less experienced in the customs of their immediate culture, were more inclined to be influenced in a subconscious manner by what was happening outside that culture. One might suppose that because of their level of education, their greater knowledge of current fads and customs from an extended culture, and their lower allegiance to their primary culture, they would be more knowledgeable and critical of an extended culture. But they were not. One hypothesis for their lack of thoughtfulness within an extended culture, and an alarming one, is that the youth were in transition between their primary culture and an extended culture. They had not learned the values and customs of their primary culture well enough and therefore did not have a strong grounding in the related cultural thoughtfulness with its scepticism and suspicion. They were more vulnerable to being influenced by an extended culture. This phenomenon also typifies other cultural groups and has been particularly noted among Native groups who have failed to learn well their primary or Native culture and only partly understand the "white man's" extended culture.

"BUT WE'RE FOUNDERING"

This expression was commonly used by older people of Bridget's Harbour to mean that support was giving way, such as when a cliff or bank of earth was slipping into the sea. It is also used to refer to a boat that ran aground on a rock or reef and that could no longer continue its course. When used to describe the situation of the people themselves, the two concepts of "support" and "not staying on course" were very significant. The people were no longer able to integrate and control literacy demands from outside their immediate context; they no longer had the support to continue their way of life. They were losing control. The cod fishery had been suspended by outside authorities (federal government); an adult education upgrading centre was established by a private developer through assistance from a federal financial compensation plan; rules about school opening and closure and curriculum (children's school) were set by a school board in a town of which very few knew the name; the church was no longer viewed as providing the leadership and support as in former times; their thinking, whether on literacy or other topics, was influenced by the media (in fact, a constant message they heard and that was reinforced by the introduction of the TAGS education upgrading program and the adult learning centre, was that they were illiterate); decisions were made about hiring of people in government, school, council, or church positions by "outside" officials or by those with "outside connections"; the community council, rather than exemplifying their cultural values and behaviours in its operations and dealings with the people, was resorting to more formal written language structures more indicative of bureaucracy and officialdom.

In Bridget's Harbour there was frustration over inaction or lack of information from the government as to what was in store for their future. They were willing to attend an adult education upgrading centre even if they had no plans to go further in their educational endeavours; they were even willing to meet in a rented house to "talk" about their future. Some were suspicious that the current situation was part of a hidden agenda to close down the inshore fishery, to place a revived fishery in the hands of big plant owners and the draggers. They felt the government was keeping them "busy" in the meantime until at some point they would "wake up to find the deed done." While the government and union were promoting the emergence of "professional" fisherpersons, no one knew (at the time of the study) what this would entail. The adult education upgrading program was not differentiated for those who hoped to return to the fishery from those who were going to opt out for work outside the fishery. In the meantime the moratorium became the source of other difficulties.

> Since the moratorium, people do not socialize as much, and the attitude towards voluntarism has changed. Some respondents attributed this change to the phenomenon that when the groundfishery was active, people came together on a daily basis, as fellow-workers in the plant or fellow-fishers on the wharves, which consequently instilled trust in each other to do things cooperatively. With more personal isolation came more distrust of each other, and apathy towards community affairs. (Canadian Institute for Research on Regional Development, 1995:186)

The respondents lacked the experience, the knowledge of organizational or bureaucratic structure, a familiarity with procedural operations, and the critical literacy necessary to situate the power within their culture, to place the resolution of matters under their control.

"THERE'S A PLOT UNDERFOOT"

Literacy/educational upgrading was offered to the fisherpersons and plant workers as a partial solution (in some cases, as a total solution, especially for those who completed a trade and left the province) to their social and economic woes. But anyone who understands literacy will know that it is best acquired in circumstances when people control their goals and purposes and when social and economic conditions are supportive rather than stressful. Granted, there were some, especially young people, who jumped at the opportunity to obtain instruction in a trade and headed off to the mainland. But there were many, including some who participated in the educational endeavours, who became more and more suspicious of rules and regulations formulated during the fishery moratorium. They felt the government knew that a revived fishery could never sustain the number of workers as in former times and they also felt that many of the rules and regulations were aimed at getting as many people as possible out of the fishery (and out of Newfoundland), especially inshore fishers. They felt there was a tug-of-war between the fishers, on one hand, and the bureaucrats, on the other. This point was aptly made by a fisherman in a letter to the editor (*Evening Telegram*, 1 May 1996).

> Never once has the incompetent way the fishery was managed by the geniuses in Ottawa been mentioned. Never once would those smart-ass bureaucrats listen to what these people were telling them that the fish stocks were declining.
>
> Never once has the destruction of small fish by draggers (and this is still going ahead today in the shrimp fishery) or the destruction caused by draggers on the spawning grounds been mentioned. Never once has the situation that exists with seals been mentioned. They are tip toeing around this issue like a bunch of pussy cats afraid some animal activist in Europe may shout at them.
>
> No, they would lead you to believe (seeing we are stupid fisherpeople) that none of these factors had any bearing on the decline of the cod stocks. It's those people in those small boats who are the problem and they have to go one way or another.

Another letter to the editor (*Evening Telegram*, 29 March 1996) had supported these comments.

> The death of the cod fishery prompted the large offshore fleets – mainly multinationals – to turn to other species and basically move to a lower rung on the fish-food chain.
>
> Presently the fishery is carried on by shrimp trawlers with equipment that is causing very large bycatches of juvenile fish of all species and wanton destruction of the sea beds. These juvenile fish are shovelled overboard in unknown thousands of biomass.

A newspaper account (*Evening Telegram*, 15 March 1996) of a meeting of more than 100 fisherpersons noted that the impact of the draggers and the use of otter trawl technology were uppermost in their minds. Fisherpeople were also worried about permitted harvesting practices they, themselves, were engaged in. One fisherman said, "The men in _____ are catching lump roe; lump roe is $3.00 a pound. But how long will this last? The roe (eggs) are taken from the female which then dies and is of no use. These eggs will never hatch; how long will this last?" They felt helpless to stop a practice they were part of. It was a source of much needed income and a continued link with the ocean.

Most of the fisherpeople had remembered an era of resettlement in the 1950s and 1960s by a former provincial government. That plan was publicly promoted. The goal was to get people out of smaller communities and into "growth centres." To most, this had been a failure. They felt a similar goal was being pursued now, and it was even worse than had happened a few decades earlier. Firstly, the "plot" was more concealed and some people refused to believe it was happening. Secondly, the displaced fishery workers from smaller rural communities were not going to "growth centres" in the province but to large urban centres in mainland Canada. It was estimated that 20 per cent of young people were leaving (*Evening Telegram*, 7 July 1996). Thirdly, they maintained the "plot" was initiated and promoted by the federal government so that the people had less power in fighting it. They felt that moves by the federal government on other fronts, such as changes in the UI regulations, were all creating added pressure for the depopulation of rural Newfoundland.

A publication by the Canadian Institute for Research on Regional Development in April 1995 contributed to this belief. This study had been partly funded by the Atlantic Canada Opportunities Agency (ACOA), an agency of the federal government. The authors of the report studied twelve communities in Atlantic Canada, six in Newfoundland and Labrador. While no specific communities were named, the study "urged Ottawa to let the truly hopeless places dwindle away" (*Evening Telegram*, 19 June 1996). The report judged the viability of communities on one criterion only – economic. The authors set up three categories of communities based on economic viability.

> (1) Communities with a solid infrastructure and some economic diversity.
> (2) Communities showing some promise for economic diversity, but having little in the way of administrative structure and support.
> (3) Communities totally reliant on the fishery in the past with precious few entrepreneurs and little in the way of administrative capacity to identify, plan, organize, and pursue new economic activities.

The report emphasized that economic viability in the fishery was only likely with modern technology and trawlers. In reference to the Great Northern Peninsula of Newfoundland, the authors said: "Certainly a growth community of 26,000 people concentrating on fishing and fish processing can be prosperous, if both activities are carried out with modern technology. Unfortunately, they are not. Only a small minority of those engaged in the fishery are using large modern trawlers" (p. 93). The report advocated the very thing that inshore fisherpeople were fighting against to keep them alive. Furthermore, the report was reminiscent of documents of the 1950s and 1960s as it advocated centralization, which according to the authors would allow the people "access to good educational, cultural, recreational, and health facilities in St. John's or Halifax" (p. 296). One woman, who said she "was fit to be tied," damned the authors for their "urban egomaniacal attitude" and said there was more "culture in rural communities in Newfoundland and Labrador than in St. John's and Halifax put together." What bothered another woman was that the report focused only on the northern cod and its disappearance. "They didn't bother to look at the other species [of fish] that we are now processing." People were aware of the value of other fish species through periodic newspaper reports. For example, the estimated market value of fish landed in the province in 1994 (during the moratorium) was $452 million, $307 million of which was for shellfish. For 1995, the total value was $588.6 million, over $450 million of which was for shellfish (*Evening Telegram*, 4 August 1996). The data for one under-utilized species, sea urchins, showed that the processing revenue for 1993-94 was $44,000, but for 1995-96 it had increased to $814,600.

As time passed, any subtleness regarding a plot to resettle people became explicit. A May 1996 review by Human Resources Development of the TAGS program (*Evening Telegram*, 20 January 1997) stated that career consultants (from Human Resources Development) "are having a tough time persuading people to take job retraining and to look for work outside the fishery" – in most cases, meaning outside Newfoundland. The reasons for this, according to the report, are: "Cultural barriers, most notably the unwillingness of many maritimers to *relocate*" (emphasis added), and "strong community ties, home ownership and an often unwavering belief that the fish stocks will return." These men and women, because of their resistance to resettlement, are considered "non-salvageable"; officials "have accepted that to some extent and concentrate on those they consider salvageable," according to the daily paper.

REGULATIONS

As part of the plot theory, people told of the many regulations from outside bureaucrats that encroached on their lives in their primary culture. A letter to the editor of the *Evening Telegram* on 1 May 1996 stated:

> These regulations are coming at us from all angles by those experts in Ottawa, the better part of whom wouldn't know a cod fish from a dory scoop. People are driven to total frustration not only with themselves but with everyone else.

In a special report in the *Evening Telegram* on 5 May 1996, the reporter noted:

> The one certain villain in the picture is the Federal Department of Fisheries and Oceans which is blamed for the anxiety and uncertainty in people's lives. Some are sure beyond doubt that government is out to destroy rural Newfoundland through draconian fishing regulations.

There were two types of regulations in which the people were continuously caught up: regulations for income support and regulations for a possible revived fishery.

Income support. The regulations for income support went through various stages, with the final stage being part of The Atlantic Groundfish Strategy (TAGS) or the "Package." Application forms had to be completed. If people failed to qualify, then they could bring their literacy skills to bear in an appeal process that extended over three levels. If they were successful in qualifying for income support, the next issue was the length of time for which they could qualify. Once again, if the qualifying period was less than anticipated, they could go through the appeals process.

It was widely known that federal government officials had underestimated the number of people who would qualify, and this only raised scorn for the way bureaucrats were "on top of things." One person felt that when this realization "hit home," the officials countered by "tightening the regulations" to make it more and more difficult to qualify. One fisherman commented, "What you have to remember is that over the last four years, with NCARP, TAGS, SEC, vessel support, we've been through hell and then some. People have got all these letters and every time those letters started coming, some people got caught on the short end of the stick" (*The Express*, 24 April 1996). People reported frustrating and heart-wrenching instances of disqualification either initially or during the income support period. One woman who was dropped from the program saw no alternative for a livelihood but welfare. She said, "The two older kids don't like the idea of me going on welfare, but what can I do? They cut me off and that's it."

Fisher/fishery classification. Two sets of regulations were aimed at streamlining a future fishery. One, directed at professionalizing fishers, was initiated by the fishers' union and endorsed at the provincial level. The second, labelled CORE (Classification of Real Enterprises), was the creation of the federal Department of Fisheries and Oceans.

There were three levels of professional classification: Apprentice fisherperson, Level 1, and Level 2. Prior to the moratorium, fisher-people were classed as full-time or part-time. While professionalization had been designed by the union to recognize the skills and knowledge of those involved in the fishery, some now felt it was going to exclude people from fishing.

CORE is directed at classifying fishing boats or enterprises. Fishers must choose one of three qualifying time periods: 1989-95, 1986-92, or 1985-91. Among other criteria, a fisher must have been the head of an active fishing enterprise for two of the last three years of the period, must have held a key fishery licence, and must have earned a minimum income from the fishery. The latter was a big concern for a number of fishers and many tales were recounted. One fisherman, now fifty-three, began fishing with his father at the age of nine, and left school at fifteen to fish full-time. He failed to qualify through CORE because his gross income fell short of the criterion. He felt penalized because he had headed a one-person operation and therefore would have had less income. Two others who failed due to the minimum income criterion stated that there was a catch failure in 1990-91 due to severe ice conditions. (All qualifying periods contained these poor income years.) The qualifications of another fisherman were questioned because during the moratorium he had earned a salary outside the fishery as an instructor for a course offered by his union. He was a veteran fisherman of twenty years.

CORE and professionalization regulations overlapped as a person had to be classified as a Level 2 professional before being classed as CORE. One of the criteria for Level 2 was to have spent at least seven years in the fishery. One person who fished with his father for six years could not qualify as CORE and purchase his father's enterprise licence so his father could not retire as planned. A big implication for many fishers is that the number of CORE fishing enterprises will be capped, and after that a Level 2 professional fisherperson can only be classed as CORE if he/she is able to buy the licence of a retiring CORE fisher.

One fisherman who felt harassed by all the regulations and implications said, "Somebody is sitting at a desk, a bureaucrat, a pencil pusher saying 'I got the answers to Newfoundland's problems'" (*Evening Telegram*, 17 March 1996).

"VENTING OUR VIEWS"

Fishers are not reticent to speak out about the intrusion on their lives by union and government, as the examples cited above show. Yet they admit that they have very little power to interrupt the planned agenda. "But nobody can ever say we didn't make a murmur," said one person. Not only were fishers, and people in general, expressing their views through talk and writing, but they also were capitalizing on a time-honoured cultural tradition – the medium of song.

Song has given voice to Newfoundlanders for centuries, not only to express emotion but to publicize their views. Because song incorporates music and rhythm with words, it constitutes a powerful way of exposing one's heart and soul about an issue in a much more poignant way than language alone could ever do. Many songs were composed and sung on the theme of "we're foundering," and songs from the 1950s and 1960s about resettlement resurfaced. Some stanzas of songs as examples of the voice of the people about government rules, regulations, and expectations, and the helplessness of the people in charting their futures, are given below. (Note: the words on paper are a poor substitute for the words as sung, whether with or without musical accompaniment. Those who know the songs will "hear" the rhythm as they read the words. For those who don't know the songs, the meaning and emotion will, unfortunately, be less.)

The first song portrays a feeling of helplessness in the face of present conditions.

Now the waters are as barren as the cliffs that guard the cove
And catch the north wind blowing on the shore
And I wonder how an ocean turns as lifeless as a stone
And I wonder can the sea revive once more
And I wonder will they lie there evermore?

Well I hear some people say we'd be better off to stay ashore
And train for jobs outside the fishery
Now wouldn't I look like a fool to go traipsing off to school
After forty years of living on the sea?

(From the song, "Will They Lie There Evermore?" from the cassette, *Gypsies and Lovers*, by the Irish Descendants.) © John Phippard, 1994. Used by permission.

The following two selections portray the feelings about resettlement and out-migration. While these songs were written and sung for an earlier time, they were revived to express people's similar feelings at this time.

They're outport people with outport ways
But there's no where to use them and now it's too late
And they curse on the one who uttered the phrase
"Resettlement now while resettlement pays."

(From the song "Outport People" from the cassette of that name, by Simani.)

Sure the government paid us for moving away
And leaving our birthplace for a better day's pay
They said that our poor lives would n'er be the same
Once we took part in the government game.

(From the song "Government Game" from the album, *Towards the Sunset*, by Pat and Joe Byrne with Baxter Wareham); Al Pittman, songwriter.

A final example confronts the choice that many people in Newfoundland are forced to consider today.

I was born down by the water
It's here I'm gonna stay
I've searched for all the reasons
Why I should go away
'Cause I haven't got the thirst
For all those modern- day toys
So I'll just take my chances
With those saltwater joys.

Part of one other stanza in this song depicts the contrast of life in rural Newfoundland with that in big cities.

Some go to where the buildings
Reach to meet the clouds
Where warm and gentle people
Turn to swarming faceless crowds.

(From the song "Saltwater Joys" from the cassette, *Flatout*, by Buddy Wasisname and the Other Fellers); Wayne Chaulk, songwriter.

A NEW LITERACY

The title of this book is *Literacy for Living* and the first section of this chapter clearly indicates that in dealing with primary culture matters, as well as many demands of an extended culture, prior to the cod moratorium the people of Bridget's Harbour (and no doubt in many other parts of the province) were sufficiently literate. But conditions changed. The extended culture encroached more on their immediate context than most people would ever have imagined. "Our lives are a bunch of forms," said one woman. They felt that they were constantly being required to demonstrate via print (literacy) to outside officials who they were and what they "were up to." Not only did the amount of print demands increase, but also the nature of such demands. They had to "make cases" for their income and argue their right to have a future in the fishery. But they also had to "come to grips" with the fact that being literate, being knowledgeable in using print as a reader and writer, did not always work. There was more than print involved in arriving at a decision (often to their disadvantage) and many were not only not prepared for this; they did not know how to deal with it.

The Power Behind the Print

The power behind print has been recognized by experts in the field of literacy. Maguire (1995) notes that each literacy act is not just a reading, or a writing, or a speaking act, but also a social, cultural, or political act. Wason-Ellam and Blunt (1995: 3) state that "Questions about literacy and society are inseparable from questions of literacy and power relations." This inseparability was well phrased by a fisherman.

> Nobody's listening to the fishermen. They're nothing, they're only fishermen. The people making decisions are bureaucrats sitting behind a desk who know nothing about the way we live. Yet they open a textbook and make a decision that affects all our lives. (*Evening Telegram*, 5 May 1996)

The power-literacy scenario surfaced in a number of ways. One was manifested in the knowledge of the local fishers versus the power of the scientists. For years past, the fishers had pointed out that the fish stocks were in serious decline, only to be ignored by officials who still sanctioned high total allowable catches (TACs). Since the moratorium the role of draggers and fishing gear was raised time and again by the fishers who documented the destruction they caused; the officials remained silent. A report in the *Sunday Telegram* (4 August 1996) pitted the knowledge of a local fisherman against a specialist over a cod spawning theory. While the scientist "believed" that the fertilized eggs rise and remain near the surface while they are hatching, the fisherman responded, "It don't happen.

If this happened the seagulls would eat every one and there would never be another fish seen." He went on to document evidence that spawning occurred near the ocean floor, noting stirred up sand and mud and the attachment of eggs to seaweed. The fisherman's theory would likely be ignored.

The power behind literacy, as a factor in a new literacy, is not just confined to matters related to the fishery. It is common throughout society. One of the most radical books delineating the power beyond literacy is Denny Taylor's *Toxic Literacies: Exposing the Injustice of Bureaucratic Texts* (1996). Taylor demonstrates how the criminal justice system, the welfare system, the health care system, and other bureaucracies control people's lives through the use of "official texts." This power manifests itself in a number of ways.

1. *Ignoring print*. If an official chooses to ignore print by not acknowledging your correspondence or responding to the issue raised, there is little you can do. One example concerns a person who was in dispute with an engineering firm. The contact person from the firm was never available by phone and did not return calls. The other person sent three faxes, which also did not produce a response. After waiting a period of time after each fax, the person would continue to try to get a response by phone. Each time when the receptionist was asked if the contact person had seen the faxes, she indicated that she couldn't recall having received a fax. Another example of the lack of the power of print relates to the recall of books at a university library, especially when the books in question have been taken out by faculty. It is not unusual for the recall to be ignored in spite of deadlines, supposedly while the faculty member decides to finish using the books.

2. *The brush-off*. This occurs in the form of vague and meaningless language. "You can be assured that we will take the matter under advisement."

3. *Blaming the victim*. The official does not only not answer the question or address the issue of the writer but attacks the writer. As an example, a person wrote CBC radio over the failure of a reporter to keep a promise about making available a tape of an interview. A CBC spokesperson, in a letter, did not address the issue of providing the tape requested by the writer based on what the reporter said, but stated that the writer was "insistent," "bullying," and "insulting." Supposedly, this alleged behaviour did not warrant his receiving a copy of the tape.

4. *Raising irrelevant issues*. This is similar to blaming the victim. The writer's case is lessened by raising matters that tend to disparage the writer's credibility, even though those matters are irrelevant

to the focal issue. Two examples come from universities. In one case, a professor requested information (under the Access to Information Act) on the travel and hosting expenses of the president and vice-presidents. A quote by a university official stated, "All of this says to me, this is a question which has a context. The context is somebody who has a file already seven feet long – and with a history of personal vendettas." The second example concerns a professor who launched an appeal against harassment by a department chairman. In an interview with the Dean, the latter asked if the professor was "antagonistic" in his behaviour towards the chairman, as if this would justify the harassment. (Note: the dictionary defines "antagonistic" as opposing, counteracting, arousing dislike.)

5. *Setting up obstacles*. The issue of the writer will only be addressed when certain obstructing conditions are met. In the case of the professor requesting expense information, the official reply indicated the information would be available for a cost of $10,561. A definition of the term "hosting expenses" would cost $81.

6. *Power of protection*. The officials protect themselves or their friends by closing out the writer. They may use some of the above forms of power in doing this, such as failing to act or using vague and ambiguous language. In one case a faculty member, as a doctoral student, had violated plagiarism guidelines as set down by the university. When this was brought to the officials' attention, the ruling made by the administration was not to do anything about it, supposedly to protect its "image."

7. *Power of authority*. The power demonstrated here seems to have no rationale except that rules made must be rules followed, even if doing so flies in the face of logic and common sense. An example comes from a woman who received income support under the TAGS agreement but according to the TAGS counsellor she had to engage in some specified activity to continue to qualify. One option was to do volunteer work, and during one interview with the counsellor she gave the following account of her current volunteer activities.

> I am president of the Dart's League, a leader with the Sparks and Brownies, a member of the Firettes, and am responsible for calling the men on my husband's roster who is a volunteer fireman. I am a member of the Winter Carnival Committee and the Summer Recreation Committee, a volunteer worker at the arena canteen, a member of my church's women's group; we meet every Wednesday. I am a member of the 1996 High School Graduation committee and I am busy making decorations for the graduation.

But according to the counsellor that was not good enough. The volunteer work had to be structured by him.

Another example of the presence of power over print comes from Revenue Canada. Responses from Revenue Canada are computer programmed so that regardless of what discussion occurs between the taxpayer and the Revenue Canada agent, nothing can be done until the previous response "works its way through the system," yet it may take a month for the taxpayer to receive the previous response. When the printed reply does arrive, the taxpayer must start again at square one with regard to the discussions previously held. By assigning several people to a person's file, it is difficult for the taxpayer to hold any one person responsible for an error in assessing the file. In one Revenue Canada office, the concept of power was further highlighted by the height of the chairs at the wickets, with the chairs for the agents being higher than those for the public – the latter were in a subservient position.

Information Overload

A new literacy must deal with increased amounts of information that continue to bombard us. The overwhelming effect of the current mass of information is highlighted by McCarthy (1991), who provides a number of examples. Among these are the realization that a typical weekday edition of the *New York Times* contains more information than the average person in the sixteenth century would encounter in *an entire lifetime*. Another is that the amount of information now doubles every five years. By the turn of the century (only a few years away), the doubling time will be every twenty months.

The cod moratorium period also provides an example of information overload. Below are listed some of the documents that fisherpeople and plant workers were expected to be familiar with.

- Northern Cod Adjustment and Recovery Program (NCARP): Canada/Newfoundland Early Retirement Program
- Northern Cod Adjustment and Recovery Program: Supplementary Information for Groundfish Licence Retirement Applicant
- Declaration Form Income Replacement Program (NCARP)
- Application Form Groundfish Licence Retirement
- Information Guide to Income Reduction (Clawback) under NCARP
- Northern Cod Adjustment and Recovery Program Work/UI Option Information Booklet
- Northern Cod Adjustment and Recovery Program Training Options Information Booklet
- Northern Cod Adjustment and Recovery Program Vessel Support – "Helping People Help Themselves": The Atlantic Groundfish Strategy Labour Adjustment Component Information Booklet

- The Atlantic Groundfish Strategy Groundfish Licence Retirement Program
- Groundfish Licence Retirement Program Bidding Form Round Two
- Amending the Fisheries Act: A Proposal for Modernization
- Summary of Changes to the Commercial Fisheries Licensing Policy for Eastern Canada
- Commercial Fishing Vessels Identification and Number Regulation
- Atlantic Licensing Policy Review: Consultation Document
- Professionalization of Newfoundland Fish Harvesters: Discussion Paper
- Professionalization of Newfoundland and Labrador Fish Harvesters: Proposal

If the above onslaught of information proves anything, it is that the federal Department of Fisheries and Oceans places little emphasis on the literacy statistics from the federal Department of Human Resources and Development, which indicate that the illiteracy rate in Newfoundland is about 44 per cent. The documents listed above are not for the illiterate. Interestingly, as women mobilized to analyse their role during the moratorium and in a future fishery, they raised a concern that they felt excluded from much of this information because men had more contacts with the bureaucracy through their being mostly the heads of fishing enterprises and the ones who had loans. (Provincial Advisory Council on the Status of Women, 1994).

As in the case of the power behind print, information overload certainly is not confined to the fisheries context. Today people speak of "surfing the net" or "travelling the information highway" and people literally spend many hours at a time absorbing information via this medium, often without much critical reflection. As well, the number of brochures, regional and community newsletters, and newspapers are on the increase, and statements from banks, the power company, and the phone company, for example, are usually accompanied by pamphlets of information.

The dissemination of information is similar in a way to the issue of power behind print. Information is power in the sense that it is expected that people will "buy into it." In fact, originators of mass information assume that people absorb rather than critically analyse. There is little time for the latter. An example of information for absorption comes from changes to the Unemployment Insurance Act. A full-page newspaper ad (*Evening Telegram*, October 1996) detailed some of the changes. It stated, "The new Employment Insurance (EI) system is aimed at getting people back into the workforce as quickly as possible." This sounds great on the surface but in the case of Newfoundland, people know there are no jobs, there is no workplace to get people into. The only way people are to get into the workplace is to leave Newfoundland, which is already happening in record numbers. The ad contained an 800-number for further information. But there was no use phoning this number for answers to specific questions. Phoning the number resulted in two more brochures regarding the UI changes being sent.

Another example where people are "fed" information comes from a brochure enclosed with a bank statement about turning changes in social structure or technology to advantage. Five opinions or suggestions by experts are provided. An assumption underlying the information is that the person undergoing the change is financially secure. The last point ends with the sentence, "All great journeys begin with a single step." One could easily add, "So do all disasters."

Not only was information thrust onto people but people were constantly asked for information. In completing the many forms for income assistance, classification, etc., the fishers and plant workers were required to submit extensive information, such as proof of their catches as far back as 1987 and cheque stubs from the past three years. The people were being forced into a pattern of living common to an extended culture, with a need for record-keeping and secretarial help.

The Façade of Literacy

A third aspect of a new literacy that must be recognized is the use of literacy as a façade. Print becomes an adornment to something; it is meant to impress but not to have meaning. One example concerns a cul-de-sac roadway on a university campus. This was closed to all vehicle traffic except buses and a sign to that effect was posted at the entrance. Yet cars continue to use this roadway, the drivers totally oblivious to the sign. And no action appears to be taken by the campus patrol.

A second example also relates to driver education. In a local newspaper, a police sergeant wrote a column on "Traffic Tips." Two tips in particular had special significance for one citizen who had been annoyed at times by their violation: "turning into a two-lane street," and "signals and lane changes." He wrote the sergeant and suggested that while the traffic tips were helpful, some stronger form of publicity or promotion was necessary. The sergeant acknowledged this in his reply. Nothing seemed to happen. In fact, not long afterwards, the citizen, on one occasion, saw a violation of the "signals and lane changes" while a police car sat on the opposite side of the intersection. The façade was great – a police sergeant writing to the public about traffic tips, but it was just that – a façade; the print was important for display and not for action.

A final example comes from a newspaper ad by a financial investment group. The ad begins, "Give us one good reason why women need financial planning." The ad then goes on to provide five such reasons. The bottom line is that women are invited to consult the investment firm for their financial planning. Pictured are twenty-one agents ready to help – all men. While the print message no doubt has validity, the picture somehow does not seem consistent with it.

MEETING NEW LITERACY CHALLENGES

Will current literacy expertise and literacy instruction adequately meet the needs of a new literacy? To think they can is to delude ourselves. Literacy no longer can be simply conceived as generating or constructing information via print. To tell learners that literacy is power is to mislead them. Literacy is used by power holders, and effective use of literacy involves knowledge of and negotiation with these power holders and the use of counter strategies if print as a medium does not lead to a satisfactory solution.

The fisherpeople and plant workers of Bridget's Harbour, and of other communities in Newfoundland and Labrador, like people in all walks of life, must meet the new literacy challenges. They cannot afford to be passive consumers of information; they must recognize literacy as façade; they must be aware of the power behind the print and map out the best strategies for dealing with this. Unless and until there is widespread involvement in a new literacy, people will feel as buffeted and helpless as the displaced fisherpeople and plant workers described in this book. People cannot allow themselves to be programmed for print consumption, to be shut out by print pronouncements. When they engage in literacy, in the use of print, they must be just as engaged in the context or culture of print.

IMPLICATIONS FOR LITERACY EDUCATORS AND POLICY-MAKERS

The intent is not to detail implications here but to refer to three major issues that hopefully will guide literacy educators and policy-makers in future literacy work. These are: perceptions of illiteracy or low-literacy, providing literacy programs, and learner involvement in literacy programs.

Perceptions of Illiteracy and Low-Literacy

We cannot afford to try to understand illiteracy or low-literacy within a deficit model, that is, promoting the notion that people with "less than desired literacy skills" are "lacking" or "deficient." This does nothing to enhance people's self-image and self-esteem; in fact, any psychology text will indicate that it is detrimental to one's learning. Furthermore, it does not reflect reality. We can all benefit from additional skill in an area, whether keeping bank records, looking after our lawn, cleaning the house, or managing time. Why should there be such a furore because a person decides that he/she can benefit from additional literacy expertise? Unfortunately, the deficit view is prevalent, as Lytle, Marmor, and Penner (1986:1) point out: "Adult learners are widely considered to have 'deficits' that require intensive prescription of skillwork to correct." It does not help when such perceptions are expressed by politicians and journalists. Think of the effect of the following perceptions on those for whom they were intended.

> The illiterate are mothers running dreadful risks in their homes because they cannot read the labels on dangerous substances or the instructions to deal with accidents to themselves or to their children. (Fairbairn, 1987: 597)

> The illiterate are farmers, failing themselves, their families and their land because they cannot keep up in an increasingly complex and technical industry where to keep abreast of change, you must read and understand. (Fairbairn, 1987: 597)

> Loss of hope for oneself is a descent into dissolution without end. It causes men to rage in fury and women to wound themselves. People who can't read come readily to view themselves as worthless junk, and many feel they must grab what they can out of life. Canada's prisons are full of men and women who can't read. (Callwood, 1990: 41)

These perceptions of the late twentieth century are not different from those of the nineteenth century when, as Street (1984: 105) points out, illiterates were perceived "as dangerous to the social order, as alien to the dominant culture, inferior and bound up in a culture of poverty. As such they represented a threat to the established order." It seems that we have not come a long way in our perceptions of illiterates and low-literate adults. But it is time to face reality. The story of the people of Bridget's Harbour and of other fishing communities should dispel the myth of the helpless and hopeless because of lack of print knowledge. We must understand literacy as relative to the cultural contexts in which people operate and must distinguish between the use of print and the power behind print in its effect on people's lives.

Providing Literacy Programs

Literacy programs must be relevant to the participants' current life situation. As Hinzen (1984) maintains, it is essential that programs be rooted in and developed from the culture rather than imposed as part of a large-scale program by good-intentioned program developers. Freire and Macedo (1987: 44) argue that since language is the essence of culture and language is the essence of literacy programs, the language of culture cannot be ignored; programs cannot "ignore the way language may confirm or deny life histories and experiences of people who use it." Literacy must be for living.

When meaningfulness is a main criterion for literacy programs, the emphasis is on whether the learner has done something thoughtful rather than on whether he/she has learned to do something correctly. Meaningfulness is not determined through periodic tests whereby the participants usually demonstrate their memory of what has been presented in the classroom. The key instructional method of a skills or traditional school approach to literacy/education is the "banking method" (Freire and Macedo, 1987), the notion of filling one up with information and knowledge. The focus is generally on learning specific information without questioning or critical analysis. This focus is also usually based on the goal of training the largest number of individuals as quickly and as inexpensively as possible (Graff, 1981).

In meeting the demands of a new literacy, the emphasis must be on critical reflection as action. "To say the world could benefit from an increase in critical thinking might not be an understatement" (Smith, 1988: 47). Rahnema (1976: 73) phrases the importance of critical thinking as follows:

> To become literate, to my mind, is to start the journey from primary critical consciousness. It is to emerge as a human being of praxis – capable of perceiving reality and transforming it for the achievement of its ends. It is to acquire an authentic voice capable of relating words to the realities of the world. It is to participate in the creation of a culture of freedom in place of a culture of silence.

Critical thinking is not finding fault with, a point highlighted by Freire and Macedo (1987). Instead, critical thinking means viewing oneself within one's own socio-economic and sociocultural context and asking meaningful questions about how an issue may affect one's living. It involves reflecting, interpreting, reinterpreting, reconciling different viewpoints, weighing ambiguities in terms of their validity, and proposing different solutions before choosing one. It is the ability to formulate what the problem is (that is, problematizing), for without knowing the problem, thinking is not directed. It is recognizing the power behind print, the façade of literacy, and the bombardment of print information.

The value of approaching literacy and education as critical thinking is that it is transferable to many issues, concerns, and tasks in a person's life. Heath (1987) reports that a survey of several hundred adult literacy programs around the world showed that after these initiatives had ended, the most successful were those that provided for sustained involvement of the participants through continued use of literacy techniques and strategies in their daily lives.

Learner Involvement in Literacy and Adult Education Programs

There is often concern about adults not enrolling in literacy and adult education programs. A wrong conclusion is that the adults are not interested. One way of understanding the involvement of learners in a literacy/education program has been proposed by Casey (1972) and is based on the work of Howard McCluskey from the University of Michigan. Casey uses the notions of *power*, *load*, and *margin* for learning. Each person has a certain "load"; this entails all the demands made on a person: job, family responsibilities, health problems, anxieties, suspicions, commitments to friends, community, etc., and the priority accorded these in a person's life. "Power" entails all the resources, stamina, time, encouragement, and so on at hand to help deal with one's load. The degree to which one's power exceeds one's load determines the "margin" for learning or the degree to which the learner can be involved in a program. This proposal is represented in diagram form in Figure 6.

In the example illustrated by this diagram, the margin for learning is small compared to the load the individual carries. When a program does not have much meaning for a learner, such as when a learner must complete worksheets on recognizing sentence types, punctuation, and types of nouns or remember the circulatory system of the body, this may in actual fact add to a person's load and thereby decrease one's commitment to the program and any positive long-term impact. While not using the terms "power" and "load," Valentine (1986:113) advocates increasing one's power while lessening one's load when he states, "Instead of moulding students to fit the type of instruction offered, teachers would tailor instruction to help learners meet the functional literacy demands they encounter,

Figure 6: A Model for Understanding Program Involvement

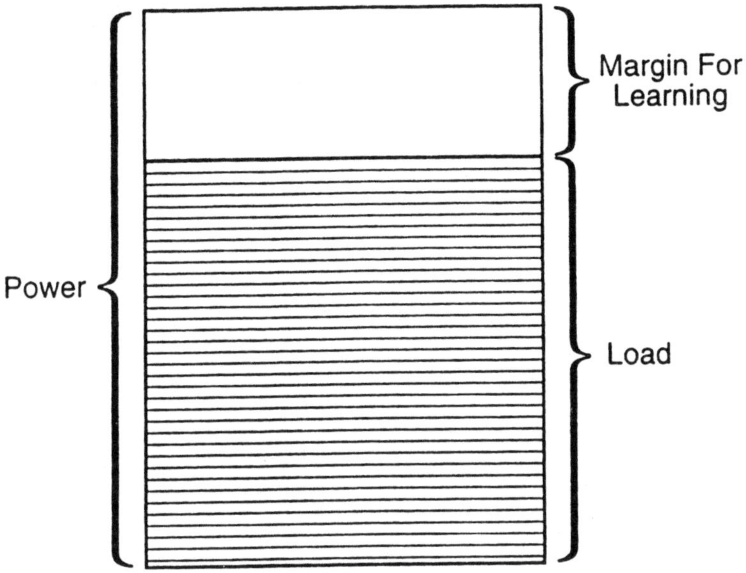

Source: Casey, 1972 49.

not in the classroom but in their adult lives." Some may enrol in a literacy or ABE program because they perceive it as extremely meaningful to their lives, whether for personal reasons or because it allows them to enter a trade that will lead to a job. Others may view the attainment of an ABE or school-leaving certificate as symbolically powerful because it is an acknowledgment of self-worth (Gowen, 1992). However, others may attend such programs because they must "toe the government line" to receive an income, while still others may resist and not attend because they are suspicious of the program intent; they may suspect it is a plot by officials to use education as a means to move people from rural areas. The meaning a program has for people is an important factor in determining their "load" and the availability of mental energy for, and commitment to, learning.

CONCLUSION

The life experiences of Bridget's Harbour respondents destroy many myths about literacy as a personal deficit or defect. They simultaneously magnify the necessity to understand a person's life context and the role of literacy within it. In addition, they highlight the significance of change within people's lives and the fact that change cannot be ignored when calculating literacy relevancy. Finally, the data point to the emergence of a new literacy in which different factors become focal, and these factors must be addressed by literacy policies and programs if literacy is to have any relationship to living.

Appendix: Exercises for Discussion and Action

CHAPTER 1

1. Choose two or three programs for adult literacy. Note the definition of literacy underlying each program. What are the implications? Choose two or three literacy programs for children. Note the definition of literacy underlying these programs. Compare these to the adult literacy definitions. What conclusions do you draw?

2. A number of descriptors of literacy have been presented in this chapter. Which of these relate to the "content" of literacy and which to the "context"?

3. What is your definition of literacy? What are the implications for program development and instruction?

4. While "kitchen talk" was a phrase coined by a respondent in this study, this concept has wider application. Give examples of its use in other aspects of society.

5. What is the role of research in literacy development?

6. The data in this study could have been reported as ethnographic description (people's lived experiences); instead, ethnographic and survey data were used to develop theoretical insights into the meaning of literacy as integral to the sociocultural context. What would have been the differences and the implications if the former method of reporting had been used?

(If you prefer, questions 5 and 6 may be left until you have read the book.

CHAPTER 2

1. As a group exercise, make a chart in which you brainstorm as many attributes of literacy as possible. Then decide whether the attributes are definitive/complete/exact/constant, that is, everyone, regardless of where they live, will think the same thing, or whether they are indefinite/variable/ relative. Form a conclusion. A start for the chart is given below:

Literacy Attributes	*Definitive*	*Indefinite*
grade level		
schooling		
reading		
etc.		

2. Using the suggested grade 9 criterion as indicative of functional literacy, list all the literacy tasks a person with grade 9 can do that a person with grade 8 can't. What is your conclusion?

3. How does a literacy task such as categorizing newspaper ads according to jobs as a classroom assignment differ from clipping or circling ads of a particular job by someone who is looking for work? What conditions would be necessary to teach this skill? Would you expect transfer from the school task to the real-life task? What conditions underlie transfer?

4. Can anyone decide for another what is functional in literacy? Discuss this from cognitive, social, ethical, political, and philosophical perspectives.

5. How could you actually know if a person needs a certain level of literacy (for example, grade 12) to perform a certain job adequately, such as waitress, plumber, nurse, tourist guide?

6. To what extent are your thoughts or beliefs original as opposed to being based on what others have said? Take each of the following concepts. Decide the basis of your meaning for each concept using the sources indicated. (Remember if it is original, you must have come up with it on your own.)

Concept	MediaTV/ radio	Authority govt/church other	Printed matter	Experiences (courses, workshops, meetings, etc.)	Original
Literacy					
Work					
Poverty					
Health					
Hunger					
Honesty					

7. For which of the above activities (nos. 1-6) would it be appropriate to make a stand, presentation, argument to some institutional authority (government, church, business, school, medical, etc.)? What would be the purpose or goal? What might be attained as a result? If you as an individual, or with others, feel inclined to follow this course of action, by all means do so.

CHAPTER 3

1. Use the framework below to discuss differences between real-life contexts and simulated contexts? Try to find as many factors as possible that would differentiate both contexts. Some simulated contexts are:

(a) Adult learners act as pretend editors of a local newspaper.
(b) Young children play house in kindergarten.
(c) A play about the downturn in the economy, such as the collapse of the fishery.
(d) A simulated parole board hearing for a jail inmate.
(e) School students taking the role of a person in a wheelchair for a day.
(f) School students fasting for a school day to empathize with hungry children in the Third World.

A framework for differentiating these contexts.

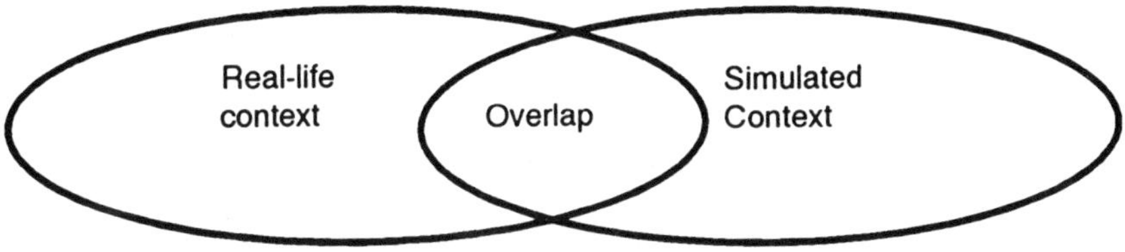

Brainstorm what the real-life context is like. Brainstorm factors unique to the simulated context. Indicate which characteristics are reflective of both. Your brainstorming should include not just description of the context but actions or events that could affect the context. For example, with regard to the students simulating people confined to wheelchairs, what would happen in both contexts if the person in the wheelchair was on the sixth floor of a building and a fire broke out? With regard to the students emulating hungry Third World children, how would their sleep patterns differ that night.

2. Take the seven functions of literacy provided by Heath (1980). Keep a log for a day and record your uses of literacy. Check the appropriate block. Detail one example each from reading, writing, and oral language and provide details of the situation, including goals. Share with your group/class.

Literacy Tasks	*Functions*						
	I	*SI*	*N*	*M*	*S*	*PR*	*C**
Reading							
Single**							
Collective							
Collaborative							
Effective							
Writing							
Single							
Collective							
Collaborative							
Effective							
Oral Language							
Single							
Collective							
Collaborative							
Effective							

* See Heath's categories in this chapter for complete words.
** "Single" means you are the only person involved; "collective" and "collaborative" are defined in the chapter; "effective" refers to whether you accomplished your goal.

3. What do you think is meant by "authentic evaluation"? From the above activity, suppose (a) someone observed what you had been doing, or (b) listened as you reported on what you had done, or (c) gave you a written test related to what you had done that was then scored. Which of these do you think is authentic evaluation? What are the pros and cons of each evaluative activity?

4. What roles do individuals play in literacy contexts and how do these affect the literacy event? In analysing roles, think of *who* the individual is, *how* this individual relates to others in terms of power, expectation, assistance, and *what* outcome(s) may result depending on role relationships and conditions? Some roles that individuals may have are:

(a) Child in a grade 3 classroom asked to read out loud from a text.

(b) Minister or priest reading/giving a sermon.
(c) A beginning (novice) broadcaster reading the news.
(d) Adult angry at an unexpected reduction in a social security income cheque writes the main office.

5. If for low-literate seniors you had to (a) recommend upgrading their literacy skills, or (b) capitalize on a supportive (family) network to ensure that reading and writing would never be a problem for them, which would you choose? Present arguments for your position. Lay out the "biases" that influence your decision.

6. Think of literacy situations in which you have been involved and in which power overrides literacy. Some examples might include: returning or getting a refund for a defective product; trying to get a government department to resolve a problem; getting the city or municipal office to correct a dangerous situation; resolving an insurance claim; getting a response from a church official as to why a certain course of action was followed, such as pertaining to the sale of church property. What is the role of literacy in these situations?

7. Think of instances when you had planned to engage in a literacy task – read a book, read the newspaper, write a letter, fill out forms – and something came up that delayed you from completing the task. Why was what came up valued more at that point in time? What factors/conditions determine what you value?

8. Sketch out a plan to teach literacy collectively in a formal literacy program.

9. For which of the above activities (nos. 1-8) would it be appropriate to make a stand, presentation, argument to some authority (government, church, business, school, medical, etc.)? What would be the purpose or goal? What might be attained as a result? If you as an individual or with others feel inclined to follow this course of action, by all means do so.

CHAPTER 4

1. "People out of work is more a matter of the economy than it is of education." Examine the truth of this statement. If possible, obtain statistics for a particular area (city, community) on (a) the number of jobs that are not filled, and (b) the number of people who wish to work but cannot find jobs. What is your conclusion?

What has been done in the area (city, community) over the past ten years to provide a higher level of education for the people? What percentage of the people have completed high school? What has been done in that period of time to create jobs? How many additional jobs were created? What is your conclusion?

2. Try to find the curriculum for a job search program, that is, how to look for a job. How is the content of this program similar to and different from the factors raised in this chapter that are considered essential to getting a job? Would you modify or change this program to make it better? If so, how?

3. How would you go about resolving the following impasses with respect to high school students:

(a) Their belief that education alone is sufficient to lead to a job.
(b) The influence of folk theory that if one's parents can live reasonably well without being gainfully employed, so can they.
((c) Experience (plus educational qualifications) is the key factor in getting a job.

4. Becker defines the human capital model as "the present value of past investment in the skills of people." Discuss this statement, focusing on how one can assess (a) present value, (b) past investment, (c) skills. Is a human capital model an appropriate model for evaluating the success of academic/trade skills instructional programs? Why or why not? For which of the following groups would a human capital model be of greater or less significance: politicians, educators, big business, social activists. Provide your rationale.

5. Choose one of the following projects.

(a) Interview (i) an employer and (ii) an instructor in a comparable trades instructional program regarding the characteristics/qualifications that a worker in that trade should possess. To what extent does the trade instructional program correspond to that of the actual job? What are the implications?

(b) Ask a work supervisor/manager to specify how a particular task is to be done (or obtain a set of directions or manual to that effect). Interview a worker for the same purpose. How are both views alike and different? What are the implications for a workplace program?

(c) Interview a trades program instructor and have him/her list as many literacy skills as possible that a learner would need to successfully master the trade. Interview a learner for the same purpose. What are the overall results? What are the implications?

6. Proposing an integrated model of an academic upgrading/literacy-trades skills instructional program is sometimes threatening to ABE/literacy instructors as they fear that their roles will be displaced. How can you allay their fears? (Consider all the goals of ABE/literacy programs.)

Propose a team teaching model (literacy/ABE and trades instructors) for an integrated model of ABE/literacy-trades skills instruction.

7. There are two approaches to workplace literacy programs:

(a) Complete a task analysis and teach the necessary work-related literacy skills, and (b) Teach developmental literacy skills as well.

What are the advantages/disadvantages of each model? Whose needs are being addressed in each one? Who should decide these needs?

8. Is the informal apprenticeship model defunct as a model for inducting people into a trade skill? Can you think of instances where this might be revived? For example, an entrepreneur recently opened a large building with provision for people who were competent to work on their vehicles to rent a bay (work area) with all the amenities of a regular garage. How could this situation have potential for an informal apprenticeship program?

9. For which of the above activities (nos. 1-8) would it be appropriate to make a stand, presentation, argument to some authority (government, church, business, school, medical, etc.)? What would be the purpose or goal? What might be attained as a result? If you as an individual or with others feel inclined to follow this course of action, by all means do so.

CHAPTER 5

1. Being "culturally thoughtful" is not to be a passive recipient of culture, but to be active, analytical, and critical. One important characteristic of being culturally thoughtful is to be able to problematize, or form problems, a first step in being culturally active. Formulate five problems that are the basis of current cultural events. Describe the event first and then formulate the problem. You may work in groups and later compare the problems you have formulated. Excerpts from local newspapers may be used to highlight events if you are not readily aware of some.

2. Ingenuity is part of survival, of functioning well under difficult circumstances. Examples are given in this chapter and we hear of

examples often in newscasts. Why is it that pride and respect are usually associated with such behaviours, but shame and sympathy are associated with resourceful literacy behaviours by those who lack the necessary literacy skills?

3. How can role models within one's culture be used to enhance educational development?

4. Discuss the concept of subjectivity and find examples in oral language and written language to illustrate. Does the concept differ in its use in both language modes? If so, how?

5. How would you develop the skill of mentally editing one's language for more formal purposes of language use (written or oral)?

6. How could you use competency in metaphor and comparison in oral language as a vehicle for transitioning oral language skill to written language skill?

7. Make a list of "potent" words (either from personal knowledge or as expressed in the media) that may engender bias. What role can language-based programs play with respect to exposing the bias of language use?

8. Find examples of computerized (e.g., voice mail recordings) versus personalized language. What are the implications for language study and language use?

9. How can oral and written language be developed and enhanced through such processes as analysis, synthesis, evaluation, prediction, and memorization? Do these processes differ in their application to both language modes?

10. How can one's self-image as a speaker of a dialect be positively reinforced (a) in school and education programs, (b) at the community level, (c) at the provincial level?

CHAPTER 6

1. Analyse conditions in your community with respect to "kultur" and "culture." These may be discussed in terms of any institution – government, school board, university, business, or church. Are there any conflicts between "kultur" and "culture" (local papers may provide information in this regard)? What are the implications?

2. What does a grade 12 or a school-leaving certificate really mean? Look up the criteria for completing grade 12 in your area. By manipulating choices, develop programs of five different profiles leading to certification. What are the implications for each program

profile for (a) literacy, (b) enrolling in university, (c) enrolling in a trade instructional program at a college or vocational institution, (d) personal growth/self-actualization?

3. What changes have you noted over a ten-year period in education in general or in an area in which you are interested? What are the implications?

4. Note the factors in Table 37 that were considered significant in reading and writing development. Which factors can the school positively influence (possibly to varying degrees) and how could the school show more direction with regard to each factor?

5. How would you work around cultural differences in fostering literacy development with regard to the following situations:

(a) If reading to/with children does not "come naturally" to parents, how could the school foster this without playing a too obvious "school-assigned" role?

(b) If fathers are unlikely to visit schools regarding their children's education, what conditions may be provided so that there is incentive to become involved?

What role can adult literacy programs play in the above two scenarios?

6. How can effective teacher-parent collaboration be developed in (a) maintaining effective and appropriate discipline in the home and school, and (b) evaluating curriculum content for possible adoption by the school? How can adult literacy programs help with respect to (b)?

7. How can parents be empowered so that when they visit their children's teachers, they can speak from their own agenda as well as acknowledging and addressing the teacher's agenda? What can be done in adult literacy classes to assist parents for this purpose?

8. A number of non-linguistic factors in the home have been mentioned as being significant in fostering literacy development. How can these factors be emphasized within the school or adult literacy program for a similar purpose? Are there other non-linguistic factors that might be promoted?

9. How can teachers/adult literacy instructors develop and encourage leisure-time reading?

10. In areas where there is no public library, how can reading material be made available to the general public?

11. Take the three categories of expectation: home, school performance, and future education. How can a teacher/adult literacy instructor better understand a student/learner by using this framework? How can teachers and adult literacy instructors develop a collaborative set of expectations with students according to the three categories?

12. For which of the above activities (nos. 1-11) would it be appropriate to make a stand, presentation, argument to some authority (government, church, business, school, medical, etc.)? What would be the purpose or goal? What might be attained as a result? If you as an individual or with others feel inclined to follow this course of action, by all means do so.

CHAPTER 7

1. "There will always be a range of education, skills, and workers." How does the meaning of this statement impact on goals that adult learners may set for themselves both for literacy and for employment? How can you as an adult literacy instructor develop recognition and respect for a range of education, skills, and workers?

2. In an initial interview with an adult learner who plans to enrol in an adult literacy program, the focus is often on the learner's functioning in literacy tasks. What are the advantages of determining the learner's quality of life? What are other indications of quality of life besides social and community involvement?

3. "One's self-image is determined by one's social reality." How do we determine the social reality of adult learners and their self-image generated from that context? Why is it that when individuals enrol in adult literacy programs, the social reality of the literacy program becomes of paramount significance and they lose sight of the broader social reality in which they may have more positive insights as to their self-worth? How can we put the literacy context in perspective with the broader social reality of learners, thereby minimizing a negative self-image they may have with respect to literacy?

4. Testimonials are popular in the adult literacy area. They usually involve stories of horrendous backgrounds and the salvation of literacy. Does this actually reflect social reality? Does literacy become the tail that wags the dog? How can testimonials (if necessary) be formulated so that a person can feel good about all successes and accomplishments in life?

5. When adults enrol in adult education and literacy classes, they often find it necessary to withdraw from participation in home and community-related activities in which they are competent. How can an adult literacy instructor help them maintain a balance in their lives between the acquisition of literacy/ABE competencies and continued involvement in the tasks in which they have a history of success?

6. You represent an educational institution currently investigating assigning credits for past learning to those entering your institution. A brochure outlining its plan states that credit will be given for learning, not for experience. Debate the merits of this statement.

7. Search for songs, particularly songs of the region or culture in which you work, that focus on social and political issues. How can these be used in adult literacy classes?

8. If possible, arrange to take adult learners to see a play that focuses on social/political issues. Prepare the learners beforehand by discussing the merits of drama as empowerment, generate some context for the issues raised, and sort out the purposes for attending and expectations. Engage in a debriefing discussion session afterwards.

9. Study a recent demonstration on picketing (unfortunately, information may be limited through TV or local paper coverage). Try to discover what efforts the organizers engaged in prior to the demonstration, how the demonstration was organized and for what purposes, and what happened after the demonstration. Analyse what makes a demonstration successful.

10. Discuss the notion of scribes with adult learners. Try to organize people from the community who are specialists in various institutional/bureaucratic areas (for example, a retired lawyer) to act as volunteer scribes for adult learners on issues related to the volunteer's expertise.

CHAPTER 8

1. The statements in Tables 53 and 54 may be presented to adult learners who are asked to rate each on a 4-point scale. How may the results be used in an adult literacy program? What would be the implications of two distinct profiles – for example, one averaging 4, and the other, 1?

2. A sense of class difference still seems to be prevalent among lower-literacy adults (this may also be a cultural influence). While

there will always be people who identify with a "higher" social class, how can this barrier to understanding and appreciating people as people be reduced?

3. What are the advantages of conceptualizing values as priorities rather than as either/or issues? Within this conceptualization, what are the implications for understanding:

(a) a high school student who does not have his homework completed?

(b) an adult learner who did not attend her adult literacy class after the fourth session?

(c) a person with very little money who stops for a beer on the way home from work?

(d) a university student rushing to class who stops to help a crying child in the university parking lot?

4. Do educators become too narrow in their prioritizing education as the key value in society? What are the implications when learners have other values rated more highly? Should educators modify the value they place on education for learners? If so, under what conditions or circumstances can this be done?

5. What are the implications in distinguishing the concept "financial security" from "work/employment" in discussing people's economic status? What are the implications for each of these economic states for adults planning on enrolling in literacy/ABE programs?

6. Encourage adult learners to retrospect/introspect on the "joys in my life," and if they so desire, to talk or write on this topic.

7. Use selected items from Tables 61 to 64 as the basis for class discussions or class writing. Develop a plan for analysing and examining each item, leading to a plan of action resulting from the advice.

CHAPTER 9

1. Draw two intersecting circles to represent immediate context (culture) and extended context (culture). Show by the overlap the extent to which you identify with both. For example, if both cultures are separate for you, you will have two distinct circles; if both are almost identical, these will be basically the one circle; there may be many other variations of overlap. Discuss your identity with each context and the implications for your current literacy functioning.

2. How can the concepts "immediate context" and "extended context" help adult literacy instructors provide meaningful instruction for adult learners?

3. Find examples of a new literacy under the headings:

(a) power behind the print
(b) information overload
(c) façade of literacy

4. What is the possible impact of negative perceptions of low-literate adults promoted by:

politicians
journalists
business
educators

What can be done to inject reality into these perceptions?

5. Look at the power-load-margin model in Figure 6. Analyse your own learning commitment/investment with respect to this model. How could this model be used to help an adult learner understand his/her situation with respect to time available for program involvement?

GENERAL

1. "The emphasis should be on whether the learner has learned to do something thoughtful rather than on whether he/she has done something right."

Analyse segments (lessons, exercises) of various literacy programs. Decide if they involve the learner in doing something "thoughtful" or "right." If the emphasis is on doing something "right," could the segments be changed to focus the learner on doing something "thoughtful"? Develop criteria for "thoughtful" and "right."

2. The concept of relevancy is difficult to define as some people argue that everything is related (relevant) to everything else, and there is some grain of truth in this. Relevancy may be understood on a number of levels: (a) the material taught makes sense in the learner's life; (b) it provides instruction in a way that ties learning to the learner's culture; and (c) it is what the educator perceives as necessary for literacy to occur. The latter is often based on theory and book knowledge and does not connect to the learner's immediate life. Analyse segments (lessons, exercises) of various literacy pro-

grams. Decide if they are relevant in terms of (a), (b), or (c) above. What are the implications?

3. Be daring! Analyse a course you are now taking in terms of its relevancy? Use the (a), (b), (c) framework in question 2 as a guide. In place of "literacy" in (c) substitute what the course is about.

4. If possible, visit an adult literacy program. What follow-up programs or activities are available for learners when they complete this program?

5. What standards (if any) are required for adult literacy instructors in your area? If there is not a common standard across programs, contact various programs to find out what training adult literacy instructors (paid and volunteer) receive?

6. One conclusion from this text is that age and the power of various groups within society rather than literacy may be more likely to engender change. What are the implications of this conclusion for literacy instructors when working with (a) children, (b) adult learners?

7. What purpose is served by governments or other power agencies by promoting a new concept that will supposedly direct future trends in an area, such as the concept of "professional fisherpersons" in this study? What concepts of this nature have occurred in your area in recent years?

References

Barnes, D. (1976). *From Communication to Curriculum.* Harmondsworth, Middlesex: Penguin Books.

Becker, A. (1991). "Responsibilities and Expectations: Interactive Home/School Factors in Literacy Development among Portuguese First Graders," in C.E. Walsh, ed., *Literacy as Praxis: Culture, Language and Pedagogy.* Norwood, N.J.: Ablex Publishing Corporation: 69-85.

Becker, G.S. (1975). *Human Capital,* 2nd ed. New York: Columbia University Press.

Biggs, D.A. (1991). "Literacy and the Betterment of Individual Life," in E.M. Jennings and A.C. Purves, eds., *Literate Systems and Individual Lives.* Albany: State University of New York Press: 117-36.

Blau, S.D. (1981). "Commentary: Literacy as a Form of Courage," *Journal of Reading,* 25: 101-05.

Blaugh, M. (1966). "Literacy and Economic Development," *School Review,* 74: 393-418.

Blaugh, M. (1985). "Where Are We Now in the Economics of Education?" *Economics of Education Review,* 4:17-28.

Bourdieu, P. (1991). "Systems of Education and Systems of Thought," in M.F.D. Young, ed., *Knowledge and Control.* London: Collier-Macmillan Publishers: 189-207.

Braddock, C. (1967). "Project 100,000," *Phi Delta Kappan,* 48: 425-28.

Brock, C. (1983). "Breaking the Failure Barrier," *Australian Journal of Reading,* 6: 105-07.

Cairns, J.C. (1988). *Adult Literacy in Canada.* Toronto: Council of Ministers of Education.

Calamai, P. (1987). *Broken Words: Why Five Million Canadians are Illiterate.* Ottawa: Southam Communications.

Callwood, J. (1990). "Reading: The Road to Freedom," *Canadian Living* (Jan.): 39-41.

Canadian Institute for Research on Regional Development (1995). *Economic Adjustment in Selected Coastal Communities.* n.p.

Carter, E. (1969). *Literacy, Libraries, and Literacy.* London: Library Association.

Casey, G.M., ed. (1972). *Public Service to the Illiterate Adult.* Detroit: Wayne State University, Office of Urban Literacy Research.

Chantraine, P. (1993). *The Last Cod Fish: Life and Death of the Newfoundland Way of Life.* St. John's: Jesperson Press.

Clark, R.A. (1984). "Definitions of Literacy: Implications for Policy and Practice," *Adult Literacy and Basic Education,* 8: 133-46.

Connell, R.W., D.J. Ashender, S. Kessler, and G.W. Dorset (1982). *Making the Difference: Schools, Families and Social Division.* London: George Allen & Unwin.

Corbett, E.P.J. (1982). "The Demands for and of Literacy," *English Quarterly,* 15: 5-16.

Cressey, D. (1983). "The Environment for Literacy: Accomplishment and Context in Seventeenth Century England and New England," in D. Resnick, ed., *Literacy in Historical Perspective.* Washington: Library of Congress.

D'Angelo, F.J. (1983). "Literacy and Cognitions: A Developmental Perspective," in R.W. Bailey and R.M. Fosham, eds., *Literacy for Life: The Demands of Reading and Writing.* New York: Modern Languages Association: 97-114.

Darling, S. (1993). "Family Literacy: An Intergenerational Approach to Education," *Viewpoints #15, Family Literacy:* 2-5 (London: ALBSU).

Darville, R. (1989). "The Language of Experience and the Literacy of Power," in M.C. Taylor and J.C. Draper, eds., *Adult Literacy Perspectives.* Toronto: Culture Concepts: 25-40.

Delattre, E.J. (1983). "The Insiders," in R.W. Bailey and R.M. Fosheim, eds., *Literacy for Life: The Demand for Reading and Writing.* New York: Modern Languages Association: 52-62.

Diehl, W.A. (1980). "Functional Literacy as a Variable Construct: An Examination of Attitudes, Behaviours, and Strategies Related to Occupational Literacy," Ph.D. dissertation, Indiana University.

Diehl, W.A., and L. Mikulecky (1980). "The Nature of Literacy at Work," *Journal of Reading,* 24: 221-27.

Doyle, W. (1983). "Academic Work," *Review of Educational Research,* 53: 159-99.

Duke, C. (1983). "Adult Education and Poverty: What Are the Connections?" *Convergence*, 16: 76-83.

Ellen, R.F. (1984). *Ethnographic Research: A Guide to General Conduct*. New York: Academic Press.

Epstein, J.L. (1986). "School and Family Connections: Toward an Integrated Theory of Family-School Relations for Student Success in School," paper presented at the American Educational Research Association annual meeting, San Francisco, April.

Erickson, F. (1984). "School Literacy, Reasoning and Civility: An Anthropologist's Perspective," *Review of Educational Research*, 54: 525-46.

The Evening Telegram, St. John's, Newfoundland: 4 February, 29 August, 5 September 1993; 4 February, 28 May, 4 June, 30 August 1994; 20, 22 August, 1 September 1995; 5 March, 17 March, 29 March, 1 May, 5 May, 19 June, 7 July, 4 August, 30 October 1996; 20 January 1997.

The Express, St. John's, Newfoundland: 20 July 1994, 24 April 1996.

Fagan, W.T. (1988). "Literacy in Canada: A Critique of the Southam Report," *Alberta Journal of Educational Research*, 34: 224-31.

Fagan, W.T. (1989). "Prisoners' and Non-institutional Adults' Perceptions of Conditions Affecting their Learning," *Journal of Correctional Education*, 40: 152-58.

Fagan, W.T. (1990). "Misconceptions about Adult Illiteracy," *Alberta Teachers' Association Magazine*, 70: 26-30.

Fagan, W.T. (1992). *A Framework for Literacy Development: Effective Program and Instructional Strategies for Reading and Writing for Low-Achieving Adults and Children*. Montreal: Les Editions de la Chenelière.

Fagan, W.T. (1993). "Literacy and Cultural Discourse: The Relativity of Print," *Canadian Journal of Educational Communication*, 22: 151-60.

Fagan, W.T. (1994a). "Empowerment: The Literacy of Song in Newfoundland," paper presented at the Canadian Society for the Study of Education Conference, Calgary.

Fagan, W.T. (1994b). "Adult Literacy Surveys: A Trans-border Comparison," *Journal of Reading*, 38: 260-69.

Fairbairn, J. (1987). "Illiteracy in Canada," *Senate Debates*. Ottawa: 11 March.

Faris, J.C. (1973). *Cat Harbour: A Newfoundland Fishing Settlement*. St. John's: Institute of Social and Economic Research, Memorial University.

Farrell, T.J. (1977). "Literacy, the Basics of All That Jazz," *College English*, 38: 443-59.

Fine, M. (1987). "Silencing in Public School," *Language Arts*, 64: 157-74.

Fingeret, A. (1983). "A Social Network: A New Perspective on Independence and Illiterate Adults," *Adult Education Quarterly*, 33: 133-46.

Fox, J., and J. Powell (1990). *A Literate World*. Paris: UNESCO.

Freire, P. (1970). "The Adult Literacy Process as Cultural Action for Freedom," *Harvard Educational Review*, 40: 205-25.

Freire, P., and D. Macedo (1987). *Literacy: Reading the Word and the World*. South Hadley, Mass.: Bergin and Garvey.

Gaffney, M.E. (1982). "Crosshanded: Work Organization and Values in a Newfoundland Fishery," Ph.D. dissertation, Ohio State University.

Galtung, J. (1975). "Literacy, Education, and Schooling - For What?" *Convergence*, 8: 39-49.

Galtung, J. (1981). "Literacy, Education, and Schooling - For What?" in H. Graff, ed., *Literacy and Social Development in the West! A Reader*. Cambridge: Cambridge University Press: 271-85.

Gearing, F. (1979). "A Reference Model for a Cultural Theory of Education and Schooling," in F. Gearing and L. Sangree, eds., *Toward a Cultural Theory of Education and Schooling*. New York: Mouton Publishers: 169-230.

Gee, J.P. (1986). "Literate America on Illiterate America," *Journal of Education*, 168: 126-40.

Gee, J.P. (1991) "What Is Literacy?" in C. Mitchell and K. Weiler, eds., *Rewriting Literacy: Culture and the Discourse of the Other*. New York: Bergin and Garvey: 3-11.

Gillin, J. (1948). *The Ways of Men*. New York: Appleton-Century Crofts.

Giroux, H.A. (1979/1980). "Mass Culture and the Rise of the New Illiteracy: Implications for Reading," *Interchange*, 10: 89-94.

Giroux, H.A. (1983). *Theory and Resistance in Education*. London: Heineman Educational Books.

Giroux, H.A. (1988). "Literacy and the Pedagogy of Voice and Political Empowerment," *Educational Theory*, 38: 61-75.

Goodman, K.S. (1985)."Commentary: On Being Literate in an Age of Information," *Journal of Reading*, 28: 388-92.

Goody, J., ed. (1968). *Literacy in Traditional Societies*. Cambridge: Cambridge University Press.

Gowen, S.G. (1992). *The Politics of Literacy: A Case Study*. New York: Teachers College Press.

Graff, H. (1981). "Introduction," in Graff, ed., *Literacy and Social Development in the West! A Reader*. Cambridge: Cambridge University Press: 1-13.

Graue, M.E. (1991). "Construction of Community and the Meaning of Being a Parent," paper presented at the annual meeting of the American Education Research Association, Chicago, April.

Griggs vs. Duke Power Company, 401 U.S. 436 (1971). 3 FEP Cases 175.

Hannon, P. (1993). "Intergenerational Literacy Intervention: Possibilities and Problems." *Viewpoints #15, Family Literacy:* 6-9 (London: ALBSU).

Harvey, B. (1993). "Faith Thrives beyond Pews," *Edmonton Journal*: B4, 5 June.

Hayes, A.S., ed. (1965). *Literacy*. Washington: Center for Applied Linguistics.

Heath, S.B. (1980). "The Functions and Uses of Literacy," *Journal of Communication*, 30: 123-33.

Heath, S.B. (1986). "Sociocultural Contexts of Language Development." In *Beyond Language: Social and Cultural Factors in Schooling Language Minority Students.* Los Angeles, CA: Evaluation, Dissemination and Assessment Center: 143-86.

Henze, R.C. (1992). "Literacy in Rural Greece: From Family to Individual," in F. Dubin and N.A. Kuhlman, eds., *Cross-cultural Literacy: Global Perspectives on Reading and Writing*. Englewood Cliffs, N.J.: Regents/Prentice-Hall: 47-62.

Herrick, C. (1974). "Migration as an Adaptive Strategy in Newfoundland," in M.A. Sterns, ed., *Perspectives on Newfoundland Society and Culture*. St. John's: Memorial University of Newfoundland: 177-80.

Hill, R.A. (1983). *The Meaning of Work and the Reality of Unemployment in the Newfoundland Context*. St. John's: Community Services Council of Newfoundland and Labrador.

Hinzen, H. (1984). Letter to *Network Literacy*, vol. 1, cited in Street (1984).

Hirshman, A.O. (1970). *Exit, Voice, and Loyalty*. London: Oxford University Press.

Holzman, M. (1986). "Opinion: The Social Context of Literacy Education," *College English*, 46: 229-38.

House, J.D. (1989). *Going Away . . . and Coming Back: Economic Life and Migration in Small Canadian Communities*. St. John's: Institute of Social and Economic Research, Memorial University.

Hunter, C.S. (1982). "Literacy for Empowerment and Social Change," *Visible Language*, 16: 137-43.

Hunter, C., and D. Harman (1979). *Adult Literacy in the United States*. New York: McGraw-Hill.

Jennings, E.M., and A.C. Purves, eds. (1991). *Literate Systems and Individual Lives*. Albany: State University of New York Press.

Jentoft. S. (1993). *Dangling Lines: The Fisheries Crisis and the Future of Coastal Communities, the Norwegian Experience*. St. John's: Institute of Social and Economic Research, Memorial University.

Kandel, I.L. (1946). "Salvation through Literacy," *School and Society*, 64: 396.

Kazemek, F.E. (1984). "Adult Literacy Education: An Ethical Endeavour," *Adult Literacy and Basic Education*, 8: 61-72.

Kazemek, F.E. (1985). "Functional Literacy Is Not Enough: Adult Literacy as a Developmental Process," *Journal of Reading*, 28: 332-35.

Kirsch, I., and J.T. Guthrie (1977/1978). "The Concept and Measurement of Functional Literacy," *Reading Research Quarterly*, 13: 485-507.

Kozol, J. (1975). *The Night Is Dark and I Am Far from Home*. Boston: Houghton Mifflin.

Langer, J.A., ed. (1987). *Language, Literacy and Culture: Issues of Society and Schooling*. Norwood, NJ: Ablex Publishing.

Lankshear, C., and M. Lawler (1987). *Literacy: Schooling and Revolution*. New York: Falmer Press.

Lather, P. (1986a). "Issues of Validity in Openly Ideological Research: Between a Rock and a Soft Place," *Interchange*, 17: 63-86.

Lather, P. (1986b). "Research as Praxis," *Harvard Educational Review*, 56, 257-77.

Lave, J.A. , M. Murtagh, and O. de la Roche (1984). "The Dialect of Arithmetic in Grocery Shopping," in B. Rogoff and J. Lave, eds., *Everyday Cognition: Its Development in Social Context*. Cambridge, Mass.: Harvard University Press: 67-94.

Lave, J., and E. Wenger (1991). *Situated Learning: Legitimate Peripheral Participation*. Cambridge: Cambridge University Press.

Levine, K. (1982). "Functional Literacy: Fond Illusions and False Economies," *Harvard Educational Review*, 52: 249-66.

Levine, K. (1986). *The Social Context of Literacy*. London: Routledge & Kegan Paul.

Levinger, L. (1978). "The Human Side of Illiteracy," *English Journal*, 67: 26-29.

Lytle, S.L. (1991). "Living Literacy: Rethinking Development in Adulthood," paper presented at the American Education Research Association annual meeting, Boston.

Lytle, S.L, and J. Landau (1987). "Introduction," in D. A. Wagner, ed., *The Future of Literacy in a Changing World*. New York: Pergamon Press: 209-15.

Lytle, S.L., T.W. Marmor and F.H. Penner (1986). "Literacy Theory in Practice: Assessing Reading and Writing of Low-Literate Adults." Paper presented at the American Education Association Annual Meeting, San Francisco.

Mace, J. (1992). *Talking about Literacy*. London: Routledge.

Maguire, M.H. (1995). "The Many Faces of Literacy," in L. Wason-Ellam, A. Blunt, and S. Robinson, eds., *Horizons of Literacy* . Canadian Council of Teachers of English Language Arts: 19-29.

Matthews, R. (1976). *There's No Better Place Than Here*. Toronto: Peter Martin.

McCarthy, M.J. (1991). *Mastering the Information Age*. Los Angeles: Jeremy P. Tarcher.

McKee-Brown, M.J. (1991). "Validity and the Problem of Reality: An Issue of Trust," paper presented at the American Education Research Association annual meeting, Chicago, April.

McPeck, J. (1981). *Critical Thinking and Education*. Oxford: Martin Robertson.

Mikulecky, L. (1985). "Literacy Task Analysis: Defining and Measuring Occupational Literacy Demands," paper presented at the American Education Research Association annual meeting, Chicago, April.

Myers, J. (1992). "The Social Contexts of School and Personal Literacy," *Reading Research Quarterly*, 27: 296-33.

Newman, A.P., and C. Beverstock (1990). *Adult Literacy: Contexts and Challenges*. Newark, Delaware: International Reading Association.

Norris, S.P., L.M. Phillips, and J.W. Bulcock (1992). *Demographic Causes of Reading Literacy Levels in Newfoundland and Labrador*. St. John's: Memorial University of Newfoundland.

Norton, M. (1992). "Metacognition and Literacy Development at Work: A Descriptive Study," Ph.D. dissertation, University of Alberta.

Ogbu, J.U. (1981). "Origins of Human Competence: A Cultural Ecological Perspective," *Child Development*, 52: 413-39.

Ogbu, J.U. (1987). "Opportunity, Structure, Cultural Boundaries and Literacy," in Langer, ed., *Language, Literacy and Culture:* 149-72.

Ogbu, J.U. (1990). "Cultural Model, Identity, and Literacy," in J.W. Stigler, R. A. Shweder, and G. Herdt, eds., *Cultural Psychology: Essays on Comparative Human Development*. Cambridge: Cambridge University Press: 520-41.

Olson, D.R. (1990). "Mythologizing Literacy," in S.P. Norris and L.M. Phillips, eds., *Foundations of Literacy Policy in Canada*. Calgary: Detselig: 15-22.

Olson, D.R., N. Torrance, and A. Hildyard (1985). *Literacy, Language and Learning: The Nature and Consequences of Reading and Writing*. Cambridge: Cambridge University Press.

Ong, W.J. (1982). "Reading, Technology and Human Consciousness," in J.C. Raymond, ed., *Literacy as a Human Problem*. University, Alabama: University of Alabama Press: 170-99.

Organization for Economic Co-operation and Development and Statistics Canada (1995). *Literacy, Economy, and Society*. Paris: Organization for Economic Co-operation/Ottawa: Statistics Canada.

O'Sullivan, J.T. (1992). *Reading Beliefs and Reading Achievement: A Development Study of Students from Low Income Families*. Report #6, Summary Reports of Paths to Literacy and Illiteracy in Newfoundland and Labrador. St. John's: Memorial University of Newfoundland.

Paris, S., and K. Wixson (1987). "The Development of Literacy: Access, Acquisition and Instruction," in D. Bloome, ed., *Literacy and Schooling*. Norwood, N.J.: Ablex Publishing: 35-54.

Port au Port Economic Development Association and Employment and Immigration Canada (1983). *Education and Employment: Building a Future*. A follow-up to the Port au Port youth survey of 1983. Port au Port, Newfoundland.

Provincial Advisory Council on the Status of Women, Newfoundland and Labrador (1994). *The Impact of the Cod Moratorium on Women in Newfoundland and Labrador: A Review of the Literature*. St. John's: Provincial Advisory Council on the Status of Women, Newfoundland and Labrador, April.

Purves, A.C. (1987). "Literacy, Culture, and Community," in D.A. Wagner, ed., *The Future of Literacy in a Changing World*. New York: Pergamon Press: 216-32.

Purves, A.C. (1990). *The Scribal Society*. White Plains, N.Y.: Longman.

Purves, A.C. (1991). "The Textual Contract: Literacy as Common Knowledge and Conventional Wisdom," in E.M. Jennings, and A.C. Purves, eds., *Literate Systems and Individual Lives*. Albany: State University of New York Press.

Rahnema, M. (1976). "Literacy: To Read the Word or the World?" *Prospects*, 6: 72-82.

Reder, S.M. (1987). "Comparative Aspects of Functional Literacy Development: Three Ethnic Communities," in D. Wagner, ed., *The Future of Literacy in a Changing World*. New York: Pergamon Press: 250-70.

Royal Commission of Inquiry into the Delivery of Programs and Services in Primary, Elementary, Secondary Education (1992). *Our Children, Our Future*. St. John's: Government of Newfoundland and Labrador.

Rush, R.T., A.J. Moe, and R.L. Storlie (1986). *Occupational Literacy Education*. Newark, Delaware: International Reading Association.

The Sacred Heart Messenger (May 1992). Dublin, Ireland: Messenger Publications.

Scribner, S. (1984). "Studying Working Intelligence," in B. Rogoff and J. Lave, eds., *Everyday Cognition: Its Development in Social Context*. Cambridge, Mass.: Harvard University Press: 9-40.

Scribner, S., and M. Cole (1978). "Literacy without Schooling: Testing for Intellectual Effects," *Harvard Educational Review*, 48: 448-61.

Scribner, S., and M. Cole (1981). *Psychology of Literacy*. Cambridge, Mass.: Harvard University Press.

Secretary's Commission on Achieving Necessary Skills (1990). *What Work Requires of Schools: A SCANS Report for America 2000*. Washington: U.S. Government Printing Office, June.

Seidenfeld, M.A. (1943). "Illiteracy - Fact and Fiction," *School and Society*, 58: 330-32.

Siefert, M. (1979). "Research: Reading on the Job," *Journal of Reading*, 22: 360-62.

Smith, D. (1986). "The Anthropology of Literacy Acquisition," in B.B. Schieffin and P. Gilmore, eds., *The Acquisition of Literacy: Ethnographic Perspectives*. Norwood, N.J.: Ablex Publishing: 261-76.

Smith, D. (1987). "Illiteracy as a Social Fault: Some Principles of Research and Some Results," in D. Bloome, ed., *Literacy and Schooling* . Norwood, N.J.: Ablex Publishing: 55-64.

Smith, F. (1988). *Joining the Literacy Club*. Portsmouth, N.H.: Heinemann.

Snow, C.E., W.S. Barnes, J. Chandler, I.F. Goodman, and L. Hemphill (1991). *Unfilled Expectations: Home and School Influences on Literacy*. Cambridge, Mass.: Harvard University Press.

Snow, C.E., and D.K. Dickinson (1991). "Skills That Aren't Basic in a New Conception of Literacy," in E.M. Jennings and A.C. Purves, eds., *Literate Systems and Individual Lives*. Albany: State University of New York Press: 179-92.

Southam Literacy Survey (1987). *Literacy in Canada: A Research Report.* Ottawa: Southam Communications (prepared by The Creative Research Group, Toronto).

Spain, D.H. (1975). *The Human Experience: Readings in Sociological Anthropology.* Homewood, Ill.: Dorsey Press.

Spradley, J.P. (1974). "Culture and the Contemporary World," in J.P. Spradley, ed., *Conformity and Conflict.* Boston: Little, Brown: 1-11.

Statistics Canada (1990). *Survey of Literacy Skills Used in Daily Activities.* Ottawa: Statistics Canada.

Sticht, T. G. (1987). "Literacy, Cognitive Robotics and General Technology: Training for Marginally Literate Adults," in D. Wagner, ed., *The Future of Literacy in a Changing World.* New York: Pergamon Press: 289-301.

Sticht, T. G. (1988/1989). "Adult Literacy Education," in E. Rothkopf, ed., *Review of Research in Education.* Washington: American Education Research Association: 59-96.

Sticht, T.G., L. Fox, R. Hauke, and D. Zaph (1977). *The Role of Reading in the Navy* (NPRDC TR 77-77). San Diego: Navy Personnel Research and Development Center.

Story, G.M., W.J. Kirwin and J.D.A. Widdowson (1990). *Dictionary of Newfoundland English: Second Edition with Supplement.* St. John's: Breakwater Books.

Street, B.V. (1984). *Literacy in Theory and Practice.* London: Cambridge University Press.

Stuckey, J.E. (1991). *The Violence of Literacy.* Portsmouth, N.H.: Boynton/Cook and Heinemann.

Swartz, M.J., and D.K. Jordan (1980). *Culture: The Anthropological Perspective.* New York: John Wiley & Sons.

Szwed, J. (1987). *Private Cultures and Public Imagery: Interpersonal Relations in a Newfoundland Peasant Society.* St. John's: Institute of Social and Economic Research, Memorial University.

Taylor, D. (1996). *Toxic Literacies: Exposing the Injustice of Bureaucratic Texts.* Portsmouth, N.H.: Heinemann.

Topping, D.M. (1992). "Literacy and Cultural Erosion in the Pacific Islands," in F. Dubin and N.A. Kuhlman, eds., *Cross-Cultural Literacy: Global Perspectives on Reading and Writing.* Englewood Cliffs, N.J.: Regents/ Prentice-Hall: 19-28.

Tough, A. (1979). "Major Learning Efforts: Recent Research and Future Directions," *Adult Education,* 28: 250-363.

Trueba, H.T. (1993). "The Dynamics of Cultural Transmission," in H.T. Trueba, C. Rodriguez, Y. Zou, and J. Cintron, eds., *Healing Multicultural America*. London: Falmer Press: 1-28.

UNESCO International Literacy Year Secretariat (1990). *International Literacy Year* (brochure). Paris: UNESCO.

Valentine, T. (1986). "Adult Functional Literacy as a Goal of Instruction," *Adult Education Quarterly*, 36: 108-13.

Venezky, R.L. (1990). "Gathering Up, Looking Ahead," in R.L. Venezky, D. A. Wagner, and B. S. Ciliberti, eds., *Toward Defining Literacy. Newark, Delaware: International Reading Association: 70-74.*

Verne, E. (1981). "Literacy and Industrialization: The Dispossession of Speech," in H. Graff, ed., *Literacy and Social Development in the West! A Reader*. Cambridge: Cambridge University Press: 286-303.

Vivelo, F.R. (1978). *Cultural Anthropology Handbook*. New York: McGraw-Hill.

Wagner, D.A. (1987). "Literacy Futures: Five Common Problems from Industrialized Countries," in D.A. Wagner, ed.,*The Future of Literacy in* a *Changing World* . New York: Pergamon Press: 3-16.

Wagner, J. (1993). "Ignorance in Educational Research, or How Can You Not Know That?" *Educational Researcher*, 22: 15-23.

Wagner, S. (1985). "Illiteracy and Adult Literacy Teaching in Canada," *Prospects*, 15: 407-17.

Walker, L. (1978.1979). "Newfoundland Dialect and Learning to Read and Spell," *English Quarterly*, 11: 37-44.

Walker, L. (1979). "Newfoundland Dialect Interference in Fourth Grade Spelling," *Alberta Journal of Educational Research*, 25: 221-33.

Wason-Ellam, L., and A. Blunt (1995). "Understanding Literacy Events," in L. Wason-Ellam, A. Blunt, and S. Robinson, eds., *Horizons of Literacy*. Canadian Council of Teachers of English Language Arts: 1-16.

Williams, S.B. (1987). "A Comparative Study of Black Dropouts and Black High School Graduates in an Urban Public School System," *Education and Urban Society*, 19: 311-19.

Willinsky, J. (1990). *The New Literacy: Redefining Reading and Writing in the Schools*. New York: Routledge, Chapman and Hall.

Windham, D.M. (1991). "Literacy, Economic Structures and Individual and Public Policy Incentives," in E.M. Jennings and A.C. Purves, eds., *Literate Systems and Individual Lives*. Albany: State University of New York Press: 23-36.

Winterowd, W.R. (1987). "Literacy: 'Kultur' and Culture," *Language Arts*, 64: 86-87.

Winterowd, W.R. (1989). *The Culture and Politics of Literacy*. Oxford: Oxford University Press.

Worsham, T. (1988). "From Cultural Literacy to Cultural Thoughtfulness," *Educational Leadership*, 46: 20-21.

Index